Rethinking
the
Western
Tradition

*The volumes in this series
seek to address the present debate
over the Western tradition
by reprinting key works of
that tradition along with essays
that evaluate each text from
different perspectives.*

The Genteel Tradition in American Philosophy
and
Character and Opinion in the United States

GEORGE SANTAYANA

Edited and with an Introduction by

James Seaton

with essays by

Wilfred M. McClay

John Lachs

James Seaton

Roger Kimball

Yale University Press

New Haven and London

Published with assistance from the Mary Cady Tew Memorial Fund.

Printed in the United States of America.

ISBN: 978-0-300-11665-6 (pbk.)

Library of Congress Control Number: 2009930169

A catalogue record for this book is available from the Library of Congress
and the British Library.

This paper meets the requirements of ANSI/NISO Z39.48-1992
(Permanence of Paper).

10 9 8 7 6 5 4 3 2 1

Contributors

Roger Kimball is co-editor and publisher of *The New Criterion* and president and publisher of Encounter Books.

John Lachs is Centennial Professor of Philosophy at Vanderbilt University.

Wilfred M. McClay holds the SunTrust Bank Chair of Excellence in Humanities at the University of Tennessee at Chattanooga, where he is also professor of history.

James Seaton is professor of English at Michigan State University.

Contents

Contributors   v

A Note on the Texts   ix

Introduction: George Santayana — The Philosopher as Cultural Critic

   James Seaton   xi

Texts

   The Genteel Tradition in American Philosophy   3

   Character and Opinion in the United States   21

   Preface   23

   Chapter I: The Moral Background   25

   Chapter II: The Academic Environment   39

   Chapter III: William James   51

   Chapter IV: Josiah Royce   64

   Chapter V: Later Speculations   81

   Chapter VI: Materialism and Idealism in American Life   92

   Chapter VII: English Liberty in America   103

Essays

   The Unclaimed Legacy of George Santayana

      Wilfred M. McClay   123

   Understanding America

      John Lachs   148

   The Genteel Tradition and English Liberty

      James Seaton   160

   Mental Hygiene and Good Manners:

   The Contribution of George Santayana

      Roger Kimball   175

Index   193

A Note on the Texts

The text of "The Genteel Tradition in American Philosophy" is taken from *The Genteel Tradition in American Philosophy: The Annual Public Address Before the Union, August 25, 1911* (Berkeley, CA: The University Press, 1911). The text was first published in the *University of California Chronicle*, 13.4 (October 11, 1911).

The text of *Character and Opinion in the United States* is taken from *Character and Opinion in the United States with Reminiscences of William James and Josiah Royce and Academic Life in America* (New York: Charles Scribner's Sons, 1920).

Introduction
George Santayana—The Philosopher as Cultural Critic

JAMES SEATON

George Santayana is best known as one of the great American philosophers, but he was also a poet, a playwright, an autobiographer, a best-selling novelist, and a cultural critic of the first rank. His writings on American culture, especially "The Genteel Tradition in American Philosophy" and *Character and Opinion in the United States,* are essential texts not merely for students of American philosophy but for anyone interested in studying American culture and society. The insights of his cultural criticism were made possible by Santayana's unusual position as both an outsider and an insider in American society. Santayana was born in Spain in 1863, his mother and father were both Spanish, and he remained a Spanish citizen all his life. He did not visit the United States during the last forty years of his life, from 1912 until his death in Rome in 1952. And yet Santayana grew up in Boston, studied and taught at Harvard for thirty years, and wrote all his works in English. As an old man he acknowledged, "It is as an American writer that I must be counted, if I am counted at all." [1]

Santayana's American connection was a result of the marriage in 1849 of his mother, Josefina Borrás, to George Sturgis, an American from a wealthy Boston family. [2] They met in the Philippines, where her father had been an official in the Spanish colonial government. After the death of George Sturgis in 1857 at forty, Josefina Borrás Sturgis married Agustín Santayana in Spain in 1861. Determined that her children should be raised and educated in the United States, she moved to Boston with the children of her first marriage in 1869, George and his father following in 1872. Agustín Santayana, unable or unwilling to adapt to Boston, returned to his family home in Avila, but his son stayed. After graduating from Boston Latin School, George Santayana entered Harvard University, where he remained as an undergraduate, graduate student, and finally professor in the Department of Philosophy. In 1912, a small inheritance from his mother made it possible for him to resign, and he left Harvard and the United States, never to return.

Santayana's ideas were formed in response to the attitudes and doctrines around him in New England and Harvard, yet his own temperament and view of the world remained Spanish and, more specifically, Castilian. In contrast to the earnest, reforming Protestantism of New England, Santayana all his life adhered to the "rather detached and skeptical philosophy" shared by "all true Castilians," "one that teaches us that all conditions are bearable, all dignities trumpery, and wisdom simply the gift of making the best of whatever is thrust upon us."[3] Although Santayana eventually became a full professor in Harvard's Department of Philosophy, he never felt entirely at home at the university or in Boston. In his autobiography, *Persons and Places,* he listed some reasons he was regarded as a suspicious character: "I had disregarded or defied public opinion by not becoming a specialist, but writing pessimistic old-fashioned verses, continuing to range superficially over literature and philosophy, being indiscernibly a Catholic or an atheist, attacking Robert Browning, prophet of the half-educated and half-believing, avoiding administrative duties, neglecting the Intelligentsia, frequenting the society of undergraduates and fashionable ladies, spending my holidays abroad, and even appearing as a witness in the disreputable Russell trial" (395).[4]

Santayana's early publications were not calculated to reassure Harvard's President Eliot and other cultural guardians about the young philosopher's moral earnestness. The three books of poetry, *Sonnets and Other Verses* (1894), *Lucifer: A Theological Tragedy* (1899), and *A Hermit of Carmel and Other Poems* (1901), were not what was expected from a professor of philosophy, while Santayana's philosophical works raised even more questions. In the introduction to *The Sense of Beauty,* he warned that his approach to aesthetics was not that of the sort of philosopher who attempted to demonstrate that "beauty is the manifestation of God to the senses."[5] He was instead one of "those that wallow in Epicurus' sty" (10), defining beauty as "pleasure regarded as the quality of a thing" (33). Worse yet, in *Interpretations of Poetry and Religion* he explained that "religion and poetry are identical in essence" and advised the champions of religions that in the interests of religion itself they "would do well to withdraw their pretension to be dealing with matters of fact."[6] Such advice was not always received with gratitude. William James, whose essay "The Will to Believe" had provided justifications for believing, under certain conditions, in the factual truth of religious doctrines, characterized *Interpretations* as "the perfection of rottenness," as Santayana himself happily pointed out, commenting that "what arrested his attention was my aestheticism, that seemed to find the highest satisfaction in essences or ideals, apart from their eventual satisfaction in matters of fact. . . . What he called rottenness was my apparent assumption that in the direction of religion and morals imagination was all, and there was nothing objective" ("Apologia," 499).

James, not for the last time, had misunderstood Santayana, but he would probably not have liked the book more if he had understood it better. If "aestheticism" in religion is taken to mean a single-minded emphasis on the beauty of rituals and doctrines apart from their relation to morality and everyday life, then Santayana's approach in *Interpretations of Poetry and Religion* was the opposite of aesthetic. He insisted that religious beliefs, including such uncompromising doctrines as eternal damnation and reward, were valuable not because they were beautiful but because they provided "apt symbols of moral truth" (4). Though the past may be forgotten, it cannot be changed, and thus the recognition that "every loss is irretrievable and every joy indestructible" (64) is an acknowledgment of hard moral truth, a truth symbolically and powerfully conveyed through the doctrine of eternal reward and punishment. On the other hand "the idea of universal salvation . . . is the expression of a feeble sentimentality, a pleasant reverie without structure or significance" (66). In a chapter entitled "The Poetry of Barbarism" Santayana criticized both Walt Whitman and Robert Browning for, among other failures, their blurring of the distinction between moral goods and evils, a distinction he believed rightly emphasized and driven home by the Christian vision of a final judgment.

While Santayana argued that "the Christian myth" provided valuable insights into human life, he rejected the claim of Christianity or any other religion to provide knowledge about the physical universe. He also rejected philosophic attempts to establish "a mythical physics, purporting to describe the structure of the universe in terms quite other than those which scientific physics could use."[7] This latter rejection set Santayana in opposition to the most influential philosophical current of his day, the idealism inaugurated by Kant, Fichte, Schelling, and Hegel and dominant in the universities of both England and the United States during Santayana's Harvard years. William James, no friend to Hegelian philosophy, commented in 1882 that it had "become quasi-official" in the United States and England.[8] Josiah Royce — like James first Santayana's teacher and then his colleague, but unlike James an admirer of Hegel's thought — was able in 1892 to declare with satisfaction that the core of "modern philosophical thought" was the notion that "the world is, in its wholeness, and in all of its real constituent parts, a world of mind or of spirit."[9] Royce and other philosophical idealists saw Darwin's theory of evolution not as a body blow against religion but as a "true empirical verification of the presence of the great active Spirit in his world." Darwin's empirical research confirmed that Hegel had been on the right track in his speculations about the movement of Spirit. Science provided support for what idealist philosophy had already proclaimed: "the immanence in nature of ideal powers, of significant tendencies, that from the beginning so moulded the atoms, so predetermined the laws of their mechanism, so endowed them with swift flight and with close affinity, that the outcome of ages of their motion has been spiritual" (289).

Evolution in the physical world was the counterpart of intellectual, moral, and spiritual evolution. Idealist philosophy was not merely in vague accord with Christianity; its conception of the relation between the individual self and the divine was actually superior to that expressed in the gospels or in the Nicene Creed. The identity between one's own "true self" and the divine Self who is God was indeed adumbrated by the early church through its "deep symbolism," but, Royce emphasized, this conception "in its fullness, only an idealistic interpretation can really and rationally express." Philosophical idealism made clear the identity between one's individual self and the Mind or Self of the universe, so that the conception of "the suffering God, who is just our own true self, who actually and in his flesh bears of the sins of the world" (470) becomes not an object of faith but the conclusion of a logical argument. Royce's philosophy thus contributed its prestige to the genteel tradition, in which the contradictory claims of idealist philosophy and Calvinist Christianity were ignored or smoothed over. Whatever was lost in intellectual clarity was more than made up for in "self-satisfaction," as Santayana pointed out in *Character and Opinion:*

> If evolution was to be taken seriously and to include moral growth, the great men of the past could only be stepping-stones to our own dignity. To grow was to contain and sum up all the good that had gone before, adding an appropriate increment. Undoubtedly some early figures were beautiful, and allowances had to be made for local influences in Palestine, a place so much more primitive and backward than Massachusetts. Jesus was a prophet more winsome and nearer to ourselves than his predecessors; but how could any one deny that the twenty centuries of progress since his time must have raised a loftier pedestal for Emerson or Channing or Phillips Brooks? It might somehow not be in good taste to put this feeling into clear words; one and perhaps two of these men would have deprecated it; nevertheless it beamed with refulgent self-satisfaction in the lives and maxims of most of their followers. (31)

Like Royce, Santayana was ready to accept the scientific validity of Darwin's theory of evolution. Unlike Royce, Santayana saw no evidence in

Darwin or elsewhere to confirm the belief of Royce and the other idealists that "the whole universe, including the physical world also, is essentially one live thing, a mind, one great Spirit" (*Spirit*, 17). Santayana instead took the view Royce identified as the polar opposite of his own, the materialistic or naturalistic view acknowledging "the ultimate existence of wholly un-spiritual realities at the basis of experience and as the genuine truth of the world" (*Spirit*, xiv).

The demise of Hegelian or Roycean idealism and the undiminished prestige of science may suggest that the differences between Royce and Santayana are no longer relevant to our contemporary situation. Neither Royce nor Santayana is a name to conjure with in the era of postmodernism, and it has become difficult even to understand how Royce could ever have reached the certainty expressed in the concluding passage of *The Spirit of Modern Philosophy*: "We have found in a world of doubt but one assurance — but one, and yet how rich! All else is hypothesis. The Logos alone is sure. The brief and seemingly so abstract creed of philosophy: '*This world is the world of the Logos*,' has answered our questions in the one sense in which we can dare to hope for an answer" (471; italics in original).

Today the certainty is all the other way. In contemporary cultural studies "logocentrism" is a sin almost as bad as racism or sexism, and indeed it is generally assumed that anybody guilty of the former is probably guilty of the latter two as well. And yet there are some ways in which the ideas of the great opponent of logocentrism, Jacques Derrida, are not so different from those of Josiah Royce. Derrida, after all, famously declared that "there is nothing outside the text," an ambiguous pronouncement which has often been taken to mean that absolutely anything and everything may be — and should be, if one is philosophically sophisticated — understood as a kind of text.[10] Any notion of a brute reality incapable of being interpreted as a text is ruled out. Derrida's assertion carries with it the sense that there is no reality outside of human experience, no "things-in-themselves," noth-ing that can be assumed to exist except as a text to be interpreted by hu-man beings. The difference between Royce's "logos" and Derrida's "text" seems to be the difference between a text that has a clear meaning, though one perhaps difficult to decipher, and a variety of texts whose meaning is unclear and unresolvable. Both, however, insist on a view of the world in which the "ultimate existence of wholly unspiritual realities at the basis of experience and as the genuine truth of the world" is ruled out or ignored. Philosophical idealists like Royce believed that thinkers like himself were able to get at the nature of reality in a way that scientists could not. Some postmodern textualists believe that their skills give them the ability to critique the natural sciences from a superior standpoint in projects such as "feminist science."[11]

Paul Gross and Norman Levitt titled their book describing what they called "the academic left and its quarrels with science" *Higher Superstition*.[12] George Santayana found that the philosophical idealism of the genteel tradition, its assent to "the remarkable conclusion that the human spirit was not so much the purpose of the universe as its seat, and the only universe there was," gave rise to a "higher superstition" that "views the world as an oracle or charade, concealing a dramatic unity, or formula, or maxim, which all experience exists to illustrate" (*Character and Opinion*, 33). The cultural constructivism that Gross and Levitt find at the heart of the contemporary "higher superstition" bears a strong resemblance to the "remarkable conclusion" noted by Santayana; in both cases theorists trained in nonscientific fields find a license to pronounce about science in the belief that there is no such thing as an external reality independent of human thought and action.[13] Those who are especially qualified to analyze human thoughts and actions on the basis of their training in the social sciences or the humanities are, so the thinking goes, likewise qualified to make judgments about findings in the natural sciences, since it is in any case human thoughts and actions that are decisive, once it is granted that there is no external reality to which one might appeal. Santayana's critique in *Reason in Science* of the pretensions of idealist philosophy to an authority beyond and superior to that of the natural sciences reads today like a critique of postmodernist claims to a similar superiority available to textualists. Raising an objection that would seem to apply to deconstructionists today, Santayana argues that idealist philosophy reveals the limitations of its view of the physical sciences "when science is systematically disparaged in favour of a method that is merely disintegrating and incapable of establishing a single positive truth" (225). Santayana's refusal to accept the authority of philosophy over the findings of scientific research remains relevant, though today one might substitute "cultural science studies" or "feminist science" for "metaphysics" in this passage: "It is impossible to base science on a deeper foundation or to override it by a higher knowledge. What is called metaphysics, if not an anticipation of natural science, is a confusion of it with dialectic or a mixture of it with myths" (229).

It was the five volumes of *The Life of Reason* (1905–1906) — *Reason in Common Sense, Reason in Society, Reason in Religion, Reason in Art,* and *Reason in Science* — that solidified Santayana's reputation and earned him a promotion to full professor. The subtitle of *The Life of Reason* was *The Phases of Human Progress,* and it is possible to read the volumes, quickly, as a vindication of the progress of secular reason against religion and metaphysics. The 1998 publication of the one-volume abridged edition by Prometheus Books seems based on such a reading; the last sentence of the blurb on the back cover asserts what is apparently meant to be taken as the moral of the work as a whole: "Hence, to take so-called religious truths as literal claims is preposterous."[14] William James, on the other hand, was delighted to find in the five volumes "a sort of Bergsonian vision of a miraculous human evolution," according to Santayana ("Apologia," 499). Santayana's devastating critique of Bergson's theory of "creative evolution" in the third chapter of *Winds of Doctrine* had not been written when James made his comment, but it should have been clear already that Santayana, though willing to accept Darwin's theory of evolution as a valid scientific hypothesis, saw no need to adopt any version of Darwinism in regard to either metaphysics or morality, unlike Bergson — or James's even more influential fellow pragmatist John Dewey.[15] Santayana later reflected that the "historical manner" employed in *The Life of Reason* lent itself to misunderstanding, especially among its first readers: "I might have seemed to favour the then popular notion that historical sequence is equivalent to moral progress," a view he not only did not hold but emphatically rejected: "from my earliest youth, this notion was my pet aversion: it seemed an insult to vanished honour and vanished beauty" ("Apologia," 557). In the chapter on Bergson Santayana commented that "the theory of evolution, taken enthusiastically, is apt to exercise an evil influence on the moral estimation of things" because it encourages the assumption "that later things are necessarily better than what they have grown out of: and this is false altogether."[16]

The success of *The Life of Reason* with both the general public and professional philosophers meant not only that the text was subjected to multiple misunderstandings but also that for the rest of his life everything else Santayana wrote was measured against *The Life of Reason*, usually with the suggestion that the later work did not live up to the standards set by the former. Irwin Edman was disappointed that "the architectonic humanism of *The Life of Reason*" eventually gave way to "the anarchic detachment of *The Realms of Being*"; Santayana's later philosophical works seemed a "post-humanism, an abdication of humanism."[17] This alleged "abdication" aroused what Santayana described as "personal animus" and "resentment" ("Apologia" 538, 560) because Edman and many others had invested so much in the secular, humanistic outlook they found in *The Life of Reason*. Santayana himself claimed that his philosophy had never changed, though his interests had altered. He had, furthermore, learned a few things after

1906, and his later writings were worth considering on their own merits. In a 1941 letter he blames the pragmatists for the over-estimation of *The Life of Reason* and the consequent under-appreciation of his other works: " . . . what annoys me is that now people should still talk about the *Life of Reason* as if it represented my whole philosophy, or was the best part of it. That is because Dewey's disciples make it a subject for their courses, and cricize [sic] it for not raising or not solving the questions that they propose to their classes. It is not me they are considering, but the convenience of having a readable book to use as a stalking horse, their own books not being readable." [18] Santayana acknowledged there was a difference of emphasis but found no contradiction between the stress on "reason" in the earlier work and on "spirit" in the later. There might be a "practical incompatibility between spirituality and humanism, between poetry and business, between sheer logic and sound sense," but there was no fundamental opposition: "the conflict is only marginal, the things are concentric." [19]

   When *The Life of Reason* was published Santayana, according to his autobiography *Persons and Places,* had already gone through the quiet transformation he calls his *metanoia,* his "change of heart." [20] Although believing that "for a poet and a lover of youth the age of thirty is itself a ground for *metanoia,*" Santayana lists three events that "helped to *disintoxicate*" his mind (423; italics in original): the death of his father, the marriage of his older sister, and the death of a friend and student, Warwick Potter. There was no religion or institution or person to which or to whom he could commit himself entirely — not Catholicism, not Harvard, and no individual. Teaching at the university "where philosophy was most modern, most deeply Protestant, most hopefully new," he could never be "a happy participator in the intellectual faith of my neighbours" (426). The young Santayana could retain his integrity only by accepting the role he was already inclined to adopt, that of an observer rather than a participant. He is careful to distinguish his own "final settlement of the moral problem" (427) from both bitter cynicism and ecstatic mysticism: "I had not been ravaged by any hostile fate; my heart had simply uttered a warning against its own weakness. It had said to me: Cultivate imagination, love it, give it endless forms, but do not let it deceive you. Enjoy the world, travel over it, and learn its ways, but do not let it hold you. Do not suffer it to oppress you with craving or with regret for the images that you may form of it. You will do the least harm and find the greatest satisfactions, if, being furnished as lightly as possible with possessions, you live freely among ideas. To possess things and persons in idea is the only pure good to be got out of them; to possess them physically or legally is a burden and a snare" (427–28).

Composing his autobiography during World War II while living in the convent of the Blue Nuns in Rome, Santayana could proudly attest that he had remained true to the way of life to which his "change of heart" had led him: "I have distributed my few possessions, eschewed chattels of every kind, a fixed residence, servants, carriages, or anything that would pin me down materially or engulf me in engagements. . . . I am happy in solitude and confinement, and the furious factions into which the world is divided inspire hatred for none of them in my heart" (422).

The strongest attachment of Santayana's life was to a British lord, John Francis Stanley Russell, Bertrand Russell's older brother and the second Earl Russell. The passages describing him in Santayana's autobiography make it clear that a large part of the fascination had to do with Russell's physical grace, all the more impressive in one who also possessed great wealth and high social standing: "He [Russell] moved deliberately, gracefully, stealthily, like a tiger well fed and with a broad margin of leisure for choosing his prey. There was precision in his indolence; and mild as he seemed, he suggested a latent capacity to leap, a latent astonishing celerity and strength, that could crush at one blow" (291). To the young Santayana every movement Russell made was impressive, including an act as routine as opening the mail: "Russell opened his letters with the tips of his strong fingers, without haste, without one needless movement or the least unnecessary force" (294). The clarity and straightforward tone of the autobiography make it clear that Santayana feels no need to either justify or conceal his feeling for Russell. Santayana exhibited the same lack of defensiveness in a conversation remembered by his assistant Daniel Cory; discussing the English poet and classical scholar A. E. Housman, Santayana commented "I suppose Housman was really what people nowadays call 'homosexual' " and added "I think I must have been that way in my Harvard days — although I was unconscious of it at the time."[21] Russell himself was at the opposite pole from Santayana in almost every way, including his athletic prowess, his social standing and personal wealth, his impulsiveness, his radical views on social and political matters, and the "excessive dominance" in his character "of the primitive male impulse to be masterful, despotic, and polygamous" (319). Throughout his life Russell exhibited what Santayana called a "headlong propensity to be re-entangled" (477), engaging in a series of affairs and marriages that sometimes ended in civil court cases, including the "disreputable Russell trial" where Santayana appeared as a witness, and once in a jail sentence for bigamy. Santayana remained loyal, no matter what. In regard to one particularly lurid scandal, Santayana commented "I wasn't going to desert Russell for that, or for anything" (299). Toward the end of his life Russell seems to have lost interest in Santayana, but even that made no difference to the philosopher: "I had lapsed into an old but unimportant acquaintance in his eyes, while in mine he remained the most interesting of mortals" (479).

For those concerned with Santayana's thought, perhaps the most important aspect of his character revealed in this relationship is his refusal to allow the strength of his feeling for Russell to affect Santayana's own independence of judgment. One of the most impressive examples of that independence occurs in a 1910 letter responding to a message in which Russell had proclaimed his sympathy for the Spanish anarchist Francisco Ferrer Guardia, accused of involvement in assassination plots. Santayana in reply not only makes clear his disagreement with Russell but goes on to take issue with Russell's congenital sympathy with rebellion in general. The passage is worth quoting at some length not only as a demonstration of Santayana's independence in relation to the man to whom he most wished to remain close but also because Santayana's reflections on the inextricability of a civilization's virtues and vices remain relevant today:

> As to the sympathy you betray, however, with Ferrer, and the present instigators and perpetrators of murder . . . I am separated from you *toto caelo.* . . . It is the presence of cowards in the government now, that encourages continued outrages and the disgraceful tone, in the revolutionary press in Spain and abroad, which makes it appear that the anarchists, who throw bombs, burn convents, and shoot at old gentlemen in railway stations, are the martyrs, and their victims the tyrants. . . . The tyrants in Spain are the anarchists and the revolutionary press; it is they that carry things with a high hand, and defend — and do — murder. . . . It is one thing to see the arbitrary and ultimately unstable character of a civilization (every civilization is essentially unstable) and another to set about destroying it by blind force. This latter system is hateful, because inspired only by hate: it has no ideal of a positive sort to inspire it, nor, if it had, could it attain that ideal merely by destroying what now exists. The want of intelligence is immense, that does not see that everything we have that makes (or might make) life worth living is an incident to the irrational, traditional civilization in which we have been reared. All things are like language, which he must use, beautify, but not worship; and your anarchists are mere blundering dumb beasts, that sputter and howl, because they find the rules of grammar absurd and inconvenient. So they are, for people too stupid or too ill-bred to use them, but that does not make these people martyrs, or heralds of progress.[22]

In August 1911 Santayana, having already decided to resign his professorship, expressed his considered judgment on the intellectual world of Harvard and Boston in a lecture at the University of California at Berkeley. "The Genteel Tradition in American Philosophy" makes use of the California setting by pointing to "your forests and your Sierras" as mute evidence that "the human distinction between good and evil" could not possibly be "the centre and pivot of the universe," in contrast to the anthropomorphic conceit of the genteel tradition. Santayana cites approvingly "a Californian" who has observed to him that "if the philosophers had lived among your mountains their systems would have been different from what they are" (19). The phrase "the genteel tradition" became popular with many who knew nothing at all about the philosophies of his colleagues William James, Josiah Royce, or, for that matter, Santayana himself. The conclusion of the lecture makes clear the difference between Santayana's own, immanent criticism of the genteel tradition and the attack on it by political and social rebels seeking to liberate their fellow citizens from sexual repression and material inequality. Santayana himself did not have any desire to adopt the pose of a rebel, any more than he was ready to join genteel philosophy in "white-washing and adoring things as they are" (17). When in his closing he called on the audience to free themselves from the genteel tradition and "be frankly human," he immediately made clear the kind of liberation he favored, adding "Let us be content to live in the mind" (20).

In "The Genteel Tradition" Santayana credits William James with having "given some rude shocks to this tradition" by expressing in philosophy "the genuine, the long silent American mind" heard otherwise only in the poetry of Walt Whitman. Santayana's most important teacher, colleague, and philosophical adversary, William James remains a major force in American culture, unlike Josiah Royce or Santayana himself. George Cotkin observed in 1990 that "the cultural and philosophical arbiters of our day increasingly turn to James for inspiration, direction, justification," and James's prestige has not declined in the twenty-first century.[23] Understanding what is at stake in Santayana's partial agreements and more significant disagreements with James goes far to clarifying some central issues in the culture wars of the twenty-first century.

One of the major sources for renewed interest in James is his ability to give philosophical support for what Cotkin calls the "Jamesian temperament of openness to difference and of tolerance for diversity" (136). James's philosophical advocacy of "openness" went beyond a defense of traditional liberal tolerance understood as the notion that views one may despise or abhor should be opposed by the advocacy of other views rather than silenced by coercion. James anticipated today's multiculturalists in arguing that it is not enough merely to acknowledge the legal right of others to hold ideas about God different from one's own. To tolerate while continuing to disapprove the religions or lifestyles of others is morally unsatisfactory according to multiculturalism; instead, one is called upon to "celebrate diversity" by learning to appreciate and value other religions or ways of life while renouncing a belief in the superiority of one's own. Similarly, when James defended "our right to adopt a believing attitude in religious matters" in his famous essay "The Will to Believe," he was not arguing for a legal right but rather for the moral and intellectual respectability of religious belief.[24] Influential thinkers such as T. H. Huxley and W. K. Clifford had argued that belief in the absence of evidence should not merely be avoided but should be condemned. James quotes Clifford's assertion that "It is wrong always, everywhere, and for anyone, to believe anything upon insufficient evidence" (462). James, however, warns against condemning anybody's belief, no matter how mistaken it may seem: "No one of us ought to issue vetoes to the other, nor should we bandy words of abuse. We ought, on the contrary, delicately and profoundly to respect one another's mental freedom—then only shall we bring about the intellectual republic; then only shall we have that spirit of inner tolerance without which all our outer tolerance is soulless, and which is empiricism's glory; then only shall we live and let live, in speculative as well as in practical things" (478). If James's conception of a "spirit of inner tolerance" against a mere "outer tolerance" that is "soulless" seems directly relevant to contemporary debates, there is reason to turn to his overall philosophy to find a principled basis for affirming the movement from tolerance to multiculturalism.

It is surely the case that multiculturalism needs some sort of philosophical justification. Though it has become the official philosophy of virtually every college and university in the United States, attempts to explicate its assumptions typically generate the sort of contradictions pointed out by Stanley Fish in his essay "Boutique Multiculturalism."[25] Fish's "boutique multiculturalism," characterized by its "superficial or cosmetic relationship to the objects of its affection" (56) is scarcely an intellectual position at all. "Strong multiculturalism," on the other hand, aims at intellectual seriousness but is eventually revealed as "not a distinct position but a somewhat deeper instance of the shallow category of boutique multiculturalism" (61). The strong version, like the shallower, eventually breaks down "because sooner or later the culture whose core values you are tolerating will reveal itself to be intolerant at that same core" (60). Fish concludes that "no one could possibly *be* a multiculturalist in any interesting or coherent sense" (63). Given such seemingly insoluble difficulties in the contemporary doctrine, we would be well-advised to return not only to James's anticipations but to the critiques Santayana offered, not only because of their intellectual merit but because they too offer a philosophical basis, and perhaps a surer one, for respecting "one another's mental freedom." James's defense of religious belief did not, Santayana observes, commit him to the actual truth of that belief: "He did not really believe; he merely believed in the right of believing that you might be right if you believed" (*Character and Opinion,* 56). So far, so good, one might say; the whole point of multiculturalism or James's "inner tolerance" is to grant the legitimacy of beliefs that you yourself do not share, to say and really feel that they are just as good as your own beliefs, even though for some reason or other you do not happen to share them. In the passage quoted from "The Will to Believe," James suggests that the "inner tolerance" he commends so highly is the fruit of his philosophical empiricism — it is "empiricism's glory" to foster respect for the ideas of others. Santayana points out, however, that James's version of empiricism carries with it a very definite view of reality that rules out any other, including orthodox religious doctrines and even the commonsense belief in the independent reality of external objects. For James "experience or mental discourse not only constituted a set of substantive facts, but the *only* substantive facts" (*Character and Opinion,* 53). His philosophy could not accept the possibility that one might find in religious doctrines what believers themselves find, "discoveries of absolute fact, which everybody else might be constrained to recognize" (55). James was more than willing to analyze religious experiences as psychological data, but his analyses never involved an inquiry as to whether the visions described in those experiences might tell the truth about the universe. Once a religious vision is reduced to a psychological case study, however, its significance as a source of knowledge about God and the afterlife is a dead issue. William James, Santayana suggests, was a sort of vivisectionist of religious experience: "He would tenderly vivisect the experiences in question, to show how living they were, though of course he could not guarantee, more than other surgeons do, that the patient would survive the operation. An operation that eventually kills may be technically successful, and the man may die cured; and so a description of religion that showed it to be madness might first show how real and how warm it was, so that if it perished, at least it would perish understood" (57).

In Santayana's view James's desire to be fair to all points of view did not prevent James from adhering to his own set of values, but it did prevent him from making those values explicit and defending them against other views,

as a philosopher should: "Aversions and fears imply principles of preference, goods acknowledged; and it is the philosopher's business to make
these goods explicit" (*Character and Opinion,* 61). James, however, refused to work out his own "principles of preference" in an explicit way,
though his writings demonstrate an unquestioning belief that, in Santayana's words, "certain thoughts and hopes — those familiar to a liberal
Protestantism — were every man's true friends in life" (59). In both his
commitment to the values of "liberal Protestantism" and in his failure to
make those values open to debate by making them explicit James remained
faithful to the genteel tradition, despite the vigor of his language and the
novelty of his pragmatism. In contrast, Santayana's commentary on American culture demonstrates his ability to make his own preferences clear
without condemning those with different preferences. Santayana has many
criticisms of American life. He objects to the democratic tendency to reduce "all things as far as possible to the common denominator of quantity"
while ignoring gradations of quality (100). It is clear that Santayana identifies himself with "the luckless American who is born a conservative, or
who is drawn to poetic subtlety, pious retreats, or gay passions" but is
doomed to have "the categorical excellence of work, growth, enterprise,
reform, and prosperity dinned into his ears" (94). Santayana could sum up
the culture of the United States as in large part "a flood of barbarism from
below" (23). And yet, despite these reservations, Santayana was also willing to consider the possibility that the American way of life, characterized
by "the spirit of free co-operation" (103) originated in England but brought
to full expression in America, "may last indefinitely, and can enlist every
reasonable man and nation in its service" (108). Santayana's analysis of
American culture in *Character and Opinion in the United States* is no
vivisection but a living portrait whose truth remains pertinent today.

What was it that was lacking in James's or Royce's philosophy but
integral to Santayana's outlook that facilitated his natural ability to sympathize with and appreciate viewpoints different from his own, while at the
same time criticizing them sharply though politely? It is an ability perhaps demonstrated most impressively in the portraits of William James and
Josiah Royce in *Character and Opinion in the United States* but observable
throughout Santayana's discussion on American culture and anywhere in
Santayana's many essays on literary and philosophical figures. Santayana's
ability to unite understanding and critique was surely fostered by his adherence to the traditional stance of the philosopher as a disinterested seeker
of truth for its own sake. In the postmodernist era a claim to seek truth for its

own sake is likely to be rejected out of hand. A study of Santayana's voluminous writings, however, suggests that he came closer than most to achieving this ideal. In Santayana's own view, the disinterested pursuit of truth is in any case not an heroic achievement but a source of pleasure, one that is always available. "Philosophers," observes Santayana, "have always had a royal road to complete satisfaction. One of the purest of pleasures, which they cultivate above all others, is the pleasure of understanding" (*Character and Opinion,* 69). Santayana rejected philosophical or mystical attempts to deny the reality of evil, but he did point out that from the point of view of the philosophical seeker of truth, all things are indeed good: "If we define the intellect as the power to see things as they are, it is clear that in so far as the philosopher is a pure intellect the universe will be a pure good to the philosopher; everything in it will give play to his exclusive passion. Wisdom counsels us therefore to become philosophers and to concentrate our lives as much as possible in pure intelligence, that we may be led by it into the ways of peace" (69).

Neither William James nor Josiah Royce was much interested in being led "into the ways of peace." Both saw the world as, in James's words, "a real fight, in which something is eternally gained for the universe by success," a battle between good and evil in which neutrality was impossible and one had to choose sides.[26] James declared that "Scepticism in moral matters is an active ally of immorality. Who is not for is against. The universe will have no neutrals in these questions."[27] For James "the deepest difference, practically, in the moral life of man is the difference between the easy-going and the strenuous mood," and for him the "strenuous mood" was the only one that made life worth living.[28] To many belief in God might seem a source of peace and consolation, but to James the practical value of belief lay in its incitement to strenuous exertion: "The capacity of the strenuous mood lies so deep down among our natural human possibilities that even if there were no metaphysical or traditional grounds for believing in a God, men would postulate one simply as a pretext for living hard, and getting out of the game of existence its keenest possibilities of zest" (616). On his account Royce found the justification for evil in the combat it incites: "The justification of the existence of my evil impulse comes just at the instant when I hate and condemn it. Condemning and conquering the evil will makes it part of a good will. . . . The good world is not innocent. It does not ignore evil; it possesses and still conquers evil" (*Spirit,* 459). Because both Royce and James saw the world as a battlefield between good and evil, they felt philosophically justified in devoting their energies and their talents to fighting for the good rather than disinterestedly seeking the truth for its own sake. Both felt an obligation to edify and inspire their students and their fellow citizens.

Santayana, on the other hand, felt no obligation to uplift or to fight for the right, and thus he was free to pursue the pleasure of understanding for its own sake. Santayana has been accused of selfishness, insensitivity, and a lack of compassion, charges that he scarcely bothered to deny, explaining "Certainly, I am profoundly selfish in the sense that I resist human contagion, except provisionally, on the surface, and in matters indifferent to me. . . . On the other hand, I am not selfish in a competitive way. I don't want to snatch money or position or pleasures from other people, nor do I attempt to dominate them, as an unselfish man would say, for their own good" (*Persons,* 515). We may leave aside the question of Santayana's personal moral standing while noting that his philosophical stance allowed him to make observations and draw conclusions that other, more committed or engaged thinkers would never have reached. One reason for Santayana's continuing relevance — if also for the undeserved neglect his works have suffered — is that his ideas cannot be enlisted by one side or the other of the culture wars without considerable distortion; he cannot be identified in any simple way as a liberal or a conservative, a progressive or a reactionary.

When Santayana left Harvard, he also left the United States for good. Traveling in Europe and England, he found himself in England at the beginning of World War I and stayed there until the end of the conflict. It was during and in the immediate aftermath of what was known to contemporaries as the Great War that Santayana wrote three works of cultural criticism, *Egotism in German Philosophy, Soliloquies in England,* and the study of American culture included in this volume. The lectures that were collected and published as *Character and Opinion in the United States* were first delivered to English audiences in the years immediately following the war. The first two chapters expand and clarify the thesis of "The Genteel Tradition in American Philosophy," while the two chapters on William James and Josiah Royce offer brilliant analyses of the extent to which the dominance of the genteel tradition prevented these two gifted philosophers from achieving the intellectual clarity they sought. Beyond the genteel tradition, Santayana finds that American society has encouraged "the disintegration of conventional categories" and "the impartial assemblage and mutual confrontation of all sorts of ideas." This refusal to take anything for granted might eventually lead to a more secure basis for philosophy, but at the present "never was the human mind master of so many facts and sure of so few principles" (90). Unlike many critics of American culture, both foreign and domestic, Santayana does not engage in wholesale condemnations or denunciations, rejecting, for example, the notion that the American's materialism is rooted in "love of the almighty dollar" (100). In his fine biography of Santayana John McCormick writes that *Character and Opinion in the United States* is "among the finest of his works . . . at once personal and objective, neither bitter nor sentimental. It offers a view of the country and a period that could not have been written by any American or foreign traveler, no matter what his gifts" (*Biography,* 246).

The impetus behind both *Egotism in German Philosophy* (1916) and *Soliloquies in England* (1922) is clearly the world war, though neither is a "war book," written to inspire one side and condemn the other. *Egotism in German Philosophy* is surely a powerful critique of German romantic idealism, and Santayana does argue that the dominant school of German philosophy encouraged a "spirit of uncompromising self-assertion and metaphysical conceit" that found expression in war.[29] Yet the book is neither a condemnation of the German people — Santayana begins by observing that "the majority of intelligent Germans hold views which German philosophy proper must entirely despise" (149) — nor even a condemnation of contemporary German policies, government, or armies, about all of which it says nothing. The book does, however, offer a persuasive case against philosophical idealism, with its tendency to reject the independent reality of things and even other people and, just as importantly, against the sort of romanticism that rejects the lessons of human experience embodied in traditional moral principles. Santayana observed that the "romantic will" takes pride in remaining "unteachable" (213), while idealism argues that there is nothing, after all, to be taught, given "the ultra-romantic and ultra-idealistic doctrine that the very notion of truth or fact is a fiction of the will, invented to satisfy our desire for some fixed point of reference in thought" (160).

Santayana's own family, including his beloved sister Susana, were, like many in Spain, hoping for a German victory, in the belief that the Germans were on the side of tradition and religion. Santayana himself preferred living in a traditional society, yet, as he writes in *Persons and Places,* "without so much as asking for a reason, my heart had been entirely on the English side in the war" (333). Just as he found much to respect about American society even though he considered the Declaration of Independence "a salad of illusions" (*Persons,* 404), so the deeply felt appreciation of English character expressed in *Soliloquies in England* was compatible with disdain for English parliamentary politics. For Santayana "what governs the Englishman is his inner atmosphere, the weather in his soul" prior to and better than any doctrines: "It gives a sense of direction in life which is virtually a code of ethics, and a religion behind religion. On the other hand, to say it was the vision of any ideal or allegiance to any princi- ple would be making it far too articulate and abstract. . . . It is a mass of dumb instincts and allegiances, the love of a certain quality of life, to be maintained manfully."[30] Santayana admired the bravery of the British sol- diers especially because he felt that they fought without the support of philosophy or ideology, "without so much as asking for a reason": "Caught by the impulse of the hour, they rose . . . cheerily, rashly, to meet the unforeseen, fatal, congenial adventure, the goal not seen, the air not mea- sured, but the firm heart steady through the fog or blinding fire, making the best of what came, trembling but ready for what might come, with a simple courage which was half joy in living and half willingness to die" (111–12).

The publication in 1923 of *Scepticism and Animal Faith* with its subtitle *Introduction to a System of Philosophy* marked the official beginning of the later phase of Santayana's philosophical career. Both earlier and later, how- ever, Santayana's goal was never to invent a philosophy of his own but to clarify and refine the "human orthodoxy" he found assumed everywhere but articulated only occasionally and partially. The introduction to *Scepti- cism and Animal Faith* immediately qualifies and almost reverses its open- ing assertion — "Here is one more system of philosophy" — by assuring the reader in declarations italicized for emphasis that *"my system is not mine, or new"* but is simply a more consistent, more explicit version of the assumptions of the unphilosophic general reader. His "system" provides *"no system of the universe"* and thus is *"not metaphysical"* (italics in original).[31] Santayana explains "I have a great respect for orthodoxy . . . for a certain shrewd orthodoxy which the sentiment and practice of laymen maintain everywhere. . . . I am animated by distrust of all high guesses, and by sympathy with the old prejudices and workaday opinions of mankind: they are ill expressed, but they are well grounded. What novelty my version of things may possess is meant simply to obviate occasions for sophistry by giving to everyday beliefs a more accurate and circumspect form" (3).

In a 1915 essay, "Philosophical Heresy," Santayana had argued that the very attempt to work out a system of philosophy was mistaken: "Viewed from a sufficient distance, all systems of philosophy are seen to be personal, temperamental, accidental, and premature. They treat partial knowledge as if it were total knowledge: they take peripheral facts for central and typical facts: they confuse the grammar of human expression, in language, logic, or moral estimation, with the substantial structure of things. In a word, they are human heresies."[32] They are heresies, that is, against the "human orthodoxy" that Santayana describes as "merely the current imagination and good sense of mankind — something traditional, conventional, incoherent, and largely erroneous . . . yet something ingenuous, practically acceptable, fundamentally sound, and capable of correcting its own innocent errors" (197–98). In 1915 he envisioned "two ways in which philosophy might be achieved without heterodoxy." One seemed impossible: the way of "comprehensive synthesis; a speculation so evenly inspired and broadly based that it should report the system or the medley of known things without twisting any of them." The more practicable alternative would lie "in confessing that a system of philosophy is a personal work of art which gives a specious unity to some chance vista in the cosmic labyrinth" (200–201). The 1915 essay insists that a system that eludes categorization as simply another heresy must "renounce all claim to be a system of the universe" (202), a renunciation Santayana does indeed make in *Scepticism and Animal Faith.*

But can a philosophy that "is a personal work of art" also be true to "human orthodoxy"? More specifically, could it be possible for a man like Santayana, seemingly so detached from ordinary human passions, with a style marked by formal elegance and writing on topics like the realm of truth or the realm of spirit, to still remain in touch with common humanity? Without attempting a definitive answer, one can observe that throughout the four volumes of *Realms of Being* Santayana repeatedly connects his ideas to the "orthodoxy" shared by non-philosophers. Thus he opens *The Realm of Truth* by declaring proudly, "An unsophisticated reader will find no difficulty in understanding the sense in which the word truth is used in this book."[33] In concluding the last volume of *Realms of Being, The Realm of Spirit,* Santayana was happy to point out the parallels between his "realms" and traditional Christian theology, despite the metaphysical gap between his materialistic naturalism and Christian doctrine. Santayana was offering only "a language," while Christianity required a "dogma"; whatever questions of fact might arise about the dogma, the last two thousand years had demonstrated that the language provided a vocabulary allowing human beings to make sense of their lives.[34]

Santayana proved his ability to speak to the general reader in his only novel, *The Last Puritan,* a Book-of-the-Month selection and a bestseller when published in the United States in 1936. Subtitled *A Memoir in the Form of a Novel,* it recreates the intellectual and emotional climate of New England before World War I. The story of Oliver Alden, the "last puritan" of the title, dramatizes what Santayana calls in the preface "the essential tragedy of the late-born Puritan" as he had seen it exemplified in the lives and early deaths of "five or six young Harvard poets in the 1880's and 1890's."[35] Santayana knew that the genteel tradition not only could not be identified with Puritanism but that it stifled what was honest and most vital in the Puritan heritage, vitiating not only religious expression but art and literature as well. He had observed in his 1911 lecture that "when a genteel tradition forbids people to confess that they are unhappy, serious poetry and profound religion are closed to them by that" (11). Oliver Alden is only able to confess his own unhappiness to himself after his marriage proposals are rejected by two women, the first time politely, the second time more emphatically — Rose Darnley asks him, " 'Can't you see that I would rather die than marry you?' " (550). Only after this humiliating rebuff is he able to come to terms with his "true life," his "deeper self" (551). Only then is he able to accept the consequences of his "dreadful inheritance . . . that I need to be honest, that I need to be true, that I need to be just." Recognizing that people like himself are "a belated phenomenon" (553), he gives up his hopes of personal happiness and of reforming the world: "Enough if at all times I practice charity, and keep myself as much as possible from complicity in wrong" (555).

Santayana found refuge from World War II in the clinic of the Blue Nuns in Rome, where he remained from 1941 until his death in 1952 a few months before his eighty-ninth birthday. Many American servicemen visited him after the liberation of Rome, apparently much to his pleasure as well as theirs. He wrote in a December 1944 letter that "A great many army men have come to see me, as the oldest living inhabitant. . . . I tell the Sisters that I was never happier in my life than I am here . . ." (*Letters* 7:112). More than a year later, visitors were still arriving: "A lot of army men have come to see me, as the oldest inhabitant of the village, and overwhelmed me with presents and other favours" (*Letters* 7:129). Santayana was apparently ready to discuss philosophical questions with anybody who wanted to talk with him, regardless of his or her professional standing. In a February 1946 letter he addresses "Lieutenant Garcia" as an intellectual equal in an ongoing conversation: "That you should think Plato good but not true, and should at the same time follow Darwin with approval would seem to indicate that you instinctively think as I think. . . . Of course, if you hanker for a physically real *good* world, you will never find it, and it may seem to you discouraging spiritually that spirit should not rule the universe. That would seem to me a pity, and a lack of caution in not keeping truth and imagination in their respective places. Is that what makes you uncomfortable?" (*Letters* 7:221).

Visiting in 1945, the literary critic Edmund Wilson was at first "nonplussed and embarrassed" to find that Santayana apparently did not know who he was, but Wilson soon realized that all Santayana "had to know about me in order to talk of himself was that I was one of his readers."[36] Santayana seemed to Wilson a contemporary example of an ancient type: "the sage who has made it his business to meet and to reflect on all kinds of men and who will talk about the purpose and practice of life with anyone who liked to discuss them — as with me, whom he didn't know from Adam — since these are matters which concern us all." Wilson found it "at the same time respect-inspiring and disturbing to one's wartime preoccupations to find this little husk of a man, at once so ascetic and so cheerful, sustaining at eighty-one so steady an intellectual energy . . . intact and unmoved by the tides of invasion and revolution that had been brawling back and forth around him" (46). Wilson's portrait of Santayana "intact and unmoved" provided a model for Wallace Stevens's even more eloquent tribute, "To an Old Philosopher in Rome," where he envisions Santayana as "The one invulnerable man among / Crude captains . . ."[37]

The high estimation of Santayana shared by Stevens and Wilson became a minority view during the quarter-century or so after the philosopher's death in 1952. It was unfortunate for Santayana's reputation that the last book published during his lifetime was his *Dominations and Powers: Reflections on Liberty, Society and Government.* Though an impressive accomplishment for a man nearing ninety, *Dominations and Powers* is not one of Santayana's strongest works; it lacks the incisive criticism from within — immanent criticism — that marks Santayana's critiques of American, English, and German culture earlier in the century. The book's failure to mention, let alone respond to, Hitler's nearly successful attempt to murder all the Jews within reach called attention to Santayana's lifelong inability to transcend the prejudice against Jews typical of his era and milieu. It is true that Santayana had never been an apologist for Nazism. He had recognized it from the first as "a sort of romanticism gone mad," as he described it in a 1934 letter to Sidney Hook,[38] and thus an extreme version of the romanticism he had analyzed and warned against in 1915 as a "false religion" giving rise to a "religious tyranny" whose "victims," Santayana declared, "in some degree, are all men" (*Egotism,* 146–47, 195). In 1925 when the American writer John Jay Chapman asked Santayana to become the president of the "Aryan Society," the philosopher declined, asking "Against whom is the Aryan Society directed?" and suggesting that if the Society truly "stood for the life of reason," it might have to be "especially directed against the Aryans," given the lack of sanity in the supposed Aryan strongholds of Europe and America. Santayana advised Chapman that "races, like nations, seem an unfortunate class of units to identify with moral ideas."[39]

Dominations and Powers was criticized, fairly enough, for its failure to address the Nazi genocide, but it was also criticized, less fairly, for the author's unwillingness to take sides on contemporary political questions. Santayana had made it clear that the book was not intended "to proclaim a political creed,"[40] but clearly many readers wanted just that from him. John Yolton's rhetorical question condemning Santayana's apparent neutrality in *Dominations and Powers* as "philosophic lassitude" was representative: "Are we to stand aside with philosophic lassitude when we see the capitalistic system making economic slaves of vast layers of our American population, when we see that same system resorting to political witch-hunts against all liberal non-conformists, when we see slavery and oppression running rampant in the eastern areas of the world?"[41]

Santayana had no wish to found a school or foster disciples. He was not interested in encouraging movements or instigating reforms. It seems impossible as well as ill-advised to reduce his thought to a series of slogans on behalf of any particular political program or doctrine, and he believed that Americans would in any case go their own way, regardless of the advice offered by philosophers. Today many would-be prophets and earnest reformers demand our attention, threatening that the fall of Western civilization will be averted only if their advice is heeded. Santayana took a different tack. In the preface to *Character and Opinion in the United States* he confronted the possibility of the dissolution of Western culture with equanimity, speculating that life would be renewed somehow. He even suggested, slyly, that the catastrophe and the renewal had already occurred — "both this destruction and this restoration have already occurred in America" (24). For what purpose, then, did Santayana work out his analysis of American culture and society? He himself claimed "I have no axe to grind, only my thoughts to burnish" (23). Whether or not we can entirely believe in such detachment, it is a relief to read an author who is not out to frighten or even to inspire but simply to tell the truth as he sees it. We may be ready to learn from a thinker who explicitly disclaimed the role of prophet or reformer but observed that "the critic and artist too have their rights, and to take as calm and as long a view as possible seems to be but another name for the love of truth" (23).

Today, more than fifty years after Santayana's death, there has been a modest revival of interest in Santayana, signaled most clearly by the progress of a new critical edition of all of Santayana's writings that so far includes *Persons and Places, The Last Puritan, The Sense of Beauty, Inter-*

pretations of Poetry and Religion, and eight books of his letters, all published by MIT Press. It should now be possible to study his works with
some of the same philosophic detachment about Santayana himself that he
commended and, to an impressive degree, practiced in regard to the world
at large. One can freely concede Santayana's flaws and limitations and yet
recognize that his unique perspective in relation to American culture in
particular allowed him insights that not only illuminate the world of his
own time but our world today. Wilfred McClay believes that Santayana's
emphasis on the importance of the life of the mind is perhaps more valuable today than when it was written as a corrective to the dominant trends in
American culture. He nevertheless warns against a "strain of irresponsibility" (139) in Santayana's outlook, notes his genteel anti-Semitism,
and points out that his judgments on contemporary politics were often
misguided, as in his partial approval of Mussolini. John Lachs finds Santayana's contrast between "absolute liberty" and "English liberty" an excellent framework for understanding why people from ethnic groups and
nations at war with one another outside the United States are able to live
at peace within its borders. Lachs argues, however, that Santayana under-
rates the importance of prosperity and material abundance and, like many
philosophers and cultural critics, overrates the importance of contempla-
tion. Roger Kimball observes that Santayana could be "naïve if not obtuse"
(185) about contemporary politics but commends both his critique of liberalism in general and his appreciative understanding of "English liberty" in
the United States. Kimball points to the contemporary relevance of Santayana's concept of a "genteel tradition," though today's version honors
neither tradition nor gentility. Similarly, my own essay argues that Santayana's critique of "The Genteel Tradition in American Philosophy" goes
far to explain the contradictions in the stance of the postmodernist left
today, with its unstable union of moral certainties and epistemological skepticism. My essay joins the others in arguing for the continuing fruitfulness of Santayana's distinction between "English liberty" and "absolute
liberty," adding that Santayana's portrait of American culture is even more
significant when contrasted with his susceptibility to considering nations
and cultures by aesthetic rather than moral and political criteria. None
of the contributors contend that Santayana's philosophy should be accepted
in its entirety, but all agree on the continuing value of Santayana as an
acute commentator on human life and a cultural critic who was at his
most perceptive in his observations on the society and culture of the United
States.

NOTES

1. George Santayana, "Apologia Pro Menta Sua," *The Philosophy of George Santayana,* ed. Paul Arthur Schlipp, The Library of Living Philosophers, Vol. II (LaSalle, IL: Open Court, 1991), 495–605, p. 603. First published in 1940. Hereafter cited as "Apologia" in the text.

2. The following biographical details are taken from John McCormick's *George Santayana: A Biography* (New York: Knopf, 1987), 3–16. Hereafter cited as *Biography.*

3. George Santayana, *Persons and Places: Fragments of Autobiography,* ed. William G. Holzberger and Herman J. Saatkamp, Jr., The Works of George Santayana, Vol. I (Cambridge, MA: MIT Press, 1987), p. 322. Hereafter cited as *Persons,* unless the context makes it clear that this title is being cited, in which case the passage will be identified by a page number in the text.

4. Santayana discusses the situation leading up to the trial and its impact on Russell in *Persons and Places,* 315–20.

5. George Santayana, *The Sense of Beauty: Being the Outlines of Aesthetic Theory,* ed. William G. Holzberger and Herman J. Saatkamp, Jr., The Works of George Santayana, Vol. II (Cambridge, MA: MIT Press, 1988), p. 9. First published in 1896. Quotations from this volume in the immediately following passage are cited by page number.

6. George Santayana, *Interpretations of Poetry and Religion,* ed. William G. Holzberger and Herman J. Saatkamp, Jr. The Works of George Santayana, Vol. III (Cambridge, MA: MIT Press, 1989), p. 3. First published in 1900. Following quotations from this volume in this paragraph and the next one are cited by page number.

7. *Reason in Science, The Life of Reason,* The Works of George Santayana, Triton Edition, Vol. V (New York: Charles Scribner's Sons, 1936), p. 74. Hereafter cited as *Reason in Science* unless the context makes it clear that this title is being cited, in which case the passage will be identified by page number.

8. William James, "On Some Hegelisms," *The Will to Believe and Other Essays in Popular Philosophy, William James: Writings 1878–1899* (New York: Literary Classics of the United States, 1992), 653–79, p. 653. "On Some Hegelisms" was first published in *Mind* in April, 1882; *The Will to Believe and Other Essays in Popular Philosophy* was first published in 1897.

9. Josiah Royce, *The Spirit of Modern Philosophy: An Essay in the Form of Lectures* (New York: Norton, 1967), pp. vi, xiv. Hereafter cited as *Spirit,* unless the context makes it clear that this title is being cited, in which case the passage will be identified by page number. *The Spirit of Modern Philosophy* was originally published in 1892.

10. Jacques Derrida, *Of Grammatology,* trans. Gayatri Chakravorty Spivak

(Baltimore: Johns Hopkins University Press, 1976), p. 158. Published as *De la Grammatologie* in 1967.

11. See, for example, Sandra G. Harding, *The Science Question in Feminism* (Ithaca, NY: Cornell University Press, 1986) and *Feminist Science Studies: A New Generation,* ed. Maralee Mayberry, Banu Subramaniam, and Lisa H. Weasel (New York: Routledge, 2001).

12. Paul R. Gross and Norman Levitt, *Higher Superstition: The Academic Left and Its Quarrels with Science* (Baltimore: Johns Hopkins University Press, 1994).

13. Santayana, on the other hand, believed that the assumption of such an external reality was the indispensable starting point of any inquiry into the nature of things: "The postulate of substance — the assumption that there are things and events prior to the discovery of them and independent of this discovery — underlies all natural knowledge." *The Realm of Matter,* The Works of George Santayana, Triton Edition, Vol. VII (New York: Charles Scribner's Sons, 1937), p. 185.

14. *The Life of Reason* (Amherst, NY: Prometheus Books, 1998), back cover.

15. For Dewey, Darwin's theory of evolution was of central importance not only for science but also for philosophy; according to Dewey, Darwin "introduced a mode of thinking that in the end was bound to transform the logic of knowledge, and hence the treatment of morals, politics, and religion" ("The Influence of Darwin on Philosophy," *The Influence of Darwin on Philosophy and Other Essays in Contemporary Though*t [New York: Peter Smith, 1951], 1–19, p. 2). Originally published in 1919.

16. George Santayana, "The Philosophy of M. Henri Bergson," *Winds of Doctrine,* The Works of George Santayana, Triton Edition, Vol. VII (New York: Charles Scribner's Sons, 1937), 49–90, pp. 50–51.

17. Irwin Edman, "Humanism and Post-Humanism in the Philosophy of Santayana," *The Philosophy of George Santayana,* ed. Paul Arthur Schlipp. The Library of Living Philosophers, Vol. II (LaSalle, IL: Open Court, 1991), 293–312, pp. 310–11. First published in 1940.

18. George Santayana, Letter to Nancy Saunders Toy, *The Letters of George Santayana,* Book Seven, 1941–1947, ed. William G. Holzberger, The Works of George Santayana, Vol. V (Cambridge, MA: MIT Press, 2006), p. 27. Hereafter cited as *Letters* 7.

19. George Santayana, "On the Unity of My Earlier and Later Philosophy," The Works of George Santayana, Triton Edition, Vol. VII (New York: Charles Scribner's Sons, 1937), vii–xv, p. xii.

20. Chapter XXV of *Persons and Places,* where Santayana describes his *metanoia,* is entitled "A Change of Heart."

21. Daniel Cory, *Santayana: The Later Years: A Portrait with Letters* (New York: George Braziller, 1963), p. 40.

22. George Santayana, Letter to John Francis Stanley Russell, *The Letters of George Santayana,* Book Two, 1910–1920, ed. William G. Holzberger, The Works of George Santayana, Vol. V (Cambridge, MA: MIT Press, 2002), p. 16.

23. George Cotkin, *William James, Public Philosopher* (Baltimore: Johns Hopkins University Press, 1990), p. 2. The following quotation from this book is cited by page number in the text.

24. William James, "The Will to Believe," *The Will to Believe and Other Essays in Popular Philosophy, William James: Writings 1878–1899* (New York: Literary Classics of the United States, 1992), 457–79, p. 457. Following quotations from this essay are cited by page number in the text.

25. Stanley Fish, "Boutique Multiculturalism," *The Trouble with Principle* (Cambridge, MA: Harvard University Press, 1999), 56–72. Following quotations from this essay are cited by page numbers in the text.

26. William James, "Is Life Worth Living?" *The Will to Believe and Other Essays in Popular Philosophy, William James: Writings 1878–1899* (New York: Literary Classics of the United States, 1992), 480–503, p. 502.

27. William James, "The Sentiment of Rationality," *The Will to Believe and Other Essays in Popular Philosophy, William James: Writings 1878–1899* (New York: Literary Classics of the United States, 1992), 504–39, p. 538.

28. William James, "The Moral Philosopher and the Moral Life," *The Will to Believe and Other Essays in Popular Philosophy, William James: Writings 1878–1899* (New York: Literary Classics of the United States, 1992), p. 615. The following quotation from this essay is cited by page number in the text.

William James's brother Henry James seems to have been less sure that the "strenuous mood" was to be preferred, though one of his protagonists believes that a similar division is the "simplest" if not the "deepest" way to distinguish between personalities. In James's 1886 novel *The Bostonians* the Southern conservative Basil Ransom competes with the feminist Olive Chancellor for the love of Verena Tarrant. In the conclusion of the novel Verena deserts Olive Chancellor to marry Ransom. Basil Ransom, the narrator informs the reader, believes "that the simplest division it is possible to make of the human race is into the people who take things hard and the people who take them easy." On meeting Olive Chancellor for the first time, he notices "very quickly that Miss Chancellor belonged to the former class. . . . He himself, by nature, took things easy" (Henry James, *The Bostonians* [New York: Penguin, 2000], p. 10).

29. George Santayana, *Egotism in German Philosophy,* The Works of George Santayana, Triton Edition, Vol. VI (New York: Charles Scribner's Sons, 1936), 143–249, p. 146. First published in 1916. Following quotations from this volume in this paragraph are cited by page number in the text. Thereafter cited as *Egotism.*

30. George Santayana, *Soliloquies in England and Later Soliloquies,* The Works

of George Santayana, Triton Edition, Vol. IX (New York: Charles Scribner's Sons, 1937), p. 36. First published in 1922. Following quotations from this volume in this paragraph are cited by page number.

31. George Santayana, *Scepticism and Animal Faith: Introduction to a System of Philosophy,* The Works of George Santayana, Triton Edition, Vol. XIII (New York: Charles Scribner's Sons, 1937), 1–275, pp. 3–4. First published in 1923. The following quotation from this volume in this paragraph is cited by page number in the text.

32. George Santayana, "Philosophical Heresy." The Works of George Santayana, Triton Edition, Vol. VIII (New York: Charles Scribner's Sons, 1937), 195–207, p. 197. First published in 1915. Following quotations from this volume in this paragraph are cited by page number in the text.

33. George Santayana, *The Realm of Truth, Realms of Being,* The Works of George Santayana, Triton Edition, Vol. XV (New York: Charles Scribner's Sons, 1940), 1–144, p. 3.

34. George Santayana, *The Realm of Spirit, Realms of Being,* The Works of George Santayana, Triton Edition, Vol. XV (New York: Charles Scribner's Sons, 1940), 145–449, p. 449.

35. George Santayana, *The Last Puritan: A Memoir in the Form of a Novel,* ed. William G. Holzberger and Herman J. Saatkamp, Jr., The Works of George Santayana, Vol. IV (Cambridge, MA: MIT Press, 1994), p. 5. Following quotations from this volume are cited by page number.

36. Edmund Wilson, "A Visit to Santayana," *Europe without Baedeker: Sketches among the Ruins of Italy, Greece, and England* (New York: Noonday, 1966), 41–55, p. 44. First published in 1947. Immediately following quotations from this essay are cited by page number in the text.

37. Wallace Stevens, "To an Old Philosopher in Rome." *The Collected Poems of Wallace Stevens* (New York: Alfred A. Knopf, 1964), 508–11, p. 510.

38. George Santayana, Letter to Sidney Hook, *The Letters of George Santayana,* Book Five, 1933–1936, ed. William G. Holzberger, The Works of George Santayana, Vol. V (Cambridge, MA: MIT Press, 2003), p. 116.

39. George Santayana, Letter to John Jay Chapman, *The Letters of George Santayana,* Book Three, 1921–1927, ed. William G. Holzberger, The Works of George Santayana, Vol. V (Cambridge, MA: MIT Press, 2002), pp. 294–95. In the same letter questioning Aryan superiority, Santayana allowed himself to "confess that I don't like the Jewish spirit, because it is worldly, seeing God in thrift and success" (p. 295). He added, "I know nothing of the blacks," an ignorance he shared with many who have not been deterred, in 1925 or later, from making sweeping, usually negative, generalizations about people of African descent. Given Santayana's dislike of what he called "the Jewish spirit" and his ignorance about

"blacks," it is all the more noteworthy that he refused to use Darwinism either to support his prejudice or to replace ignorance with specious science at a time (the 1920s) when many at both ends of the political spectrum were doing both.

40. George Santayana, *Dominations and Powers: Reflections on Liberty, Society, and Government* (New Brunswick, NJ: Transaction Publishers, 1995), p. 461. Originally published in 1950.

41. John W. Yolton, "The Psyche as Social Determinant," *Journal of Philosophy,* Vol. XLIX, No. 7 (March 27, 1952), 232–39, p. 238.

The Genteel Tradition in
American Philosophy

THE GENTEEL TRADITION
IN AMERICAN PHILOSOPHY*

Ladies and Gentlemen: The privilege of addressing you to-day is very welcome to me, not merely for the honor of it, which is great, nor for the pleasures of travel, which are many, when it is California that one is visiting for the first time, but also because there is something I have long wanted to say which this occasion seems particularly favorable for saying. America is still a young country, and this part of it is especially so; and it would have been nothing extraordinary if, in this young country, material preoccupations had altogether absorbed people's minds, and they had been too much engrossed in living to reflect upon life, or to have any philosophy. The opposite, however, is the case. Not only have you already found time to philosophize in California, as your society proves, but the eastern colonists from the very beginning were a sophisticated race. As much as in clearing the land and fighting the Indians they were occupied, as they expressed it, in wrestling with the Lord. The country was new, but the race was tried, chastened, and full of solemn memories. It was an old wine in new bottles; and America did not have to wait for its present universities, with their departments of academic philosophy, in order to possess a living philosophy, — to have a distinct vision of the universe and definite convictions about human destiny.

Now this situation is a singular and remarkable one, and has many consequences, not all of which are equally fortunate. America is a young country with an old mentality: it has enjoyed the advantages of a child carefully brought up, and thoroughly indoctrinated; it has been a wise child. But a wise child, an old head on young shoulders, always has a comic and an unpromising side. The wisdom is a little thin and verbal, not aware of its full meaning and grounds; and physical and emotional growth may be stunted by it, or even deranged. Or when the child is too vigorous for that, he will develop a fresh mentality of his own, out of his observations and actual instincts; and this fresh mentality will interfere with the traditional

*Address delivered before the Philosophical Union, Aug. 25, 1911.

mentality, and tend to reduce it to something perfunctory, conventional, and perhaps secretly despised. A philosophy is not genuine unless it inspires and expresses the life of those who cherish it. I do not think the hereditary philosophy of America has done much to atrophy the natural activities of the inhabitants; the wise child has not missed the joys of youth or of manhood; but what has happened is that the hereditary philosophy has grown stale, and that the academic philosophy afterwards developed has caught the stale odor from it. America is not simply, as I said a moment ago, a young country with an old mentality: it is a country with two mentalities, one a survival of the beliefs and standards of the fathers, the other an expression of the instincts, practice, and discoveries of the younger generations. In all the higher things of the mind — in religion, in literature, in the moral emotions — it is the hereditary spirit that still prevails, so much so that Mr. Bernard Shaw finds that America is a hundred years behind the times. The truth is that that one-half of the American mind, that not occupied intensely in practical affairs, has remained, I will not say high-and-dry, but slightly becalmed; it has floated gently in the backwater, while, alongside, in invention and industry and social organization the other half of the mind was leaping down a sort of Niagara Rapids. This division may be found symbolized in American architecture: a neat reproduction of the colonial mansion — with some modern comforts introduced surreptitiously — stands beside the sky-scraper. The American Will inhabits the sky-scraper; the American Intellect inhabits the colonial mansion. The one is the sphere of the American man; the other, at least predominantly, of the American woman. The one is all aggressive enterprise; the other is all genteel tradition.

Now, with your permission, I should like to analyze more fully how this interesting situation has arisen, how it is qualified, and whither it tends. And in the first place we should remember what, precisely, that philosophy was which the first settlers brought with them into the country. In strictness there was more than one; but we may confine our attention to what I will call Calvinism, since it is on this that the current academic philosophy has been grafted. I do not mean exactly the Calvinism of Calvin, or even of Jonathan Edwards; for in their systems there was much that was not pure philosophy, but rather faith in the externals and history of revelation. Jewish and Christian revelation was interpreted by these men, however, in the spirit of a particular philosophy, which might have arisen under any sky, and been associated with any other religion as well as with Protestant Christianity. In fact, the philosophical principle of Calvinism appears also in the Koran, in Spinoza, and in Cardinal Newman; and persons with no very distinctive

Christian belief, like Carlyle or like Professor Royce, may be nevertheless, philosophically, perfect Calvinists. Calvinism, taken in this sense, is an expression of the agonized conscience. It is a view of the world which an agonized conscience readily embraces, if it takes itself seriously, as, being agonized, of course it must. Calvinism, essentially, asserts three things: that sin exists, that sin is punished, and that it is beautiful that sin should exist to be punished. The heart of the Calvinist is therefore divided between tragic concern at his own miserable condition, and tragic exultation about the universe at large. He oscillates between a profound abasement and a paradoxical elation of the spirit. To be a Calvinist philosophically is to feel a fierce pleasure in the existence of misery, especially of one's own, in that this misery seems to manifest the fact that the Absolute is irresponsible or infinite or holy. Human nature, it feels, is totally depraved: to have the instincts and motives that we necessarily have is a great scandal, and we must suffer for it; but that scandal is requisite, since otherwise the serious importance of being as we ought to be would not have been vindicated.

To those of us who have not an agonized conscience this system may seem fantastic and even unintelligible; yet it is logically and intently thought out from its emotional premises. It can take permanent possession of a deep mind here and there, and under certain conditions it can become epidemic. Imagine, for instance, a small nation with an intense vitality, but on the verge of ruin, ecstatic and distressful, having a strict and minute code of laws, that paint life in sharp and violent chiaroscuro, all pure righteousness and black abominations, and exaggerating the consequences of both perhaps to infinity. Such a people were the Jews after the exile, and again the early Protestants. If such a people is philosophical at all, it will not improbably be Calvinistic. Even in the early American communities many of these conditions were fulfilled. The nation was small and isolated; it lived under pressure and constant trial; it was acquainted with but a small range of goods and evils. Vigilance over conduct and an absolute demand for personal integrity were not merely traditional things, but things that practical sages, like Franklin and Washington, recommended to their countrymen, because they were virtues that justified themselves visibly by their fruits. But soon these happy results themselves helped to relax the pressure of external circumstances, and indirectly the pressure of the agonized conscience within. The nation became numerous; it ceased to be either ecstatic or distressful; the high social morality which on the whole it preserved took another color; people remained honest and helpful out of good sense and good will rather than out of scrupulous adherence to any fixed principles. They retained their instinct for order, and often created order with surprising quickness; but the sanctity of law, to be obeyed for its own sake, began to escape them; it seemed too unpractical a notion, and not quite serious. In fact, the second and native-born American mentality began to take shape. The sense of sin totally evaporated. Nature, in the words of Emerson, was all beauty and commodity; and while operating on it laboriously, and drawing quick returns, the American began to drink in inspiration from it aesthetically. At the same time, in so broad a continent, he had elbow-room. His neighbors helped more than they hindered him; he wished their number to increase. Good-will became the great American virtue; and a passion arose for counting heads, and square miles, and cubic feet, and minutes saved — as if there had been anything to save them for. How strange to the American now that saying of Jonathan Edwards, that men are naturally God's enemies! Yet that is an axiom to any intelligent Calvinist, though the words he uses may be different. If you told the modern American that he is totally depraved, he would think you were joking, as he himself usually is. He is convinced that he always has been, and always will be, victorious and blameless.

Calvinism thus lost its basis in American life. Some emotional natures, indeed, reverted in their religious revivals or private searchings of heart to the sources of the tradition; for any of the radical points of view in philosophy may cease to be prevalent, but none can case to be possible. Other natures, more sensitive to the moral and literary influences of the world, preferred to abandon parts of their philosophy, hoping thus to reduce the distance which should separate the remainder from real life.

Meantime, if anybody arose with a special sensibility or a technical genius, he was in great straits; not being fed sufficiently by the world, he was driven in upon his own resources. The three American writers whose personal endowment was perhaps the finest — Poe, Hawthorne, and Emerson — had all a certain starved and abstract quality. They could not retail the genteel tradition; they were too keen, too perceptive, and too independent for that. But life offered them little digestible material, nor were they naturally voracious. They were fastidious, and under the circumstances they were starved. Emerson, to be sure, fed on books. There was a great catholicity in his reading; and he showed a fine tact in his comments, and in his way of appropriating what he read. But he read transcendentally, not historically, to learn what he himself felt, not what others might have felt before him. And to feed on books, for a philosopher or a poet, is still to starve. Books can help him to acquire form, or to avoid pitfalls; they cannot supply him with substance, if he is to have any. Therefore the genius of Poe and Hawthorne, and even of Emerson, was employed on a sort of inner play, or digestion of vacancy. It was a refined labor, but it was in danger of being morbid, or tinkling, or self-indulgent. It was a play of intra-mental rhymes. Their mind was like an old music-box, full of tender echoes and quaint fancies. These fancies expressed their personal genius sincerely, as dreams may; but they were arbitrary fancies in comparison with what a real observer would have said in the premises. Their manner, in a word, was subjective. In their own persons they escaped the mediocrity of the genteel tradition, but they supplied nothing to supplant it in other minds.

The churches, likewise, although they modified their spirit, had no philosophy to offer save a selection or a new emphasis on parts of what Calvinism contained. The theology of Calvin, we must remember, had much in it besides philosophical Calvinism. A Christian tenderness, and a hope of grace for the individual, came to mitigate its sardonic optimism; and it was these evangelical elements that the Calvinistic churches now emphasized, seldom and with blushes referring to hell-fire or infant damnation. Yet philosophic Calvinism, with a theory of life that would perfectly justify hell-fire and instant damnation if they happened to exist, still dominates the traditional metaphysics. It is an ingredient, and the decisive ingredient, in what calls itself idealism. But in order to see just what part Calvinism plays in current idealism, it will be necessary to distinguish the other chief element in that complex system, namely, transcendentalism.

Transcendentalism is the philosophy which the romantic era produced in Germany, and independently, I believe, in America also. Transcendentalism proper, like romanticism, is not any particular set of dogmas about what things exist; it is not a system of the universe regarded as a fact, or as a collection of facts. It is a method, a point of view, from which any world, no matter what it might contain, could be approached by a self-conscious observer. Transcendentalism is systematic subjectivism. It studies the perspectives of knowledge, as they radiate from the self; it is a plan of those avenues of inference by which our ideas of things must be reached, if they are to afford any systematic or distant vistas. In other words, transcendentalism is the critical logic of science. Knowledge, it says, has a station, as in a watch-tower; it is always seated here and now, in the self of the moment. The past and the future, things inferred and things conceived, lie around it, painted as upon a panorama. They cannot be lighted up save by some centrifugal ray of attention and present interest, by some active operation of the mind.

This is hardly the occasion for developing or explaining this delicate insight; suffice it to say, lest you should think later that I disparage transcendentalism, that as a method I regard it as correct and, when once suggested, unforgettable. I regard it as the chief contribution made in modern times to speculation. But it is a method only, an attitude we may always assume if we like and that will always be legitimate. It is no answer, and involves no particular answer, to the question: What exists; in what order is what exists produced; what is to exist in the future? This question must be answered by observing the object, and tracing humbly the movement of the object. It cannot be answered at all by harping on the fact that this object, if discovered, must be discovered by somebody, and by somebody who has an interest in discovering it. Yet the Germans who first gained the full transcendental insight were romantic people; they were more or less frankly poets; they were colossal egotists, and wished to make not only their own knowledge but the whole universe center about themselves. And full as they were of their romantic isolation and romantic liberty, it occurred to them to imagine that all reality might be a transcendental self and a romantic dreamer like themselves; nay, that it might be just their own transcendental self and their own romantic dreams extended indefinitely. Transcendental logic, the method of discovery for the mind, was to become also the method of evolution in nature and history. Transcendental method, so abused, produced transcendental myth. A conscientious critique of knowledge was turned into a sham system of nature. We must therefore distinguish sharply the transcendental grammar of the intellect, which is significant and potentially correct, from the various transcendental systems of the universe, which are chimeras.

In both its parts, however, transcendentalism had much to recommend it to American philosophers, for the transcendental method appealed to the individualistic and revolutionary temper of their youth, while transcendental myths enabled them to find a new status for their inherited theology, and to give what parts of it they cared to preserve some semblance of philosophical backing. This last was the use to which the transcendental method was put by Kant himself, who first brought it into vogue, before the terrible weapon had got out of hand, and become the instrument of pure romanticism. Kant came, he himself said, to remove knowledge in order to make room for faith, which in his case meant faith in Calvinism. In other words, he applied the transcendental method to matters of fact, reducing them thereby to human ideas, in order to give to the Calvinistic postulates of conscience a metaphysical validity. For Kant had a genteel tradition of his own, which he wished to remove to a place of safety, feeling that the empirical world had become too hot for it; and this place of safety was the region of transcendental myth. I need hardly say how perfectly this expedient suited the needs of philosophers in America, and it is no accident if the influence of Kant soon became dominant here. To embrace this philosophy was regarded as a sign of profound metaphysical insight, although the most mediocre minds found no difficulty in embracing it. In truth it was a sign of having been brought up in the genteel tradition, of feeling it weak, and of wishing to save it.

But the transcendental method, in its way, was also sympathetic to the American mind. It embodied, in a radical form, the spirit of Protestantism as distinguished from its inherited doctrines; it was autonomous, undismayed, calmly revolutionary; it felt that Will was deeper than Intellect; it focused everything here and now, and asked all things to show their credentials at the bar of the young self, and to prove their value for this latest born moment. These things are truly American; they would be characteristic of any young society with a keen and discursive intelligence, and they are strikingly exemplified in the thought and in the person of Emerson. They constitute what he called self-trust. Self-trust, like other transcendental attitudes, may be expressed in metaphysical fables. The romantic spirit may imagine itself to be an absolute force, evoking and molding the plastic world to express its varying moods. But for a pioneer who is actually a world-builder this metaphysical illusion has a partial warrant in historical fact; far more warrant than it could boast of in the fixed and articulated society of Europe, among the moonstruck rebels and sulking poets of the romantic era. Emerson was a shrewd Yankee, by instinct on the winning side; he was a cheery, child-like soul, impervious to the evidence of evil, as of everything that it did not suit his transcendental individuality to appreciate or to notice. More, perhaps, than anybody that has ever lived, he practiced the transcendental method in all its purity. He had no system. He opened his eyes on the world every morning with a fresh sincerity, marking how things seemed to him then, or what they suggested to his spontaneous fancy. This fancy, for being spontaneous, was not always novel; it was guided by the habits and training of his mind, which were those of a preacher. Yet he never insisted on his notions so as to turn them into settled dogmas; he felt in his bones that they were myths. Sometimes, indeed, the bad example of other transcendentalists, less true than he to their method, or the pressing questions of unintelligent people, or the instinct we all have to think our ideas final, led him to the very verge of system-making; but he stopped short. Had he made a system out of his notion of compensation, or the over-soul, or spiritual laws, the result would have been as thin and forced as it is in other transcendental systems. But he coveted truth; and he returned to experience, to history, to poetry, to the natural science of his day, for new starting-points and hints toward fresh transcendental musings.

To covet truth is a very distinguished passion. Every philosopher says he is pursuing the truth, but this is seldom the case. As Mr. Bertrand Russell has observed, one reason why philosophers often fail to reach the truth is that often they do not desire to reach it. Those who are genuinely concerned in discovering what happens to be true are rather the men of science, the naturalists, the historians; and ordinarily they discover it, according to their lights. The truths they find are never complete, and are not always important; but they are integral parts of the truth, facts and circumstances that help to fill in the picture, and that no later interpretation can invalidate or afford to contradict. But professional philosophers are usually only scholastics: that is, they are absorbed in defending some vested illusion or some eloquent idea. Like lawyers or detectives, they study the case for which they are retained, to see how much evidence or semblance of evidence they can gather for the defense, and how much prejudice they can raise against the witnesses for the prosecution; for they know they are defending prisoners suspected by the world, and perhaps by their own good sense, of falsification. They do not covet truth, but victory and the dispelling of their own doubts. What they defend is some system, that is, some view about the totality of things, of which men are actually ignorant. No system would ever have been framed if people had been simply interested in knowing what is true, whatever it may be. What produces systems is the interest in maintaining against all comers that some favorite or inherited idea of ours is sufficient and right. A system may contain an account of many things which, in detail, are true enough; but as a system, covering infinite possibilities that neither our experience nor our logic can prejudge, it must be a work of imagination, and a piece of human soliloquy. It may be expressive of human experience, it may be poetical; but how should any one who really coveted truth suppose that it was true?

Emerson had no system; and his coveting truth had another exceptional consequence: he was detached, unworldly, contemplative. When he came out of the conventicle or the reform meeting, or out of the rapturous close atmosphere of the lecture-room, he heard nature whispering to him: "Why so hot, little sir?" No doubt the spirit or energy of the world is what is acting in us, as the sea is what rises in every little wave; but it passes through us, and cry out as we may, it will move on. Our privilege is to have perceived it as it moves. Our dignity is not in what we do, but in what we understand. The whole world is doing things. We are turning in that vortex; yet within us is silent observation, the speculative eye before which all passes, which bridges the distances and compares the combatants. On this side of his genius Emerson broke away from all conditions of age or country and represented nothing except intelligence itself.

There was another element in Emerson, curiously combined with transcendentalism, namely, his love and respect for Nature. Nature, for the transcendentalist, is precious because it is his own work, a mirror in which he looks at himself and says (like a poet relishing his own verses), "What a genius I am! Who would have thought there was such stuff in me?" And the philosophical egotist finds in his doctrine a ready explanation of whatever beauty and commodity nature actually has. No wonder, he says to himself, that nature is sympathetic, since I made it. And such a view, one-sided and even fatuous as it may be, undoubtedly sharpens the vision of a poet and a moralist to all that is inspiriting and symbolic in the natural world. Emerson was particularly ingenious and clear-sighted in feeling the spiritual uses of fellowship with the elements. This is something in which all Teutonic poetry is rich and which forms, I think, the most genuine and spontaneous part of modern taste, and especially of American taste. Just as some people are naturally enthralled and refreshed by music, so others are by landscape. Music and landscape make up the spiritual resources of those who cannot or dare not express their unfulfilled ideals in words. Serious poetry, profound religion (Calvinism, for instance) are the joys of an unhappiness that confesses itself; but when a genteel tradition forbids people to confess that they are unhappy, serious poetry and profound religion are closed to them by that; and since human life, in its depths, cannot then express itself openly, imagination is driven for comfort into abstract arts, where human circumstances are lost sight of, and human problems dissolve in a purer medium. The pressure of care is thus relieved, without its quietus being found in intelligence. To understand oneself is the classic form of consolation; to elude oneself is the romantic. In the presence of music or landscape human experience eludes itself; and thus romanticism is the bond between transcendental and naturalistic sentiment.

Have there been, we may ask, any successful efforts to escape from the genteel tradition, and to express something worth expressing behind its back? This might well not have occurred as yet; but America is so precocious, it has been trained by the genteel tradition to be so wise for its years, that some indications of a truly native philosophy and poetry are already to be found. I might mention the humorists, of whom you here in California have had your share. The humorists, however, only half escape the genteel tradition; their humor would lose its savor if they had wholly escaped it. They point to what contradicts it in the facts; but not in order to abandon the genteel tradition, for they have nothing solid to put in its place. When they point out how ill many facts fit into it, they do not clearly conceive that this militates against the standard, but think it a funny perversity in the facts. Of course, did they earnestly respect the genteel tradition, such an incongruity would seem to them sad, rather than ludicrous. Perhaps the prevalence of humor in America, in and out of season, may be taken as one more evidence that the genteel tradition is present pervasively, but everywhere weak. Similarly in Italy, during the Renaissance, the Catholic tradition could not be banished from the intellect, since there was nothing articulate to take its place; yet its hold on the heart was singularly relaxed. The consequence was that humorists could regale themselves with the foibles of monks and of cardinals, with the credulity of fools, and the bogus miracles of the saints; not intending to deny the theory of the church, but caring for it so little at heart, that they could find it infinitely amusing that it should be contradicted in men's lives, and that no harm should come of it. So when Mark Twain says, "I was born of poor but dishonest parents," the humor depends on the parody of the genteel Anglo-Saxon convention that it is disreputable to be poor; but to hint at the hollowness of it would not be amusing if it did not remain at bottom one's habitual conviction.

The one American writer who has left the genteel tradition entirely behind is perhaps Walt Whitman. For this reason educated Americans find him rather an unpalatable person, who they sincerely protest ought not to be taken for a representative of their culture; and he certainly should not, because their culture is so genteel and traditional. But the foreigner may sometimes think otherwise, since he is looking for what may have arisen in America to express, not the polite and conventional American mind, but the spirit and the inarticulate principles that animate the community, on which its own genteel mentality seems to sit rather lightly. When the foreigner opens the pages of Walt Whitman, he thinks that he has come at last upon something representative and original. In Walt Whitman democracy is carried into psychology and morals. The various sights, moods, and emotions are given each one vote; they are declared to be all free and equal, and the innumerable commonplace moments of life are suffered to speak like the others. Those moments formerly reputed great are not excluded, but they are made to march in the ranks with their companions, — plain foot-soldiers and servants of the hour. Nor does the refusal to discriminate stop there; we must carry our principle further down, to the animals, to inanimate nature, to the cosmos as a whole. Whitman became a pantheist; but his pantheism, unlike that of the Stoics and of Spinoza, was unintellectual, lazy, and self-indulgent; for he simply felt jovially that everything real was good enough, and that he was good enough himself. In him Bohemia rebelled against the genteel tradition; but the reconstruction that alone can justify revolution did not ensue. His attitude, in principle, was utterly disintegrating; his poetic genius fell back to the lowest level, perhaps, to which it is possible for poetic genius to fall. He reduced his imagination to a passive sensorium for the registering of impressions. No element of construction remained in it, and therefore no element of penetration. But his scope was wide; and his lazy, desultory apprehension was poetical. His work, for the very reason that it is so rudimentary, contains a beginning, or rather many beginnings, that might possibly grow into a noble moral imagination, a worthy filling for the human mind. An American in the nineteenth century who completely disregarded the genteel tradition could hardly have done more.

But there is another distinguished man, lately lost to this country, who has given some rude shocks to this tradition and who, as much as Whitman, may be regarded as representing the genuine, the long silent American mind — I mean William James. He and his brother Henry were as tightly swaddled in the genteel tradition as any infant geniuses could be, for they were born in Cambridge, and in a Swedenborgian household. Yet they burst those bands almost entirely. The ways in which the two brothers freed themselves, however, are interestingly different. Mr. Henry James has done it by adopting the point of view of the outer world, and by turning the genteel American tradition, as he turns everything else, into a subject-matter for analysis. For him it is a curious habit of mind, intimately comprehended, to be compared with other habits of mind, also well known to him. Thus he has overcome the genteel tradition in the classic way, by understanding it. With William James too this infusion of worldly insight and European sympathies was a potent influence, especially in his earlier days; but the chief source of his liberty was another. It was his personal spontaneity, similar to that of Emerson, and his personal vitality, similar to that of nobody else. Convictions and ideas came to him, so to speak, from the subsoil. He had a prophetic sympathy with the dawning sentiments of the age, with the moods of the dumb majority. His scattered words caught fire in many parts of the world. His way of thinking and feeling represented the true America, and represented in a measure the whole ultra-modern, radical world. Thus he eluded the genteel tradition in the romantic way, by continuing it into its opposite. The romantic mind, glorified in Hegel's dialectic (which is not dialectic at all, but a sort of tragi-comic history of experience), is always rendering its thoughts unrecognizable through the infusion of new insights, and through the insensible transformation of the moral feeling that accompanies them, till at last it has completely reversed its old judgments under cover of expanding them. Thus the genteel tradition was led a merry dance when it fell again into the hands of a genuine and vigorous romanticist, like William James. He restored their revolutionary force to its neutralized elements, by picking them out afresh, and emphasizing them separately, according to his personal predilections.

For one thing, William James kept his mind and heart wide open to all that might seem, to polite minds, odd, personal, or visionary in religion and philosophy. He gave a sincerely respectful hearing to sentimentalists, mystics, spiritualists, wizards, cranks, quacks, and impostors — for it is hard to draw the line, and James was not willing to draw it prematurely. He thought, with his usual modesty, that any of these might have something to teach him. The lame, the halt, the blind, and those speaking with tongues could come to him with the certainty of finding sympathy; and if they were not healed, at least they were comforted, that a famous professor should take them so seriously; and they began to feel that after all to have only one leg, or one hand, or one eye, or to have three, might be in itself no less beauteous than to have just two, like the stolid majority. Thus William James became the friend and helper of those groping, nervous, half-educated, spiritually disinherited, emotionally hungry individuals of which America is full. He became, at the same time, their spokesman and representative before the learned world; and he made it a chief part of his vocation to recast what the learned world has to offer, so that as far as possible it might serve the needs and interests of these people.

Yet the normal practical masculine American, too, had a friend in William James. There is a feeling abroad now, to which biology and Darwinism lend some color, that theory is simply an instrument for practice, and intelligence merely a help toward material survival. Bears, it is said, have fur and claws, but poor naked man is condemned to be intelligent, or he will perish. This feeling William James embodied in that theory of thought and of truth which he called pragmatism. Intelligence, he thought, is no miraculous, idle faculty, by which we mirror passively any or every thing that happens to be true, reduplicating the real world to no purpose. Intelligence has its roots and its issue in the context of events; it is one kind of practical adjustment, an experimental act, a form of vital tension. It does not essentially serve to picture other parts of reality, but to connect them. This view was not worked out by William James in its psychological and historical details; unfortunately he developed it chiefly in controversy against its opposite, which he called intellectualism, and which he hated with all the hatred of which his kind heart was capable. Intellectualism, as he conceived it, was pure pedantry; it impoverished and verbalized everything, and tied up nature in red tape. Ideas and rules that may have been occasionally useful, it put in the place of the full-blooded irrational movement of life which had called them into being; and these abstractions, so soon obsolete, it strove to fix and to worship forever. Thus all creeds and theories and all formal precepts sink in the estimation of the pragmatist to a local and temporary grammar of action; a grammar that must be changed slowly by time, and may be changed quickly by genius. To know things as a whole, or as they are eternally, if there is anything eternal in them, is not only beyond our powers, but would prove worthless, and perhaps even fatal to our lives. Ideas are not mirrors, they are weapons; their function is to prepare us to meet events, as future experience may unroll them. Those ideas that disappoint us are false ideas; those to which events are true are true themselves.

This may seem a very utilitarian view of the mind; and I confess I think it a partial one, since the logical force of beliefs and ideas, their truth or falsehood as assertions, has been overlooked altogether, or confused with the vital force of the material processes which these ideas express. It is an external view only, which marks the place and conditions of the mind in nature, but neglects its specific essence; as if a jewel were defined as a round hole in a ring. Nevertheless, the more materialistically we interpret the pragmatist theory of what the mind is, the more vitalistic our theory of nature will have to become. If the intellect is a device produced in organic bodies to expedite their processes, these organic bodies must have interests and a chosen direction in their life; otherwise their life could not be expedited, nor could anything be useful to it. In other words — and this is a third point at which the philosophy of William James has played havoc with the genteel tradition, while ostensibly defending it — nature must be conceived anthropomorphically and in psychological terms. Its purposes are not to be static harmonies, self-unfolding destinies, the logic of spirit, the spirit of logic, or any other formal method and abstract law; its purposes are to be concrete endeavors, finite efforts of souls living in an environment which they transform and by which they, too, are affected. A spirit, the divine spirit as much as the human, as this new animism conceives it, is a romantic adventurer. Its future is undetermined. Its scope, its duration, and the quality of its life, are all contingent. The spirit grows; it buds and sends forth feelers, sounding the depths around for such other centers of force or life as may exist there. It has a vital momentum, but no predetermined goal. It uses its past as a stepping-stone, or rather as a diving-board, but has an absolutely fresh will at each moment to plunge this way or that into the unknown. The universe is an experiment; it is unfinished. It has no ultimate or total nature, because it has no end. It embodies no formula or statable law; any formula is at best a poor abstraction, describing what, in some region and for some time, may be the most striking characteristic of existence; the law is a description *a posteriori* of the habit things have chosen to acquire, and which they may possibly throw off altogether. What a day may bring forth is uncertain; uncertain even to God. Omniscience is impossible; time is real; what had been omniscience hitherto might discover something more to-day. "There shall be news," William James was fond of saying with rapture, quoting from the unpublished poem of an obscure friend, "there shall be news in heaven!" There is almost certainly, he thought, a God now; there may be several gods, who might exist together, or one after the other. We might, by our conspiring sympathies, help to make a new one. Much in us is doubtless immortal; we survive death for some time in a recognizable form; but what our career and transformations may be in the sequel, we cannot tell, although we may help to determine them by our daily choices. Observation must be continual, if our ideas are to remain true. Eternal vigilance is the price of knowledge; perpetual hazard, perpetual experiment keep quick the edge of life.

This is, so far as I know, a new philosophical vista; it is a conception never before presented, although implied, perhaps, in various quarters, as in Norse and even Greek mythology. It is a vision radically empirical and radically romantic; and as William James himself used to say, the vision and not the arguments of a philosopher is the interesting and influential thing about him. William James, rather too generously, attributed this vision to M. Bergson, and regarded him in consequence as a philosopher of the first rank, whose thought was to be one of the turning-points in history. M. Bergson had killed intellectualism. It was his book on creative evolution, said James with humorous emphasis, that had come at last to "*écraser l'infâme.*" We may suspect, notwithstanding, that intellectualism, infamous and crushed, will survive the blow; and if the author of the Book of Ecclesiastes were now alive, and heard that there shall be news in heaven, he would doubtless say that there may possibly be news there, but that under the sun there is nothing new — not even radical empiricism or radical romanticism, which from the beginning of the world has been the philosophy of those who as yet had had little experience; for to the blinking little child it is not merely something in the world that is new daily, but everything is new all day.

I am not concerned with the rights and wrongs of that controversy; my point is only that William James, in this genial evolutionary view of the world, has given a rude shock to the genteel tradition. What! The world a gradual improvization? Creation unpremeditated? God a sort of young poet or struggling artist? William James is an advocate of theism; pragmatism adds one to the evidences of religion; that is excellent. But is not the cool abstract piety of the genteel getting more than it asks for? This empirical naturalistic God is too crude and positive a force; he will work miracles, he will answer prayers, he may inhabit distinct places, and have distinct conditions under which alone he can operate; he is a neighboring being, whom we can act upon, and rely upon for specific aids, as upon a personal friend, or a physician, or an insurance company. How disconcerting! Is not this new theology a little like superstition? And yet how interesting, how exciting, if it should happen to be true! I am far from wishing to suggest that such a view seems to me more probable than conventional idealism or than Christian orthodoxy. All three are in the region of dramatic system-making and myth, to which probabilities are irrelevant. If one man says the moon is sister to the sun, and another that she is his daughter, the question is not which notion is more probable, but whether either of them is at all expressive. The so-called evidences are deviced afterwards, when faith and imagination have prejudged the issue. The force of William James's new theology, or romantic cosmology, lies only in this: that it has broken the spell of the genteel tradition, and enticed faith in a new direction, which on second thoughts may prove no less alluring than the old. The important fact is not that the new fancy might possibly be true — who shall know that? — but that it has entered the heart of a leading American to conceive and to cherish it. The genteel tradition cannot be dislodged by these insurrections; there are circles to which it is still congenial, and where it will be preserved. But it has been challenged and (what is perhaps more insidious) it has been discovered. No one need be brow-beaten any longer into accepting it. No one need be afraid, for instance, that his fate is sealed because some young prig may call him a dualist; the pint would call the quart a dualist, if you tried to pour the quart into him. We need not be afraid of being less profound, for being direct and sincere. The intellectual world may be traversed in many directions; the whole has not been surveyed; there is a great career in it open to talent. That is a sort of knell, that tolls the passing of the genteel tradition. Something else is now in the field; something else can appeal to the imagination, and be a thousand times more idealistic than academic idealism, which is often simply a way of white-washing and adoring things as they are. The illegitimate monopoly which the genteel tradition had established over what ought to be assumed and what ought to be hoped for has been broken down by the first-born of the family, by the genius of the race. Henceforth there can hardly be the same peace and the same pleasure in hugging the old proprieties. Hegel will be to the next generation what Sir William Hamilton was to the last. Nothing will have been disproved, but everything will have been abandoned. An honest man has spoken, and the cant of the genteel tradition has become harder for young lips to repeat.

With this I have finished such a sketch as I am here able to offer you of the genteel tradition in American philosophy. The subject is complex, and calls for many an excursus and qualifying footnote; yet I think the main outlines are clear enough. The chief fountains of this tradition were Calvinism and transcendentalism. Both were living fountains; but to keep them alive they required, one an agonized conscience, and the other a radical subjective criticism of knowledge. When these rare metaphysical preoccupations disappeared—and the American atmosphere is not favorable to either of them—the two systems ceased to be inwardly understood; they subsisted as sacred mysteries only; and the combination of the two in some transcendental system of the universe (a contradiction in principle) was doubly artificial. Besides, it could hardly be held with a single mind. Natural science, history, the beliefs implied in labor and invention, could not be disregarded altogether; so that the transcendental philosopher was condemned to a double allegiance, and to not letting his left hand know the bluff that his right hand was putting up. Nevertheless, the difficulty in bringing practical inarticulate convictions to expression is very great, and the genteel tradition has subsisted in the academic mind, for want of anything equally academic to take its place.

The academic mind, however, has had its flanks turned. On the one side came the revolt of the Bohemian temperament, with its poetry of crude naturalism; on the other side came an impassioned empiricism, welcoming popular religious witnesses to the unseen, reducing science to an instrument of success in action, and declaring the universe to be wild and young, and not to be harnessed by the logic of any school.

This revolution, I should think, might well find an echo among you, who live in a thriving society, and in the presence of a virgin and prodigious world. When you transform nature to your uses, when you experiment with her forces, and reduce them to industrial agents, you cannot feel that nature was made by you or for you, for then these adjustments would have been pre-established. You must feel, rather, that you are an offshoot of her life; one brave little force among her immense forces. When you escape, as you love to do, to your forests and your Sierras, I am sure again that you do not feel you made them, or that they were made for you. They have grown, as you have grown, only more massively and more slowly. In their non-human

beauty and peace they stir the sub-human depths and the superhuman possibilities of your own spirit. It is no transcendental logic that they teach; and
they give no sign of any deliberate morality seated in the world. It is rather
the vanity and superficiality of all logic, the needlessness of argument, the
finitude of morals, the strength of time, the fertility of matter, the variety,
the unspeakable variety, of possible life. Everything is measurable and
conditioned, indefinitely repeated, yet, in repetition, twisted somewhat
from its old form. Everywhere is beauty and nowhere permanence, everywhere an incipient harmony, nowhere an intention, nor a responsibility, nor
a plan. It is the irresistible suasion of this daily spectacle, it is the daily
discipline of contact with things, so different from the verbal discipline of
the schools, that will, I trust, inspire the philosophy of your children. A
Californian whom I had recently the pleasure of meeting observed that, if
the philosophers had lived among your mountains their systems would have
been different from what they are. Certainly, I should say, very different
from what those systems are from which the European genteel tradition has
handed down since Socrates; for these systems are egotistical; directly or
indirectly they are anthropocentric, and inspired by the conceited notion
that man, or human reason, or the human distinction between good and evil,
is the center and pivot of the universe. That is what the mountains and the
woods should make you at last ashamed to assert. From what, indeed, does
the society of nature liberate you, that you find it so sweet? It is hardly (is
it?) that you wish to forget your past, or your friends, or that you have any
secret contempt for your present ambitions. You respect these, you respect
them perhaps too much; you are not suffered by the genteel tradition to
criticize or to reform them at all radically. No; it is the yoke of this genteel
tradition itself, your tyrant from the cradle to the grave, that these primeval
solitudes lift from your shoulders. They suspend your forced sense of your
own importance not merely as individuals, but even as men. They allow
you, in one happy moment, at once to play and to worship, to take your-
selves simply, humbly, for what you are, and to salute the wild, indifferent,
non-censorious infinity of nature. You are admonished that what you can do
avails little materially, and in the end nothing. At the same time, through
wonder and pleasure, you are taught speculation. You learn what you are
really fitted to do, and where lie your natural dignity and joy, namely, in
representing many things, without being them, and in letting your imagination, through sympathy, celebrate and echo their life. Because the peculiarity of man is that his machinery for reaction on external things has
involved an imaginative transcript of these things, which is preserved and

suspended in his fancy; and the interest and beauty of this inward land-scape, rather than any fortunes that may await his body in the outer world, constitute his proper happiness. By their mind, its scope, quality, and temper, we estimate men, for by the mind only do we exist as men, and are more than so many storage-batteries for material energy. Let us therefore be frankly human. Let us be content to live in the mind.

Character and Opinion in the United States

PREFACE

The major part of this book is composed of lectures originally addressed to British audiences. I have added a good deal, but I make no apology, now that the whole may fall under American eyes, for preserving the tone and attitude of a detached observer. Not at all on the ground that "to see ourselves as others see us" would be to see ourselves truly; on the contrary, I agree with Spinoza where he says that other people's idea of a man is apt to be a better expression of their nature than of his. I accept this principle in the present instance, and am willing it should be applied to the judgements contained in this book, in which the reader may see chiefly expressions of my own feelings and hints of my own opinions. Only an American — and I am not one except by long association* — can speak for the heart of America. I try to understand it, as a family friend may who has a different temperament; but it is only my own mind that I speak for at bottom, or wish to speak for. Certainly my sentiments are of little importance compared with the volume and destiny of the things I discuss here: yet the critic and artist too have their rights, and to take as calm and as long a view as possible seems to be but another name for the love of truth. Moreover, I suspect that my feelings are secretly shared by many people in America, natives and foreigners, who may not have the courage or the occasion to express them frankly. After all, it has been acquaintance with America and American philosophers that has chiefly contributed to clear and to settle my own mind. I have no axe to grind, only my thoughts to burnish, in the hope that some part of the truth of things may be reflected there; and I am confident of not giving serious offence to the judicious, because they will feel that it is affection for the American people that makes me wish that what is best and most beautiful should not be absent from their lives.

Civilisation is perhaps approaching one of those long winters that overtake it from time to time. A flood of barbarism from below may soon level

*Perhaps I should add that I have not been in the United States since January 1912. My observations stretched, with some intervals, through the forty years preceding that date.

all the fair works of our Christian ancestors, as another flood two thousand years ago levelled those of the ancients. Romantic Christendom — picturesque, passionate, unhappy episode — may be coming to an end. Such a catastrophe would be no reason for despair. Nothing lasts for ever; but the elasticity of life is wonderful, and even if the world lost its memory it could not lose its youth. Under the deluge, and watered by it, seeds of all sorts would survive against the time to come, even if what might eventually spring from them, under the new circumstances, should wear a strange aspect. In a certain measure, and unintentionally, both this destruction and this restoration have already occurred in America. There is much forgetfulness, much callow disrespect for what is past or alien; but there is a fund of vigour, goodness, and hope such as no nation ever possessed before. In what sometimes looks like American greediness and jostling for the front place, all is love of achievement, nothing is unkindness; it is a fearless people, and free from malice, as you might see in their eyes and gestures, even if their conduct did not prove it. This soil is propitious to every seed, and tares must needs grow in it; but why should it not also breed clear thinking, honest judgement, and rational happiness? These things are indeed not necessary to existence, and without them America might long remain rich and populous like many a barbarous land in the past; but in that case its existence would be hounded, like theirs, by falsity and remorse. May Heaven avert the omen, and make the new world a better world than the old! In the classical and romantic tradition of Europe, love, of which there was very little, was supposed to be kindled by beauty, of which there was a great deal: perhaps moral chemistry may be able to reverse this operation, and in the future and in America it may breed beauty out of love.

CHAPTER I

THE MORAL BACKGROUND

About the middle of the nineteenth century, in the quiet sunshine of provincial prosperity, New England had an Indian summer of the mind; and an agreeable reflective literature showed how brilliant that russet and yellow season could be. There were poets, historians, orators, preachers, most of whom had studied foreign literatures and had travelled; they demurely kept up with the times; they were universal humanists. But it was all a harvest of leaves; these worthies had an expurgated and barren conception of life; theirs was the purity of sweet old age. Sometimes they made attempts to rejuvenate their minds by broaching native subjects; they wished to prove how much matter for poetry the new world supplied, and they wrote "Rip van Winkle," "Hiawatha," or "Evangeline"; but the inspiration did not seem much more American than that of Swift or Ossian or Châteaubriand. These cultivated writers lacked native roots and fresh sap because the American intellect itself lacked them. Their culture was half a pious survival, half an intentional acquirement; it was not the inevitable flowering of a fresh experience. Later there have been admirable analytic novelists who have depicted American life as it is, but rather bitterly, rather sadly; as if the joy and the illusion of it did not inspire them, but only an abstract interest in their own art. If any one, like Walt Whitman, penetrated to the feelings and images which the American scene was able to breed out of itself, and filled them with a frank and broad afflatus of his own, there is no doubt that he misrepresented the conscious minds of cultivated Americans; in them the head as yet did not belong to the trunk.

Nevertheless, *belles-lettres* in the United States — which after all stretch beyond New England — have always had two points of contact with the great national experiment. One point of contact has been oratory, with that sort of poetry, patriotic, religious, or moral, which has the function of oratory. Eloquence is a republican art, as conversation is an aristocratic one. By eloquence at public meetings and dinners, in the pulpit or in the press, the impulses of the community could be brought to expression; consecrated maxims could be reapplied; the whole latent manliness and shrewdness of the nation could be mobilised. In the form of oratory reflection, rising out of the problems of action, could be turned to guide or to sanction action, and sometimes could attain, in so doing, a notable elevation of thought. Although Americans, and many other people, usually say that thought is for the sake of action, it has evidently been in these high moments, when action became incandescent in thought, that they have been most truly alive, intensively most active, and although *doing* nothing, have found at last that their existence was worth while. Reflection is itself a turn, and the top turn, given to life. Here is the second point at which literature in America has fused with the activities of the nation: it has paused to enjoy them. Every animal has his festive and ceremonious moments, when he poses or plumes himself or thinks; sometimes he even sings and flies aloft in a sort of ecstasy. Somewhat in the same way, when reflection in man becomes dominant, it may become passionate; it may create religion or philosophy — adventures often more thrilling than the humdrum experience they are supposed to interrupt.

This pure flame of mind is nothing new, superadded, or alien in America. It is notorious how metaphysical was the passion that drove the Puritans to those shores; they went there in the hope of living more perfectly in the spirit. And their pilgrim's progress was not finished when they had founded their churches in the wilderness; an endless migration of the mind was still before them, a flight from those new idols and servitudes which prosperity involves, and the eternal lure of spiritual freedom and truth. The moral world always contains undiscovered or thinly peopled continents open to those who are more attached to what might or should be than to what already is. Americans are eminently prophets; they apply morals to public affairs; they are impatient and enthusiastic. Their judgements have highly speculative implications, which they often make explicit; they are men with principles, and fond of stating them. Moreover, they have an intense self-reliance; to exercise private judgement is not only a habit with them but a conscious duty. Not seldom personal conversions and mystical experiences throw their ingrained faith into novel forms, which may be very bold and radical. They are traditionally exercised about religion, and adrift on the subject more than any other people on earth; and if religion is a dreaming philosophy, and philosophy a waking religion, a people so wide awake and so religious as the old Yankees ought certainly to have been rich in philosophers.

In fact, philosophy in the good old sense of curiosity about the nature of things, with readiness to make the best of them, has not been absent from the practice of Americans or from their humorous moods; their humour and shrewdness are sly comments on the shortcomings of some polite conven-tion that everybody accepts tacitly, yet feels to be insecure and contrary to the principles on which life is actually carried on. Nevertheless, with the shyness which simple competence often shows in the presence of conven-tional shams, these wits have not taken their native wisdom very seriously. They have not had the leisure nor the intellectual scope to think out and defend the implications of their homely perceptions. Their fresh insight has been whispered in parentheses and asides; it has been humbly banished, in alarm, from their solemn moments. What people have respected have been rather scraps of official philosophy, or entire systems, which they have inherited or imported, as they have respected operas and art museums. To be on speaking terms with these fine things was a part of social respectabil-ity, like having family silver. High thoughts must be at hand, like those candlesticks, probably candleless, sometimes displayed as a seemly orna-ment in a room blazing with electric light. Even in William James, sponta-neous and stimulating as he was, a certain underlying discomfort was dis-cernible; he had come out into the open, into what should have been the sunshine, but the vast shadow of the temple still stood between him and the sun. He was worried about what *ought* to be believed and the awful depriva-tions of disbelieving. What he called the cynical view of anything had first to be brushed aside, without stopping to consider whether it was not the true one; and he was bent on finding new and empirical reasons for clinging to free-will, departed spirits, and tutelary gods. Nobody, except perhaps in this last decade, has tried to bridge the chasm between what he believes in daily life and the "problems" or philosophy. Nature and science have not been ignored, and "practice" in some schools has been constantly referred to; but instead of supplying philosophy with its data they have only constituted its difficulties; its function has been not to build on known facts but to explain them away. Hence a curious alternation and irrelevance, as between weekdays and Sabbaths, between American ways and American opinions.

That philosophy should be attached to tradition would be a great advan-tage, conducive to mutual understanding, to maturity, and to progress, if the tradition lay in the highway of truth. To deviate from it in that case would be to betray the fact that, while one might have a lively mind, one was not master of the subject. Unfortunately, in the nineteenth century, in America as elsewhere, the ruling tradition was not only erratic and far from the highway of truth, but the noonday of this tradition was over, and its classic forms were outgrown. A philosophy may have a high value, other than its truth to things, in its truth to method and to the genius of its author; it may be a feat of synthesis and imagination, like a great poem, expressing one of the eternal possibilities of being, although one which the creator happened to reject when he made this world. It is possible to be a master in false philosophy — easier, in fact, than to be a master in the truth, because a false philosophy can be made as simple and consistent as one pleases. Such had been the masters of the tradition prevalent in New England — Calvin, Hume, Fichte, not to mention others more relished because less pure; but one of the disadvantages of such perfection in error is that the illusion is harder to transmit to another age and country. If Jonathan Edwards, for instance, was a Calvinist of pristine force and perhaps the greatest *master* in false philosophy that America has yet produced, he paid the price by being abandoned, even in his lifetime, by his own sect, and seeing the world turn a deaf ear to his logic without so much as attempting to refute it. One of the peculiarities of recent speculation, especially in America, is that ideas are abandoned in virtue of a mere change of feeling, without any new evidence or new arguments. We do not nowadays refute our predecessors, we pleasantly bid them good-bye. Even if all our principles are unwittingly traditional we do not like to bow openly to authority. Hence masters like Calvin, Hume, or Fichte rose before their American admirers like formidable ghosts, foreign and unseizable. People refused to be encumbered with any system, even one of their own; they were content to imbibe more or less of the spirit of a philosophy and to let it play on such facts as happened to attract their attention. The originality even of Emerson and of William James was of this incidental character; they found new approaches to old beliefs or new expedients in old dilemmas. They were not in a scholastic sense pupils of anybody or masters in anything. They hated the scholastic way of saying what they meant, if they had heard of it; they insisted on a personal freshness of style, refusing to make their thought more precise than it happened to be spontaneously; and they lisped their logic, when the logic came.

We must remember that ever since the days of Socrates, and especially after the establishment of Christianity, the dice of thought have been loaded. Certain pledges have preceded inquiry and divided the possible conclusions beforehand into the acceptable and the inacceptable, the edifying and the shocking, the noble and the base. Wonder has no longer been the root of philosophy, but sometimes impatience at having been cheated and sometimes fear of being undeceived. The marvel of existence, in which the luminous and the opaque are so romantically mingled, no longer lay like a sea open to intellectual adventure, tempting the mind to conceive some bold and curious system of the universe on the analogy of what had been so far discovered. Instead, people were confronted with an orthodoxy — though not always the same orthodoxy — whispering mysteries and brandishing anathemas. Their wits were absorbed in solving traditional problems, many of them artificial and such as the ruling orthodoxy had created by its gratuitous assumptions. Difficulties were therefore found in some perfectly obvious truths; and obvious fables, if they were hallowed by association, were seriously weighed in the balance against one another or against the facts; and many an actual thing was proved to be impossible, or was hidden under a false description. In conservative schools the student learned and tried to fathom the received solutions; in liberal schools he was perhaps invited to seek solutions of his own, but still to the old questions. Freedom, when nominally allowed, was a provisional freedom; if your wanderings did not somehow bring you back to orthodoxy you were a misguided being, no matter how disparate from the orthodox might be the field from which you fetched your little harvest; and if you could not be answered you were called superficial. Most spirits are cowed by such disparagement; but even those who snap their fingers at it do not escape; they can hardly help feeling that in calling a spade a spade they are petulant and naughty; or if their inspiration is too genuine for that, they still unwittingly shape their opinions in contrast to those that claim authority, and therefore on the same false lines — a terrible tax to pay to the errors of others; and it is only here and there that a very great and solitary mind, like that of Spinoza, can endure obloquy without bitterness or can pass through perverse controversies without contagion.

Under such circumstances it is obvious that speculation can be frank and happy only where orthodoxy has receded, abandoning a larger and larger field to unprejudiced inquiry; or else (as has happened among liberal Protestants) where the very heart of orthodoxy has melted, has absorbed the most alien substances, and is ready to bloom into anything that anybody finds attractive. This is the secret of that extraordinary vogue which the transcendental philosophy has had for nearly a century in Great Britain and America; it is a method which enables a man to renovate all his beliefs, scientific and religious, from the inside, giving them a new status and interpretation as phases of his own experience or imagination; so that he does not seem to himself to reject anything, and yet is bound to nothing, except to his creative self. Many too who have no inclination to practise this transcendental method — a personal, arduous, and futile art, which requires to be renewed at every moment — have been impressed with the results or the maxims of this or that transcendental philosopher, such as that every opinion leads on to another that reinterprets it, or every evil to some higher good that contains it; and they have managed to identify these views with what still seemed to them vital in religion.

In spite of this profound mutation at the core, and much paring at the edges, traditional belief in New England retained its continuity and its priestly unction; and religious teachers and philosophers could slip away from Calvinism and even from Christianity without any loss of elevation or austerity. They found it so pleasant and easy to elude the past that they really had no quarrel with it. The world, they felt, was a safe place, watched over by a kindly God, who exacted nothing but cheerfulness and good-will from his children; and the American flag was a sort of rainbow in the sky, promising that all storms were over. Or if storms came, such as the Civil War, they would not be harder to weather than was necessary to test the national spirit and raise it to a new efficiency. The subtler dangers which we may now see threatening America had not yet come in sight — material restlessness was not yet ominous, the pressure of business enterprises was not yet out of scale with the old life or out of key with the old moral harmonies. A new type of American had not appeared — the untrained, pushing, cosmopolitan orphan, cock-sure in manner but not too sure in his morality, to whom the old Yankee, with his sour integrity, is almost a foreigner. Was not "increase," in the Bible, a synonym for benefit? Was not "abundance" the same, or almost the same, as happiness?

Meantime the churches, a little ashamed of their past, began to court the good opinion of so excellent a world. Although called evangelical, they were far, very far, from prophesying its end, or offering a refuge from it, or preaching contempt for it; they existed only to serve it, and their highest divine credential was that the world needed them. Irreligion, dissoluteness, and pessimism — supposed naturally to go together — could never prosper; they were incompatible with efficiency. That was the supreme test. "Be Christians," I once heard a president of Yale College cry to his assembled pupils, "be Christians and you will be successful." Religion was indispensable and sacred, when not carried too far; but theology might well be unnecessary. Why distract this world with talk of another? Enough for the day was the good thereof. Religions should be disentangled as much as possible from history and authority and metaphysics, and made to rest honestly on one's fine feelings, on one's indomitable optimism and trust in life. Revelation was nothing miraculous, given once for all in some remote age and foreign country; it must come to us directly, and with greater authority now than ever before. If evolution was to be taken seriously and to include moral growth, the great men of the past could only be stepping-stones to our own dignity. To grow was to contain and sum up all the good that had gone before, adding an appropriate increment. Undoubtedly some early figures were beautiful, and allowances had to be made for local influences in Palestine, a place so much more primitive and backward than Massachusetts. Jesus was a prophet more winsome and nearer to ourselves than his predecessors; but how could any one deny that the twenty centuries of progress since his time must have raised a loftier pedestal for Emerson or Channing or Phillips Brooks? It might somehow not be in good taste to put this feeling into clear words; one and perhaps two of these men would have deprecated it; nevertheless it beamed with refulgent self-satisfaction in the lives and maxims of most of their followers.

All this liberalism, however, never touched the centre of traditional orthodoxy, and those who, for all their modernness, felt that they inherited the faith of their fathers and were true to it were fundamentally right. There was still an orthodoxy among American highbrows at the end of the nineteenth century, dissent from which was felt to be scandalous; it consisted in holding that the universe exists and is governed for the sake of man or of the human spirit. This persuasion, arrogant as it might seem, is at bottom an expression of impotence rather than of pride. The soul is originally vegetative; it feels the weal and woe of what occurs within the body. With locomotion and the instinct to hunt and to flee, animals begin to notice external things also; but the chief point noticed about them is whether they are good or bad, friendly or hostile, far or near. The station of the animal and his interests thus become the measure of all things for him, in so far as he knows them; and this aspect of them is, by a primitive fatality, the heart of them to him. It is only reason that can discount these childish perspectives, neutralise the bias of each by collating it with the others, and masterfully conceive the field in which their common objects are deployed, discovering also the principle of foreshortening or projection which produces each perspective in turn. But reason is a later comer into this world, and weak; against its suasion stands the mighty resistance of habit and of moral presumption. It is in their interest, and to rehabilitate the warm vegetative autonomy of the primitive soul, that orthodox religion and philosophy labour in the western world — for the mind of India cannot be charged with this folly. Although inwardly these systems have not now a good conscience and do not feel very secure (for they are retrograde and sin against the light), yet outwardly they are solemn and venerable; and they have incorporated a great deal of moral wisdom with their egotism or humanism — more than the Indians with their respect for the infinite. In deifying human interests they have naturally studied and expressed them justly, whereas those who perceive the relativity of human goods are tempted to scorn them — which is itself unreasonable — and to sacrifice them all to the single passion of worship or of despair. Hardly anybody, except possibly the Greeks at their best, has realised the sweetness and glory of being a rational animal.

The Jews, as we know, had come to think that it was the creator of the world, the God of the universe, who had taken them for his chosen people. Christians in turn had asserted that it was God in person who, having become a man, had founded their church. According to this Hebraic tradition, the dignity of man did not lie in being a mind (which he undoubtedly is) but in being a creature materially highly favoured, with a longer life and a brighter destiny than other creatures in the world. It is remarkable how deep, in the Hebraic religions, is this interest in material existence; so deep that we are surprised when we discover that, according to the insight of other races, this interest is the essence of irreligion. Some detachment from existence and from hopes of material splendour has indeed filtered into Christianity through Platonism. Socrates and his disciples admired this world, but they did not particularly covet it, or wish to live long in it, or expect to improve it; what they cared for was an idea or a good which they found expressed in it, something outside it and timeless, in which the contemplative intellect might be literally absorbed. This philosophy was no less humanistic than that of the Jews, though in a less material fashion: if it did not read the universe in terms of thrift, it read it in terms of art. The pursuit of a good, such as is presumably aimed at in human action, was supposed to inspire every movement in nature; and this good, for the sake of which the very heavens revolved, was akin to the intellectual happiness of a Greek sage. Nature was a philosopher in pursuit of an idea. Natural science then took a moralising turn which it has not yet quite outgrown. Socrates required of astronomy, if it was to be true science, that it should show why *it was best* that the sun and moon should be as they are; and Plato, refining on this, assures us that the eyes are placed in front of the head, rather than at the back, because the front is the nobler quarter, and that the intestines are long in order that we may have leisure between meals to study philosophy. Curiously enough, the very enemies of final causes sometimes catch this infection and attach absolute values to facts in an opposite sense and in an inhuman interest; and you often hear in America that whatever is is right. These naturalists, while they rebuke the moralists for thinking that nature is ruled magically for our good, think her adorable for being ruled, in scorn of us, only by her own laws; and thus we oscillate between egotism and idolatry.

The Reformation did not reform this belief in the cosmic supremacy of man, or the humanity of God; on the contrary, it took it (like so much else) in terrible German earnest, not suffering it any longer to be accepted somewhat lightly as a classical figure of speech or a mystery resting on revelation. The human race, the chosen people, the Christian elect were like tabernacle within tabernacle for the spirit; but in the holy of holies was the spirit itself, one's own spirit and experience, which was the centre of everything. Protestant philosophy, exploring the domain of science and history with confidence, and sure of finding the spirit walking there, was too conscientious to misrepresent what it found. As the terrible facts could not be altered they had to be undermined. By turning psychology into metaphysics this could be accomplished, and we could reach the remarkable conclusion that the human spirit was not so much the purpose of the universe as its seat, and the only universe there was.

This conclusion, which sums up idealism on its critical or scientific side, would not of itself give much comfort to religious minds, that usually crave massive support rather than sublime independence; it leads to the heroic egotism of Fichte or Nietzsche rather than to any green pastures beside any still waters. But the critical element in idealism can be used to destroy belief in the natural world; and by so doing it can open the way to another sort of idealism, not at all critical, which might be called the higher superstition. This views the world as an oracle or charade, concealing a dramatic unity, or formula, or maxim, which all experience exists to illustrate. The habit of regarding existence as a riddle, with a surprising solution which we think we have found, should be the source of rather mixed emotions; the facts remain as they were, and rival solutions may at any time suggest themselves; and the one we have hit on may not, after all, be particularly comforting. The Christian may find himself turned by it into a heathen, the humanist into a pantheist, and the hope with which we instinctively faced life may be chastened into mere conformity. Nevertheless, however chilling and inhuman our higher superstition may prove, it will make us feel that we are masters of a mystical secret, that we have a faith to defend, and that, like all philosophers, we have taken a ticket in a lottery in which if we hit on the truth, even if it seems a blank, we shall have drawn the first prize.

Orthodoxy in New England, even so transformed and attenuated, did not of course hold the field alone. There are materialists by instinct in every age and country; there are always private gentlemen whom the clergy and the professors cannot deceive. Here and there a medical or scientific man, or a man of letters, will draw from his special pursuits some hint of the nature of things at large; or a political radical will nurse undying wrath against all opinions not tartly hostile to church and state. But these clever people are not organised, they are not always given to writing, nor speculative enough to make a system out of their convictions. The enthusiasts and the pedagogues naturally flock to the other camp. The very competence which scientific people and connoisseurs have in their special fields disinclines them to generalise, or renders their generalisations one-sided; so that their speculations are extraordinarily weak and stammering. Both by what they represent and by what they ignore they are isolated and deprived of influence, since only those who are at home in a subject can feel the force of analogies drawn from that field, whereas any one can be swayed by sentimental and moral appeals, by rhetoric and unction. Furthermore, in America the materialistic school is without that support from popular passions which it draws in many European countries from its association with anticlericalism or with revolutionary politics; and it also lacks the maturity, self-confidence, and refinement proper in older societies to the great body of Epicurean and disenchanted opinion, where for centuries wits, critics, minor philosophers, and men of the world have chuckled together over their Horace, their Voltaire, and their Gibbon. The horror which the theologians have of infidelity passes therefore into the average American mind unmitigated by the suspicion that anything pleasant could lie in that quarter, much less the open way to nature and truth and a secure happiness.

There is another handicap, of a more technical sort, under which naturalistic philosophy labours in America, as it does in England; it has been crossed by scepticism about the validity of perception and has become almost identical with psychology. Of course, for any one who thinks naturalistically (as the British empiricists did in the beginning, like every unsophisticated mortal), psychology is the description of a very superficial and incidental complication in the animal kingdom: it treats of the curious sensibility and volatile thoughts awakened in the mind by the growth and fortunes of the body. In noting these thoughts and feelings, we can observe how far they constitute true knowledge of the world in which they arise, how far they ignore it, and how far they play with it, by virtue of the poetry and the syntax of discourse which they add out of their own exuberance; for fancy is a very fertile treacherous thing, as every one finds when he dreams. But dreams run over into waking life, and sometimes seem to permeate and to underlie it; and it was just this suspicion that he might be dreaming awake, that discourse and tradition might be making a fool of him, that prompted the hard-headed Briton, even before the Reformation, to appeal from conventional beliefs to "experience." He was anxious to clear away those sophistries and impostures of which he was particularly apprehensive, in view of the somewhat foreign character of his culture and religion. Experience, he thought, would bear unimpeachable witness to the nature of things; for by experience he understood knowledge produced by direct contact with the object. Taken in this sense, experience is a method of discovery, an exercise of intelligence; it is the same observation of things, strict, cumulative, and analytic, which produces the natural sciences. It rests on naturalistic assumptions (since we know when and where we find our data) and could not fail to end in materialism. What prevented British empiricism from coming to this obvious conclusion was a peculiarity of the national temperament. The Englishman is not only distrustful of too much reasoning and too much theory (and science and materialism involve a good deal of both), but he is also fond of musing and of withdrawing into his inner man. Accordingly his empiricism took an introspective form; like Hamlet he stopped at the *how;* he began to think about thinking. His first care was now to arrest experience as he underwent it; though its presence could not be denied, it came in such a questionable shape that it could not be taken at its word. This mere presence of experience, this ghostly apparition to the inner man, was all that empirical philosophy could now profess to discover. Far from being an exercise of intelligence, it retracted all understanding, all interpretation, all instinctive faith; far from furnishing a sure record of the truths of nature, it furnished a set of pathological facts, the passive subject-matter of psychology. These now seemed the only facts admissible, and psychology, for the philosophers, became the only science. Experience could discover nothing, but all discoveries had to be retracted, so that they should revert to the fact of experience and terminate there. Evidently when the naturalistic background and meaning of experience have dropped out in this way, empiricism is a form of idealism, since whatever objects we can come upon will all be *a priori* and *a fortiori* and *sensu eminentiori* ideal in the mind. The irony of logic actually made English empiricism, understood in this psychological way, the starting-point for transcendentalism and for German philosophy.

Between these two senses of the word experience, meaning sometimes contact with things and at other times absolute feeling, the empirical school in England and America has been helplessly torn, without ever showing the courage or the self-knowledge to choose between them. I think we may say that on the whole their view has been this: that feelings or ideas were absolute atoms of existence, without any ground or source, so that the elements of their universe were all mental; but they conceived these psychical elements to be deployed in a physical time and even (since there were many simultaneous series of them) in some sort of space. These philosophers were accordingly idealists about substance but naturalists about the order and relations of existences; and experience on their lips meant feeling when they were thinking of particulars, but when they were thinking broadly, in matters of history or science, experience meant the universal nebula or cataract which these feelings composed — itself no object of experience, but one believed in and very imperfectly presented in imagination. These men believed in nature, and were materialists at heart and to all practical purposes; but they were shy intellectually, and seemed to think they ran less risk of error in holding a thing covertly than in openly professing it.

If any one, like Herbert Spencer, kept psychology in its place and in that respect remained a pure naturalist, he often forfeited this advantage by enveloping the positive information he derived from the sciences in a whirlwind of generalisations. The higher superstition, the notion that nature dances to the tune of some comprehensive formula or some magic rhyme, thus reappeared among those who claimed to speak for natural science. In their romantic sympathy with nature they attributed to her an excessive sympathy with themselves; they overlooked her infinite complications and continual irony, and candidly believed they could measure her with their thumb-rules. Why should philosophers drag a toy-net of words, fit to catch butterflies, through the sea of being, and expect to land all the fish in it? Why not take note simply of what the particular sciences can as yet tell us of the world? Certainly, when put together, they already yield a very wonderful, very true, and very sufficient picture of it. Are we impatient of knowing everything? But even if science was much enlarged it would have limits, both in penetration and in extent; and there would always remain, I will not say an infinity of unsolved problems (because "problems" are created by our impatience or our contradictions), but an infinity of undiscovered facts. Nature is like a beautiful woman that may be as delightfully and as truly known at a certain distance as upon a closer view; as to knowing her through and through, that is nonsense in both cases, and might not reward our pains. The love of all-inclusiveness is as dangerous in philosophy as in art. The savour of nature can be enjoyed by us only through our own senses and insight, and an outline map of the entire universe, even if it was not fabulously concocted, would not tell us much that was worth knowing about the outlying parts of it. Without suggesting for a moment that the proper study of mankind is man only — for it may be landscape or mathematics — we may safely say that their proper study is what lies within their range and is interesting to them. For this reason the moralists who consider principally human life and paint nature only as a background to their figures are apt to be better philosophers than the speculative naturalists. In human life we are at home, and our views on it, if one-sided, are for that very reason expressive of our character and fortunes. An unfortunate peculiarity of naturalistic philosophers is that usually they have but cursory and wretched notions of the inner life of the mind; they are dead to patriotism and to religion, they hate poetry and fancy and passion and even philosophy itself; and therefore (especially if their science too, as often happens, is borrowed and vague) we need not wonder if the academic and cultivated world despises them, and harks back to the mythology of Plato or Aristotle or Hegel, who at least were conversant with the spirit of man.

Philosophers are very severe towards other philosophers because they expect too much. Even under the most favourable circumstances no mortal can be asked to seize the truth in its wholeness or at its centre. As the senses open to us only partial perspectives, taken from one point of view, and report the facts in symbols which, far from being adequate to the full nature of what surrounds us, resemble the coloured signals of danger or of free way which a railway engine-driver peers at in the night, so our speculation, which is a sort of panoramic sense, approaches things peripherally and expresses them humanly. But how doubly dyed in this subjectivity must our thought be when an orthodoxy dominant for ages has twisted the universe into the service of moral interests, and when even the heretics are entangled in a scepticism so partial and arbitrary that it substitutes psychology, the most derivative and dubious of sciences, for the direct intelligent reading of experience! But this strain of subjectivity is not in all respects an evil; it is a warm purple dye. When a way of thinking is deeply rooted in the soil, and embodies the instincts or even the characteristic errors of a people, it has a value quite independent of its truth; it constitutes a phase of human life and can powerfully affect the intellectual drama in which it figures. It is a value of this sort that attaches to modern philosophy in general, and very particularly to the American thinkers I am about to discuss. There would be a sort of irrelevance and unfairness in measuring them by the standards of pure science or even of a classic sagacity, and reproaching them for not having reached perfect consistency or fundamental clearness. Men of intense feeling — and others will hardly count — are not mirrors but lights. If pure truth happened to be what they passionately desired, they would seek it single-mindedly, and in matters within their competence they would probably find it; but the desire for pure truth, like any other, must wait to be satisfied until its organ is ripe and the conditions are favourable. The nineteenth

century was not a time and America was not a place where such an achievement could be expected. There the wisest felt themselves to be, as they
were, questioners and apostles rather than serene philosophers. We should
not pay them the doubtful compliment of attributing to them merits alien to
their tradition and scope, as if the nobleness they actually possessed — their
conscience, vigour, timeliness, and influence — were not enough.

CHAPTER II

THE ACADEMIC ENVIRONMENT

During some twenty-five years — from about 1885 to 1910 — there was at Harvard College an interesting congregation of philosophers. Why at Harvard in particular? So long as philosophy is the free pursuit of wisdom, it arises wherever men of character and penetration, each with his special experience or hobby, look about them in this world. That philosophers should be professors is an accident, and almost an anomaly. Free reflection about everything is a habit to be imitated, but not a subject to expound; and an original system, if the philosopher has one, is something dark, perilous, untested, and not ripe to be taught, nor is there much danger that any one will learn it. The genuine philosopher — as Royce liked to say, quoting the Upanishads — wanders alone like the rhinoceros. He may be followed, as he may have been anticipated; and he may even be accompanied, though there is as much danger as stimulus to him in flying with a flock. In his disputations, if he is drawn into them, he will still be soliloquising, and meeting not the arguments persuasive to others, but only such a version of them as his own thought can supply. The value of his questions and answers, as Socrates knew so well, will lie wholly in the monition of the argument developing within him and carrying him whithersoever it will, like a dream or like a god. If philosophers must earn their living and not beg (which some of them have thought more consonant with their vocation), it would be safer for them to polish lenses like Spinoza, or to sit in a black skull-cap and white beard at the door of some unfrequented museum, selling the catalogues and taking in the umbrellas; these innocent ways of earning their bread-card in the future republic would not prejudice their meditations and would keep their eyes fixed, without undue affection, on a characteristic bit of that real world which it is their business to understand. Or if, being mild and bookish, it is thought they ought to be teachers, they might teach something else than philosophy; or if philosophy is the only thing they are competent to teach, it might at least not be their own, but some classic system with which, and against which, mankind is already inoculated — preferably the civilised ethics and charming myths of Plato and Aristotle, which everybody will be the better for knowing and few the worse for believing. At best, the true philosopher can fulfil his mission very imperfectly, which is to pilot himself, or at most a few voluntary companions who may find themselves in the same boat. It is not easy for him to shout, or address a crowd; he must be silent for long seasons; for he is watching stars that move slowly and in courses that it is possible though difficult to foresee; and he is crushing all things in his heart as in a winepress, until his life and their secret flow out together.

The tendency to gather and to breed philosophers in universities does not belong to ages of free and humane reflection: it is scholastic and proper to the Middle Ages and to Germany. And the reason is not far to seek. When there is a philosophical orthodoxy, and speculation is expected to be a reasoned defence of some funded inspiration, it becomes itself corporate and traditional, and requires centres of teaching, endowment, and propaganda. Fundamental questions have been settled by the church, the government, or the Zeitgeist, and the function of the professor, himself bred in that school, is to transmit its lore to the next generation, with such original touches of insight or eloquence as he may command. To maintain and elucidate such a tradition, all the schools and universities of Christendom were originally founded; and if philosophy seemed sometimes to occupy but a small place in them — as for instance in the old-fashioned American college — it was only because the entire discipline and instruction of the place were permeated with a particular system of faith and morals, which it was almost superfluous to teach in the abstract. In those universities where philosophical controversy is rife, its traditional and scholastic character is no less obvious; it lives less on meditation than on debate, and turns on proofs, objections, paradoxes, or expedients for seeming to re-establish everything that had come to seem clearly false, by some ingenious change of front or some twist of dialectic. Its subject-matter is not so much what is known of the world, as what often very ignorant philosophers have said in answer to one another; or else, when the age is out of patience with scholasticism, orthodoxy may take refuge in intuition, and for fear of the letter without the spirit, may excuse itself from considering at all what is logical or probable, in order to embrace whatever seems most welcome and comforting. The sweet homilies of the professors then become clerical, genteel, and feminine.

Harvard College had been founded to rear puritan divines, and as Calvinism gradually dissolved, it left a void there and as it were a mould, which a philosophy expressing the same instincts in a world intellectually transformed could flow into and fill almost without knowing it. Corporate bodies are like persons, long vaguely swayed by early impressions they may have forgotten. Even when changes come over the spirit of their dream, a sense of the mission to which they were first dedicated lingers about them, and may revive, like the antiquarian and poetic Catholicism of Oxford in the nineteenth century. In academic America the Platonic and Catholic traditions had never been planted; it was only the Calvinistic tradition, when revived in some modern disguise, that could stir there the secret cord of reverence and enthusiasm. Harvard was the seminary and academy for the inner circle of Bostonians, and naturally responded to all the liberal and literary movements of which Boston was the centre. In religion it became first unitarian and afterwards neutral; in philosophy it might long have been satisfied with what other New England colleges found sufficient, namely such lofty views as the president, usually a clergyman, could introduce into his baccalaureate sermons, or into the course of lectures he might give for seniors on the evidences of Christianity or on the theory of evolution. Such philosophical initiation had sufficed for the distinguished literary men of the middle of the century, and even for so deep a sage as Emerson. But things cannot stand still, and Boston, as is well known, is not an ordinary place. When the impulse to domestic literary expression seemed to be exhausted, intellectual ambition took other forms. It was an age of science, of philology, of historical learning, and the laurels of Germany would not let Boston sleep. As it had a great public library, and hoped to have a great art museum, might it not have a great university? Harvard in one sense was a university already, in that the college (although there was only one) was surrounded by a group of professional schools, notably those of law and medicine, in which studies requisite for the service of the community, and leading potentially to brilliant careers, were carried on with conspicuous success. The number of these professional schools might have been enlarged, as has been actually done later, until training in all the professions had been provided. But it happens that the descriptive sciences, languages, mathematics, and philosophy are not studies useful for any profession, except that of teaching these very subjects over again; and there was no practical way of introducing them into the Harvard system except to graft them upon the curriculum of the college; otherwise neither money nor students could have been found for so much ornamental learning.

This circumstance, external and irrelevant as it may seem, I think had a great influence over the temper and quality of the Harvard philosophers; for it mingled responsibility for the education of youth, and much labour in it, with their pure speculation. Teaching is a delightful paternal art, and especially teaching intelligent and warm-hearted youngsters, as most American collegians are; but it is an art like acting, where the performance, often rehearsed, must be adapted to an audience hearing it only once. The speaker must make concessions to their impatience, their taste, their capacity, their prejudices, their ultimate good; he must neither bore nor perplex nor demoralise them. His thoughts must be such as can flow daily, and be set down in notes; they must come when the bell rings and stop appropriately when the bell rings a second time. The best that is in him, as Mephistopheles says in *Faust,* he dare not tell them; and as the substance of this possession is spiritual, to withhold is often to lose it. For it is not merely a matter of fearing not to be understood, or giving offence; in the presence of a hundred youthful upturned faces a man cannot, without diffidence, speak in his own person, of his own thoughts; he needs support, in order to exert influence with a good conscience; unless he feels that he is the vehicle of a massive tradition, he will become bitter, or flippant, or aggressive; if he is to teach with good grace and modesty and authority, it must not be he that speaks, but science or humanity that is speaking in him.

Now the state of Harvard College, and of American education generally, at the time to which I refer, had this remarkable effect on the philosophers there: it made their sense of social responsibility acute, because they were consciously teaching and guiding the community, as if they had been clergymen; and it made no less acute their moral loneliness, isolation, and forced self-reliance, because they were like clergymen without a church, and not only had no common philosophic doctrine to transmit, but were expected not to have one. They were invited to be at once genuine philosophers and popular professors; and the degree to which some of them managed to unite these contraries is remarkable, especially if we consider the character of the academic public they had to serve and to please. While the sentiments of most Americans in politics and morals, if a little vague, are very conservative, their democratic instincts, and the force of circumstances, have produced a system of education which anticipates all that the most extreme revolution could bring about; and while no one dreams of forcibly suppressing private property, religion, or the family, American education ignores these things, and proceeds as much as possible as if they did not exist. The child passes very young into a free school, established and managed by the municipal authorities; the teachers, even for the older boys, are chiefly unmarried women, sensitive, faithful, and feeble; their influence helps to establish that separation which is so characteristic of America between things intellectual, which remain wrapped in a feminine veil and, as it were, under glass, and the rough business and passions of life. The lessons are ambitious in range, but are made as easy, as interesting, and as optional as possible; the stress is divided between what the child likes now and what he is going to need in his trade or profession. The young people are sympathetically encouraged to instruct themselves and to educate one another. They romp and make fun like young monkeys, they flirt and have their private "brain-storms" like little supermen and superwomen. They are tremendously in earnest about their college intrigues and intercollegiate athletic wars. They are fond, often compassionately fond, of their parents, and home is all the more sacred to them in that they are seldom there. They enjoy a surprising independence in habits, friendships, and opinions. Brothers and sisters often choose different religions. The street, the school, the young people's club, the magazine, the popular novel, furnish their mental pabulum. The force of example and of passing custom is all the more irresistible in this absence of authority and tradition; for this sort of independence rather diminishes the power of being original, by supplying a slenderer basis and a thinner soil from which originality might spring. Uniformity is established spontaneously without discipline, as in the popular speech and ethics of every nation. Against this tendency to uniformity the efforts of a cultivated minority to maintain a certain distinction and infuse it into their lives and minds are not very successful. They have secondary schools for their boys in which the teachers are men, and even boarding-schools in the country, more or less Gothic in aspect and English in regimen; there are other semi-foreign institutions and circles, Catholic or Jewish, in which religion is the dominant consideration. There is also the society of the very rich, with cosmopolitan leanings and a vivacious interest in artistic undertakings and personalities. But all these distinctions, important as they may seem to those who cultivate them, are a mere shimmer and ripple on the surface of American life; and for an observer who sees things in perspective they almost disappear. By a merciful dispensation of nature, the pupils of these choice establishments, the moment they plunge into business or politics, acquire the protective colouring of their environment and become indistinguishable from the generic American. Their native disposition was after all the national one, their attempted special education was perfunctory, and the influence of their public activities and surroundings is overwhelming. American life is a powerful solvent. As it stamps the immigrant, almost before he can speak English, with an unmistakable muscular tension, cheery self-confidence and habitual challenge in the voice and eyes, so it seems to neutralise every intellectual element, however tough and alien it may be, and to fuse it in the native good-will, complacency, thoughtlessness, and optimism.

Consider, for instance, the American Catholics, of whom there are nominally many millions, and who often seem to retain their ancestral faith sincerely and affectionately. This faith took shape during the decline of the Roman empire; it is full of large disillusions about this world and minute illusions about the other. It is ancient, metaphysical, poetic, elaborate, ascetic, autocratic, and intolerant. It confronts the boastful natural man, such as the American is, with a thousand denials and menaces. Everything in American life is at the antipodes to such a system. Yet the American Catholic is entirely at peace. His tone in everything, even in religion, is cheerfully American. It is wonderful how silently, amicably, and happily he lives in a community whose spirit is profoundly hostile to that of his religion. He seems to take stock in his church as he might in a gold mine — sure it is a grand, dazzling, unique thing; and perhaps he masks, even to himself, his purely imaginative ardour about it, with the pretext that it is sure to make his fortune both in this life and in the next. His church, he will tell you, is a first-rate church to belong to; the priests are fine fellows, like the policemen; the Sisters are dear noble women, like his own sisters; his parish is flourishing, and always rebuilding its church and founding new schools, orphan asylums, sodalities, confraternities, perpetual adoration societies. No parish can raise so much money for any object, or if there are temporary troubles, the fact still remains that America has three Cardinals and that the Catholic religion is the biggest religion on earth. Attachment to his church in such a temper brings him into no serious conflict with his Protestant neighbours. They live and meet on common ground. Their respective religions pass among them for family matters, private and sacred, with no political implications.

Such was the education and such the atmosphere of intellectual innocence which prevailed in the public — mostly undergraduates — to which the Harvard philosophers adapted their teaching and to some extent their philosophy. The students were intelligent, ambitious, remarkably able to "do things"; they were keen about the matters that had already entered into their lives, and invincibly happy in their ignorance of everything else. A gentle contempt for the past permeated their judgements. They were not accustomed to the notion of authority, nor aware that it might have legitimate grounds; they instinctively disbelieved in the superiority of what was out of reach. About high questions of politics and religion their minds were open but vague; they seemed not to think them of practical importance; they acquiesced in people having any views they liked on such subjects; the fluent and fervid enthusiasms so common among European students, prophesying about politics, philosophy, and art, were entirely unknown among them. Instead they had absorbing local traditions of their own, athletic and social, and their college life was their true education, an education in friendship, co-operation, and freedom. In the eighteen-eighties a good deal of old-fashioned shabbiness and jollity lingered about Harvard. Boston and Cambridge in those days resembled in some ways the London of Dickens: the same dismal wealth, the same speechifying, the same anxious respectability, the same sordid back streets, with their air of shiftlessness and decay, the same odd figures and loud humour, and, to add a touch of horror, the monstrous suspicion that some of the inhabitants might be secretly wicked. Life, for the undergraduates, was full of droll incidents and broad farce; it drifted good-naturedly from one commonplace thing to another. Standing packed in the tinkling horse-car, their coat-collars above their ears and their feet deep in the winter straw, they jogged in a long half-hour to Boston, there to enjoy the delights of female society, the theatre, or a good dinner. And in the summer days, for Class Day and Commencement, feminine and elderly Boston would return the visit, led by the governor of Massachusetts in his hired carriage-and-four, and by the local orators and poets, brimming with jokes and conventional sentiments, and eager not so much to speed the youngsters on their career, as to air their own wit, and warm their hearts with punch and with collective memories of youth. It was an idyllic, haphazard, humoristic existence, without fine imagination, without any familiar infusion of scholarship, without articulate religion: a flutter of intelligence in a void, flying into trivial play, in order to drop back, as soon as college days were over, into the drudgery of affairs. There was the love of beauty, but without the sight of it; for the bits of pleasant landscape or the works of art which might break the ugliness of the foreground were a sort of aesthetic miscellany, enjoyed as one enjoys a museum; there was nothing in which the spirit of beauty was deeply interfused, charged with passion and discipline and intricate familiar associations with delicate and noble things. Of course, the sky is above every country, and New England had brilliant sunsets and deep snows, and sea and woods were at hand for the holidays; and it was notable how much even what a homely art or accident might have done for the towns was studied and admired. Old corners were pointed out where the dingy red brick had lost its rigidity and taken on a mossy tinge, and where here and there a pane of glass, surviving all tenants and housemaids, had turned violet in the sunlight of a hundred years; and most precious of all were the high thin elms, spreading aloft, looped and drooping over old streets and commons. And yet it seemed somehow as if the sentiment lavished on these things had been intended by nature for something else, for something more important. Not only had the mind of the nation been originally somewhat chilled and impoverished by

Protestantism, by migration to a new world, by absorption in material tasks, but what fine sensibility lingered in an older generation was not easily transmitted to the young. The young had their own ways, which on principle were to be fostered and respected; and one of their instincts was to associate only with those of their own age and calibre. The young were simply young, and the old simply old, as among peasants. Teachers and pupils seemed animals of different species, useful and well-disposed towards each other, like a cow and a milkmaid; periodic contributions could pass between them, but not conversation. This circumstance shows how much American intelligence is absorbed in what is not intellectual. Their tasks and their pleasures divide people of different ages; what can unite them is ideas, impersonal interests, liberal arts. Without these they cannot forget their mutual inferiority.

Certainly those four college years, judged by any external standard, were trivial and wasted; but Americans, although so practical in their adult masculine undertakings, are slow to take umbrage at the elaborate playfulness of their wives and children. With the touching humility of strength, they seem to say to themselves, "Let the dear creatures have their fling, and be happy: what else are we old fellows slaving for?" And certainly the joy of life is the crown of it; but have American ladies and collegians achieved the joy of life? Is that the summit?

William James had a theory that if some scientific widower, with a child about to learn to walk, could be persuaded to allow the child's feet to be blistered, it would turn out, when the blisters were healed, that the child would walk as well as if he had practised and had many a fall; because the machinery necessary for walking would have matured in him automatically, just as the machinery for breathing does in the womb. The case of the old-fashioned American college may serve to support this theory. It blistered young men's heads for four years and prevented them from practising anything useful; yet at the end they were found able to do most things as well, or twice as well, as their contemporaries who had been all that time apprenticed and chained to a desk. Manhood and sagacity ripen of themselves; it suffices not to repress or distort them. The college liberated the young man from the pursuit of money, from hypocrisy, from the control of women. He could grow for a time according to his nature, and if this growth was not guided by much superior wisdom or deep study, it was not warped by any serious perversion; and if the intellectual world did not permanently entice him, are we so sure that in philosophy, for instance, it had anything to offer that was very solid in itself, or humanly very important? At least he learned that such things existed, and gathered a shrewd notion of what they could do for a man, and what they might make of him.

When Harvard was reformed — and I believe all the colleges are reformed now — the immediate object was not to refine college life or render it more scholarly, though for certain circles this was accomplished incidentally; the object was rather to extend the scope of instruction, and make it more advanced. It is natural that every great city, the capital of any nation or region, should wish to possess a university in the literal sense of the word — an encyclopædic institute, or group of institutes, to teach and foster all the professions, all the arts, and all the sciences. Such a university need have nothing to do with education, with the transmission of a particular moral and intellectual tradition. Education might be courteously presupposed. The teacher would not be a man with his hand on a lad's shoulder, his son or young brother; he would be an expert in some science, delivering lectures for public instruction, while perhaps privately carrying on investigations with the aid of a few disciples whom he would be training in his specialty. There would be no reason why either the professors or the auditors in such an institution should live together or should have much in common in religion, morals, or breeding, or should even speak the same language. On the contrary, if only each was competent in his way, the more miscellaneous their types the more perfect would these render their *universitas*. The public addressed, also, need not be restricted, any more than the public at a church or a theatre or a town library, by any requirements as to age, sex, race, or attainments. They would come on their own responsibility, to pursue what studies they chose, and so long as they found them profitable. Nor need there be any limit as to the subjects broached, or any division of them into faculties or departments, except perhaps for convenience in administration. One of the functions of professors would be to invent new subjects, because this world is so complex, and the play of the human mind upon it is so external and iridescent, that, as men's interests and attitude vary, fresh unities and fresh aspects are always discernible in everything.

As Harvard University developed, all these characteristics appeared in it in a more or less marked degree; but the transformation was never complete. The centre of it remained a college, with its local constituency and rooted traditions, and its thousand or two thousand undergraduates needing to be educated. Experts in every science and money to pay them were not at hand, and the foreign talent that could be attracted did not always prove morally or socially digestible. The browsing undergraduate could simply range with a looser tether, and he was reinforced by a fringe of graduates who had not yet had enough, or who were attracted from other colleges. These graduates came to form a sort of normal school for future professors, stamped as in Germany with a Ph.D.; and the teachers in each subject became a committee charged with something of the functions of a registry office, to find places for their nurslings. The university could thus acquire a national and even an international function, drawing in distinguished talent and youthful ambition from everywhere, and sending forth in various directions its apostles of light and learning.

I think it is intelligible that in such a place and at such a crisis philosophy should have played a conspicuous part, and also that it should have had an ambiguous character. There had to be, explicit or implicit, a philosophy for the college. A place where all polite Boston has been educated for centuries cannot bely its moral principles and religious questionings; it must transmit its austere, faithful, reforming spirit. But at the same time there had now to be a philosophy for the university. A chief part of that traditional faith was the faith in freedom, in inquiry; and it was necessary, in the very interests of the traditional philosophy, to take account of all that was being said in the world, and to incorporate the spirit of the times in the spirit of the fathers. Accordingly, no single abstract opinion was particularly tabooed at Harvard; granted industry, sobriety, and some semblance of theism, no professor was expected to agree with any other. I believe the authorities would have been well pleased, for the sake of completeness, to have added a Buddhist, a Moslem, and a Catholic scholastic to the philosophical faculty, if only suitable sages could have been found, house-trained, as it were, and able to keep pace with the academic machine and to attract a sufficient number of pupils. But this official freedom was not true freedom, there was no happiness in it. A slight smell of brimstone lingered in the air. You might think what you liked, but you must consecrate your belief or your unbelief to the common task of encouraging everybody and helping everything on. You might almost be an atheist, if you were troubled enough about it. The atmosphere was not that of intelligence nor of science, it was that of duty.

In the academic life and methods of the university there was the same incomplete transformation. The teaching required was for the most part college teaching, in college subjects, such as might well have been entrusted to tutors; but it was given by professors in the form of lectures, excessive in number and too often repeated; and they were listened to by absent-minded youths, ill-grounded in the humanities, and not keenly alive to intellectual interests. The graduates (like the young ladies) were more attentive and anxious not to miss anything, but they were no better prepared and often less intelligent; and there is no dunce like a mature dunce. Ac-

cordingly, the professor of philosophy had to swim against rather a powerful current. Sometimes he succumbed to the reality; and if, for instance, he
happened to mention Darwin, and felt a blank before him, he would add in
a parenthesis, "Darwin, Charles, author of the *Origin of Species,* 1859;
epoch-making work." At other times he might lose himself altogether in the
ideal and imagine that he was publishing immortal thoughts to the true
university, to the world at large, and was feeling an exhilarating contact
with masses of mankind, themselves quickened by his message. He might
see in his mind's eye rows of learned men and women before him, familiar
with every doubt, hardened to every conflict of opinion, ready for any
revolution, whose minds nothing he could say could possibly shock, or
disintegrate any further; on the contrary, the naked truth, which is gentle in
its austerity, might come to them as a blessed deliverance, and he might
fancy himself for a moment a sort of hero from the realms of light descend-
ing into the nether regions and throwing a sop of reason into the jaws of
snarling prejudice and frantic error. Or if the class was small, and only two
or three were gathered together, he might imagine instead that he was
sowing seeds of wisdom, warmed by affection, in the minds of genuine
disciples, future tabernacles of the truth. It is possible that if the reality had
corresponded more nearly with these dreams, and Harvard had actually
been an adult university, philosophers there might have distilled their doctrines into a greater purity. As it was, Harvard philosophy had an opposite
merit: it represented faithfully the complex inspiration of the place and
hour. As the university was a local puritan college opening its windows to
the scientific world, so at least the two most gifted of its philosophers were
men of intense feeling, religious and romantic, but attentive to the facts of
nature and the currents of worldly opinion; and each of them felt himself
bound by two different responsibilities, that of describing things as they are,
and that of finding them propitious to certain preconceived human desires.
And while they shared this doubled allegiance, they differed very much in
temper, education, and taste. William James was what is called an empiricist, Josiah Royce an idealist; they were excellent friends and greatly influenced each other, and the very diversity between them rendered their con-
junction typical of the state of philosophy in England and America, divided
between the old British and the German schools. As if all this intellectual
complication had not been enough, they were obliged to divide their energies externally, giving to their daily tasks as professors and pedagogues
what duty demanded, and only the remainder to scholarship, reflection, and
literary work. Even this distracting circumstance, however, had its compen-
sations. College work was a human bond, a common practical interest; it

helped to keep up that circulation of the blood which made the whole Harvard school of philosophy a vital unit, and co-operative in its freedom. There was a general momentum in it, half institutional, half moral, a single troubled, noble, exciting life. Every one was labouring with the contradiction he felt in things, and perhaps in himself; all were determined to find some honest way out of it, or at least to bear it bravely. It was a fresh morning in the life of reason, cloudy but brightening.

CHAPTER III

WILLIAM JAMES

William James enjoyed in his youth what are called advantages: he lived among cultivated people, travelled, had teachers of various nationalities. His father was one of those somewhat obscure sages whom early America produced: mystics of independent mind, hermits in the desert of business, and heretics in the churches. They were intense individualists, full of veneration for the free souls of their children, and convinced that every one should paddle his own canoe, especially on the high seas. William James accordingly enjoyed a stimulating if slightly irregular education: he never acquired that reposeful mastery of particular authors and those safe ways of feeling and judging which are fostered in great schools and universities. In consequence he showed an almost physical horror of club sentiment and of the stifling atmosphere of all officialdom. He had a knack for drawing, and rather the temperament of the artist; but the unlovely secrets of nature and the troubles of man preoccupied him, and he chose medicine for his profession. Instead of practising, however, he turned to teaching physiology, and from that passed gradually to psychology and philosophy.

In his earlier years he retained some traces of polyglot student days at Paris, Bonn, Vienna, or Geneva; he slipped sometimes into foreign phrases, uttered in their full vernacular; and there was an occasional afterglow of Bohemia about him, in the bright stripe of a shirt or the exuberance of a tie. On points of art or medicine he retained a professional touch and an unconscious ease which he hardly acquired in metaphysics. I suspect he had heartily admired some of his masters in those other subjects, but had never seen a philosopher whom he would have cared to resemble. Of course there was nothing of the artist in William James, as the artist is sometimes conceived in England, nothing of the æsthete, nothing affected or limp. In person he was short rather than tall, erect, brisk, bearded, intensely masculine. While he shone in expression and would have wished his style to be noble if it could also be strong, he preferred in the end to be spontaneous, and to leave it at that; he tolerated slang in himself rather than primness. The rough, homely, picturesque phrase, whatever was graphic and racy, recommended itself to him; and his conversation outdid his writing in this respect. He believed in improvisation, even in thought; his lectures were not minutely prepared. Know your subject thoroughly, he used to say, and trust to luck for the rest. There was a deep sense of insecurity in him, a mixture of humility with romanticism: we were likely to be more or less wrong anyhow, but we might be wholly sincere. One moment should respect the insight of another, without trying to establish too regimental a uniformity. If you corrected yourself tartly, how could you know that the correction was not the worse mistake? All of our opinions were born free and equal, all children of the Lord, and if they were not consistent that was the Lord's business, not theirs. In reality, James was consistent enough, as even Emerson (more extreme in this sort of irresponsibility) was too. Inspiration has its limits, sometimes very narrow ones. But James was not consecutive, not insistent; he turned to a subject afresh, without egotism or pedantry; he dropped his old points, sometimes very good ones; and he modestly looked for light from others, who had less light than himself.

His excursions into philosophy were accordingly in the nature of raids, and it is easy for those who are attracted by one part of his work to ignore other parts, in themselves perhaps more valuable. I think that in fact his popularity does not rest on his best achievements. His popularity rests on three somewhat incidental books, *The Will to Believe, Pragmatism,* and *The Varieties of Religious Experience,* whereas, as it seems to me, his best achievement is his *Principles of Psychology.* In this book he surveys, in a way which for him is very systematic, a subject made to his hand. In its ostensible outlook it is a treatise like any other, but what distinguishes it is the author's gift for evoking vividly the very life of the mind. This is a work of imagination; and the subject as he conceived it, which is the flux of immediate experience in men in general, requires imagination to read it at all. It is a literary subject, like autobiography or psychological fiction, and can be treated only poetically; and in this sense Shakespeare is a better psychologist than Locke or Kant. Yet this gift of imagination is not merely literary; it is not useless in divining the truths of science, and it is invaluable in throwing off prejudice and scientific shams. The fresh imagination and vitality of William James led him to break through many a false convention. He saw that experience, as we endure it, is not a mosaic of distinct sensations, nor the expression of separate hostile faculties, such as reason and the passions, or sense and the categories; it is rather a flow of mental discourse, like a dream, in which all divisions and units are vague and shifting, and the whole is continually merging together and drifting apart. It fades gradually in the rear, like the wake of a ship, and bites into the future, like the bow cutting the water. For the candid psychologist, carried bodily on this voyage of discovery, the past is but a questionable report, and the future wholly indeterminate; everything is simply what it is experienced as being.

At the same time, psychology is supposed to be a science, a claim which would tend to confine it to the natural history of man, or the study of behaviour, as is actually proposed by Auguste Comte and by some of James's own disciples, more jejune if more clear-headed than he. As matters now stand, however, psychology as a whole is not a science, but a branch of philosophy; it brings together the literary description of mental discourse and the scientific description of material life, in order to consider the relation between them, which is the nexus of human nature.

What was James's position on this crucial question? It is impossible to reply unequivocally. He approached philosophy as mankind originally approached it, without having a philosophy, and he lent himself to various hypotheses in various directions. He professed to begin his study on the assumptions of common sense, that there is a material world which the animals that live in it are able to perceive and to think about. He gave a congruous extension to this view in his theory that emotion is purely bodily sensation, and also in his habit of conceiving the mind as a total shifting sensibility. To pursue this path, however, would have led him to admit that nature was automatic and mind simply cognitive, conclusions from which every instinct in him recoiled. He preferred to believe that mind and matter had independent energies and could lend one another a hand, matter operating by motion and mind by intention. This dramatic, amphibious way of picturing causation is natural to common sense, and might be defended if it were clearly defined; but James was insensibly carried away from it by a subtle implication of his method. This implication was that experience or mental discourse not only constituted a set of substantive facts, but the *only* substantive facts; all else, even that material world which his psychology had postulated, could be nothing but a verbal or fantastic symbol for sensations in their experienced order. So that while nominally the door was kept open to any hypothesis regarding the conditions of the psychological flux, in truth the question was prejudged. The hypotheses, which were parts of this psychological flux, could have no object save other parts of it. That flux itself, therefore, which he could picture so vividly, was the fundamental existence. The *sense* of bounding over the waves, the *sense* of being on an adventurous voyage, was the living fact; the rest was dead reckoning. Where one's gift is, there will one's faith be also; and to this poet appearance was the only reality.

This sentiment, which always lay at the back of his mind, reached something like formal expression in his latest writings, where he sketched what he called radical empiricism. The word experience is like a shrapnel shell, and bursts into a thousand meanings. Here we must no longer think of its setting, its discoveries, or its march; to treat it radically we must abstract its immediate objects and reduce it to pure data. It is obvious (and the sequel has already proved) that experience so understood would lose its romantic signification, as a personal adventure or a response to the shocks of fortune. "Experience" would turn into a cosmic dance of absolute entities created and destroyed *in vacuo* according to universal laws, or perhaps by chance. No minds would gather this experience, and no material agencies would impose it; but the immediate objects present to any one would simply be parts of the universal fireworks, continuous with the rest, and all the parts, even if not present to anybody, would have the same status. Experience would then not at all resemble what Shakespeare reports or what James himself had described in his psychology. If it could be experienced as it flows in its entirety (which is fortunately impracticable), it would be a perpetual mathematical nightmare. Every whirling atom, every changing relation, and every incidental perspective would be a part of it. I am far from wishing to deny for a moment the scientific value of such a cosmic system, if it can be worked out; physics and mathematics seem to me to plunge far deeper than literary psychology into the groundwork of this world; but human experience is the stuff of literary psychology; we cannot reach the stuff of physics and mathematics except by arresting or even hypostatising some elements of appearance, and expanding them on an abstracted and hypothetical plane of their own. Experience, as memory and literature re-hearse it, remains nearer to us than that: it is something dreamful, passion-ate, dramatic, and significative.

Certainly this personal human experience, expressible in literature and in talk, and no cosmic system however profound, was what James knew best and trusted most. Had he seen the developments of his radical empiri-cism, I cannot help thinking he would have marvelled that such logical mechanisms should have been hatched out of that egg. The principal prob-lems and aspirations that haunted him all his life long would lose their meaning in that cosmic atmosphere. The pragmatic nature of truth, for instance, would never suggest itself in the presence of pure data; but a romantic mind soaked in agnosticism, conscious of its own habits and assuming an environment the exact structure of which can never be ob-served, may well convince itself that, for experience, truth is nothing but a happy use of signs — which is indeed the truth of literature. But if we once accept *any* system of the universe as literally true, the value of convenient signs to prepare us for such experience as is yet absent cannot be called truth: it is plainly nothing but a necessary inaccuracy. So, too, with the question of the survival of the human individual after death. For radical empiricism a human individual is simply a certain cycle or complex of terms, like any other natural fact; that some echoes of his mind should recur after the regular chimes have ceased, would have nothing paradoxical about it. A mathematical world is a good deal like music, with its repetitions and transpositions, and a little trill, which you might call a person, might well peep up here and there all over a vast composition. Something of that sort may be the truth of spiritualism; but it is not what the spiritualists imagine. Their whole interest lies not in the experiences they have, but in the inter-pretation they give to them, assigning them to troubled spirits in another world; but both another world and a spirit are notions repugnant to a radical empiricism.

I think it is important to remember, if we are not to misunderstand William James, that his radical empiricism and pragmatism were in his own mind only methods; his doctrine, if he may be said to have had one, was agnosticism. And just because he was an agnostic (feeling instinctively that beliefs and opinions, if they had any objective beyond themselves, could never be sure they had attained it), he seemed in one sense so favourable to credulity. He was not credulous himself, far from it; he was well aware that the trust he put in people or ideas might betray him. For that very reason he was respectful and pitiful to the trustfulness of others. Doubtless they were wrong, but who were we to say so? In his own person he was ready enough to face the mystery of things, and whatever the womb of time might bring forth; but until the curtain was rung down on the last act of the drama (and it might have no last act!) he wished the intellectual cripples and the moral hunchbacks not to be jeered at; perhaps they might turn out to be the heroes of the play. Who could tell what heavenly influences might not pierce to these sensitive half-flayed creatures, which are lost on the thick-skinned, the sane, and the duly goggled? We must not suppose, however, that James meant these contrite and romantic suggestions dogmatically. The agnostic, as well as the physician and neurologist in him, was never quite eclipsed. The hope that some new revelation might come from the lowly and weak could never mean to him what it meant to the early Christians. For him it was only a right conceded to them to experiment with their special faiths; he did not expect such faiths to be discoveries of absolute fact, which every-body else might be constrained to recognise. If any one had made such a claim, and had seemed to have some chance of imposing it universally, James would have been the first to turn against him; not, of course, on the ground that it was *impossible* that such an orthodoxy should be true, but with a profound conviction that it was to be feared and distrusted. No: the degree of authority and honour to be accorded to various human faiths was a moral question, not a theoretical one. All faiths were what they were experienced as being, in their capacity of faiths; these faiths, not their objects, were the hard facts we must respect. We cannot pass, except under the illusion of the moment, to anything firmer or on a deeper level. There was accordingly no sense of security, no joy, in James's apology for personal religion. He did not really believe; he merely believed in the right of believing that you might be right if you believed.

It is this underlying agnosticism that explains an incoherence which we might find in his popular works, where the story and the moral do not seem to hang together. Professedly they are works of psychological observation; but the tendency and suasion in them seems to run to disintegrating the idea of truth, recommending belief without reason, and encouraging superstition. A psychologist who was not an agnostic would have indicated, as far as possible, whether the beliefs and experiences he was describing were instances of delusion or of rare and fine perception, or in what measure they were a mixture of both. But James — and this is what gives such romantic warmth to these writings of his — disclaims all antecedent or superior knowledge, listens to the testimony of each witness in turn, and only by accident allows us to feel that he is swayed by the eloquence and vehemence of some of them rather than of others. This method is modest, generous, and impartial; but if James intended, as I think he did, to picture the *drama* of human belief, with its risks and triumphs, the method was inadequate. Dramatists never hesitate to assume, and to let the audience perceive, who is good and who bad, who wise and who foolish, in their pieces; otherwise their work would be as impotent dramatically as scientifically. The tragedy and comedy of life lie precisely in the contrast between the illusions or passions of the characters and their true condition and fate, hidden from them at first, but evident to the author and the public. If in our diffidence and scrupulous fairness we refuse to take this judicial attitude, we shall be led to strange conclusions. The navigator, for instance, trusting his "experience" (which here, as in the case of religious people, means his imagination and his art), insists on believing that the earth is spherical; he has sailed round it. That is to say, he has seemed to himself to steer westward and westward, and has seemed to get home again. But how should he know that home is now where it was before, or that his past and present impressions of it come from the same, or from any, material object? How should he know that space is as trim and tri-dimensional as the discredited Euclidians used to say it was? If, on the contrary, my worthy aunt, trusting to her longer and less ambiguous experience of her garden, insists that the earth is flat, and observes that the theory that it is round, which is only a theory, is much less often tested and found useful than her own perception of its flatness, and that moreover that theory is pedantic, intellectualistic, and a product of academies, and a rash dogma to impose on mankind for ever and ever, it might seem that on James's principle we ought to agree with her. But no; on James's real principles we need not agree with her, nor with the navigator either. Radical empiricism, which is radical agnosticism, delivers us from so benighted a choice. For the quarrel becomes unmeaning when we remember that the earth is *both* flat and round, if it is experienced as being both. The substantive fact is not a single object on which both the perception and the theory are expected to converge; the substantive facts are the theory and the perception themselves. And we may note in passing that empiricism, when it ceases to value experience as a means of discovering external things, can give up its ancient prejudice in favour of sense as against imagination, for imagination and thought are immediate experiences as much as sensation is: they are therefore, for absolute empiricism, no less actual ingredients of reality.

In *The Varieties of Religious Experience* we find the same apologetic intention running through a vivid account of what seems for the most part (as James acknowledged) religious disease. Normal religious experience is hardly described in it. Religious experience, for the great mass of mankind, consists in simple faith in the truth and benefit of their religious traditions. But to James something so conventional and rationalistic seemed hardly experience and hardly religious; he was thinking only of irruptive visions and feelings as interpreted by the mystics who had them. These interpretations he ostensibly presents, with more or less wistful sympathy for what they were worth; but emotionally he wished to champion them. The religions that had sprung up in America spontaneously — communistic, hysterical, spiritistic, or medicinal — were despised by select and superior people. You might inquire into them, as you might go slumming, but they remained suspect and distasteful. This picking up of genteel skirts on the part of his acquaintance prompted William James to roll up his sleeves — not for a knock-out blow, but for a thorough clinical demonstration. He would tenderly vivisect the experiences in question, to show how living they were, though of course he could not guarantee, more than other surgeons do, that the patient would survive the operation. An operation that eventually kills may be technically successful, and the man may die cured; and so a description of religion that showed it to be madness might first show how real and how warm it was, so that if it perished, at least it would perish understood.

I never observed in William James any personal anxiety or enthusiasm for any of these dubious tenets. His conception even of such a thing as free-will, which he always ardently defended, remained vague; he avoided defining even what he conceived to be desirable in such matters. But he wished to protect the weak against the strong, and what he hated beyond everything was the *non possumus* of any constituted authority. Philosophy for him had a Polish constitution; so long as a single vote was cast against the majority, nothing could pass. The suspense of judgement which he had imposed on himself as a duty, became almost a necessity. I think it would have depressed him if he had had to confess that any important question was finally settled. He would still have hoped that something might turn up on the other side, and that just as the scientific hangman was about to despatch the poor convicted prisoner, an unexpected witness would ride up in hot haste, and prove him innocent. Experience seems to most of us to lead to conclusions, but empiricism has sworn never to draw them.

In the discourse on "The Energies of Men," certain physiological marvels are recorded, as if to suggest that the resources of our minds and bodies are infinite, or can be infinitely enlarged by divine grace. Yet James would not, I am sure, have accepted that inference. He would, under pressure, have drawn in his mystical horns under his scientific shell; but he was not naturalist enough to feel instinctively that the wonderful and the natural are all of a piece, and that only our degree of habituation distinguishes them. A nucleus, which we may poetically call the soul, certainly lies within us, by which our bodies and minds are generated and controlled, like an army by a government. In this nucleus, since nature in a small compass has room for anything, vast quantities of energy may well be stored up, which may be tapped on occasion, or which may serve like an electric spark to let loose energy previously existing in the grosser parts. But the absolute autocracy of this central power, or its success in imposing extraordinary trials on its subjects, is not an obvious good. Perhaps, like a democratic government, the soul is at its best when it merely collects and coordinates the impulses coming from the senses. The inner man is at times a tyrant, parasitical, wasteful, and voluptuous. At other times he is fanatical and mad. When he asks for and obtains violent exertions from the body, the question often is, as with the exploits of conquerors and conjurers, whether the impulse to do such prodigious things was not gratuitous, and the things nugatory. Who would wish to be a mystic? James himself, who by nature was a spirited rather than a spiritual man, had no liking for sanctimonious transcendentalists, visionaries, or ascetics; he hated minds that run thin. But he hastened to correct this manly impulse, lest it should be unjust, and forced himself to overcome his repugnance. This was made easier when the unearthly phenomenon had a healing or saving function in the everyday material world; miracle then re-established its ancient identity with medicine, and both of them were humanised. Even when this union was not attained, James was reconciled to the miracle-workers partly by his great charity, and partly by his hunter's instinct to follow a scent, for he believed discoveries to be imminent. Besides, a philosopher who is a teacher of youth is more concerned to give people a right start than a right conclusion. James fell in with the hortatory tradition of college sages; he turned his psychology, whenever he could do so honestly, to purposes of edification; and his little sermons on habit, on will, on faith, and this on the latent capacities of men, were fine and stirring, and just the sermons to preach to the young Christian soldier. He was much less sceptical in morals than in science. He seems to have felt sure that certain thoughts and hopes — those familiar to a liberal Protestantism — were every man's true friends in life. This assumption would have been hard to defend if he or those he habitually addressed had ever questioned it; yet his whole argument for voluntarily cultivating these beliefs rests on this assumption, that they are beneficent. Since, whether we will or no, we cannot escape the risk of error, and must succumb to some human or pathological bias, at least we might do so gracefully and in the form that would profit us most, by clinging to those prejudices which help us to lead what we all feel is a good life. But what is a good life? Had William James, had the people about him, had modern philosophers anywhere, any notion of that? I cannot think so. They had much experience of personal goodness, and love of it; they had standards of character and right conduct; but as to what might render human existence good, excellent, beautiful, happy, and worth having as a whole, their notions were utterly thin and barbarous. They had forgotten the Greeks, or never known them.

This argument accordingly suffers from the same weakness as the similar argument of Pascal in favour of Catholic orthodoxy. You should force yourself to believe in it, he said, because if you do so and are right you win heaven, while if you are wrong you lose nothing. What would Protestants, Mohammedans, and Hindus say to that? Those alternatives of Pascal's are not the sole nor the true alternatives; such a wager — betting on the improbable because you are offered big odds — is an unworthy parody of the real choice between wisdom and folly. There is no heaven to be won in such a spirit, and if there was, a philosopher would despise it. So William James would have us bet on immortality, or bet on our power to succeed, because if we win the wager we can live to congratulate ourselves on our true instinct, while we lose nothing if we have made a mistake; for unless you have the satisfaction of finding that you have been right, the dignity of having been right is apparently nothing. Or if the argument is rather that these beliefs, whether true or false, make life better in this world, the thing is simply false. To be boosted by an illusion is not to live better than to live in harmony with the truth; it is not nearly so safe, not nearly so sweet, and not nearly so fruitful. These refusals to part with a decayed illusion are really an infection to the mind. Believe, certainly; we cannot help believing; but believe rationally, holding what seems certain for certain, what seems probable for probable, what seems desirable for desirable, and what seems false for false.

In this matter, as usual, James had a true psychological fact and a generous instinct behind his confused moral suggestions. It is a psychological fact that men are influenced in their beliefs by their will and desires; indeed, I think we can go further and say that in its essence belief is an expression of impulse, of readiness to act. It is only peripherally, as our action is gradually adjusted to things, and our impulses to our possible or necessary action, that our ideas begin to hug the facts, and to acquire a true, if still a symbolic, significance. We do not need a will to believe; we only need a will to study the object in which we are inevitably believing. But James was thinking less of belief in what we find than of belief in what we hope for: a belief which is not at all clear and not at all necessary in the life of mortals. Like most Americans, however, only more lyrically, James felt the call of the future and the assurance that it could be made far better, totally other, than the past. The pictures that religion had painted of heaven or the millennium were not what he prized, although his Swedenborgian connection might have made him tender to them, as perhaps it did to familiar spirits. It was the moral succour offered by religion, its open spaces, the possibility of miracles *in extremis,* that must be retained. If we recoiled at the thought of being dupes (which is perhaps what nature intended us to be), were we less likely to be dupes in disbelieving these sustaining truths than in believing them? Faith was needed to bring about the reform of faith itself, as well as all other reforms.

In some cases faith in success could nerve us to bring success about, and so justify itself by its own operation. This is a thought typical of James at his worst — a worst in which there is always a good side. Here again psychological observation is used with the best intentions to hearten oneself and other people; but the fact observed is not at all understood, and a moral twist is given to it which (besides being morally questionable) almost amounts to falsifying the fact itself. Why does belief that you can jump a ditch help you to jump it? Because it is a symptom of the fact that you *could* jump it, that your legs were fit and that the ditch was two yards wide and not twenty. A rapid and just appreciation of these facts has given you your confidence, or at least has made it reasonable, manly, and prophetic; otherwise you would have been a fool and got a ducking for it. Assurance is contemptible and fatal unless it is self-knowledge. If you had been rattled you might have failed, because that would have been a symptom of the fact that you were out of gear; you would have been afraid because you trembled, as James at his best proclaimed. You would never have quailed if your system had been reacting smoothly to its opportunities, any more than you would totter and see double if you were not intoxicated. Fear is a sensation of actual nervousness and disarray, and confidence a sensation of actual readiness; they are not disembodied feelings, existing for no reason, the devil Funk and the angel Courage, one or the other of whom may come down arbitrarily into your body, and revolutionise it. That is childish mythology, which survives innocently enough as a figure of speech, until a philosopher is found to take that figure of speech seriously. Nor is the moral suggestion here less unsound. What is good is not the presumption of power, but the possession of it: a clear head, aware of its resources, not a fuddled optimism, calling up spirits from the vasty deep. Courage is not a virtue, said Socrates, unless it is also wisdom. Could anything be truer both of courage in doing and of courage in believing? But it takes tenacity, it takes *reasonable* courage, to stick to scientific insights such as this of Socrates or that of James about the emotions; it is easier to lapse into the traditional manner, to search natural philosophy for miracles and moral lessons, and in morals proper, in the reasoned expression of preference, to splash about without a philosophy.

William James shared the passions of liberalism. He belonged to the left, which, as they say in Spain, is the side of the heart, as the right is that of the liver; at any rate there was much blood and no gall in his philosophy. He was one of those elder Americans still disquieted by the ghost of tyranny, social and ecclesiastical. Even the beauties of the past troubled him; he had a puritan feeling that they were tainted. They had been cruel and frivolous, and must have suppressed far better things. But what, we may ask, might these better things be? It may do for a revolutionary politician to say: "I may not know what I want — except office — but I know what I don't want"; it will never do for a philosopher. Aversions and fears imply principles of preference, goods acknowledged; and it is the philosopher's business to make these goods explicit. Liberty is not an art, liberty must be used to bring some natural art to fruition. Shall it be simply eating and drinking and wondering what will happen next? If there is some deep and settled need in the heart of man, to give direction to his efforts, what else should a philosopher do but discover and announce what that need is?

There is a sense in which James was not a philosopher at all. He once said to me: "What a curse philosophy would be if we couldn't forget all about it!" In other words, philosophy was not to him what it has been to so many, a consolation and sanctuary in a life which would have been unsatisfying without it. It would be incongruous, therefore, to expect of him that he should build a philosophy like an edifice to go and live in for good. Philosophy to him was rather like a maze in which he happened to find himself wandering, and what he was looking for was the way out. In the presence of theories of any sort he was attentive, puzzled, suspicious, with a certain inner prompting to disregard them. He lived all his life among them, as a child lives among grown-up people; what a relief to turn from those stolid giants, with their prohibitions and exactions and tiresome talk, to another real child or a nice animal! Of course grown-up people are useful, and so James considered that theories might be; but in themselves, to live with, they were rather in the way, and at bottom our natural enemies. It was well to challenge one or another of them when you got a chance; perhaps that challenge might break some spell, transform the strange landscape, and simplify life. A theory while you were creating or using it was like a story you were telling yourself or a game you were playing; it was a warm, self-justifying thing then; but when the glow of creation or expectation was over, a theory was a phantom, like a ghost, or like the minds of other people. To all other people, even to ghosts, William James was the soul of courtesy; and he was civil to most theories as well, as to more or less interesting strangers that invaded him. Nobody ever recognised more heartily the chance that others had of being right, and the right they had to be different. Yet when it came to understanding what they meant, whether they were theories or persons, his intuition outran his patience; he made some brilliant impressionistic sketch in his fancy and called it by their name. This sketch was as often flattered as distorted, and he was at times the dupe of his desire to be appreciative and give the devil his due; he was too impulsive for exact sympathy; too subjective, too romantic, to be just. Love is very penetrating, but it penetrates to possibilities rather than to facts. The logic of opinions, as well as the exact opinions themselves, were not things James saw easily, or traced with pleasure. He liked to take things one by one, rather than to put two and two together. He was a mystic, a mystic in love with life. He was comparable to Rousseau and to Walt Whitman; he expressed a generous and tender sensibility, rebelling against sophistication, and preferring daily sights and sounds, and a vague but indomitable faith in fortune, to any settled intellectual tradition calling itself science or philosophy.

A prophet is not without honour save in his own country; and until the return wave of James's reputation reached America from Europe, his pupils and friends were hardly aware that he was such a distinguished man. Everybody liked him, and delighted in him for his generous, gullible nature and brilliant sallies. He was a sort of Irishman among the Brahmins, and seemed hardly imposing enough for a great man. They laughed at his erratic views and his undisguised limitations. Of course a conscientious professor ought to know everything he professes to know, but then, they thought, a dignified professor ought to seem to know everything. The precise theologians and panoplied idealists, who exist even in America, shook their heads. What sound philosophy, said they to themselves, could be expected from an irresponsible doctor, who was not even a college graduate, a crude empiricist, and vivisector of frogs? On the other hand, the solid men of business were not entirely reassured concerning a teacher of youth who seemed to have no system in particular — the ignorant rather demand that the learned should have a system in store, to be applied at a pinch; and they could not quite swallow a private gentleman who dabbled in hypnotism, frequented mediums, didn't talk like a book, and didn't write like a book, except like one of his own. Even his pupils, attached as they invariably were to his person, felt some doubts about the profundity of one who was so very natural, and who after some interruption during a lecture — and he said life was a series of interruptions — would slap his forehead and ask the man in the front row "What *was* I talking about?" Perhaps in the first years of his teaching he felt a little in the professor's chair as a military man might feel when obliged to read the prayers at a funeral. He probably conceived what he said more deeply than a more scholastic mind might have conceived it; yet he would have been more comfortable if some one else had said it for him. He liked to open the window, and look out for a moment. I think he was glad when the bell rang, and he could be himself again until the next day. But in the midst of this routine of the class-room the spirit would sometimes come upon him, and, leaning his head on his hand, he would let fall golden words, picturesque, fresh from the heart, full of the knowledge of good and evil. Incidentally there would crop up some humorous characterisation, some candid confession of doubt or of instinctive preference, some pungent scrap of learning; radicalisms plunging sometimes into the sub-soil of all human philosophies; and, on occasion, thoughts of simple wisdom and wistful piety, the most unfeigned and manly that anybody ever had.

CHAPTER IV

JOSIAH ROYCE

Meantime the mantle of philosophical authority had fallen at Harvard upon other shoulders. A young Californian, Josiah Royce, had come back from Germany with a reputation for wisdom; and even without knowing that he had already produced a new proof of the existence of God, merely to look at him you would have felt that he was a philosopher; his great head seemed too heavy for his small body, and his portentous brow, crowned with thick red hair, seemed to crush the lower part of his face. "Royce," said William James of him, "has an indecent exposure of forehead." There was a suggestion about him of the benevolent ogre or the old child, in whom a preternatural sharpness of insight lurked beneath a grotesque mask. If you gave him any cue, or even without one, he could discourse broadly on any subject; you never caught him napping. Whatever the text-books and encyclopædias could tell him, he knew; and if the impression he left on your mind was vague, that was partly because, in spite of his comprehensiveness, he seemed to view everything in relation to something else that remained untold. His approach to anything was oblique; he began a long way off, perhaps with the American preface of a funny story; and when the point came in sight, it was at once enveloped again in a cloud of qualifications, in the parliamentary jargon of philosophy. The tap once turned on, out flowed the stream of systematic disquisition, one hour, two hours, three hours of it, according to demand or opportunity. The voice, too, was merciless and harsh. You felt the overworked, standardised, academic engine, creaking and thumping on at the call of duty or of habit, with no thought of sparing itself or any one else. Yet a sprightlier soul behind this performing soul seemed to watch and laugh at the process. Sometimes a merry light would twinkle in the little eyes, and a bashful smile would creep over the uncompromising mouth. A sense of the paradox, the irony, the inconclusiveness of the whole argument would pierce to the surface, like a white-cap bursting here and there on the heavy swell of the sea.

His procedure was first to gather and digest whatever the sciences or the devil might have to say. He had an evident sly pleasure in the degustation and savour of difficulties; biblical criticism, the struggle for life, the latest German theory of sexual insanity, had no terrors for him; it was all grist for the mill, and woe to any tender thing, any beauty or any illusion, that should get between that upper and that nether millstone! He seemed to say: If I were not Alexander how gladly would I be Diogenes, and if I had not a system to defend, how easily I might tell you the truth. But after the sceptic had ambled quizzically over the ground, the prophet would mount the pulpit to survey it. He would then prove that in spite of all those horrors and contradictions, or rather because of them, the universe was absolutely perfect. For behind that mocking soul in him there was yet another, a devout and heroic soul. Royce was heir to the Calvinistic tradition; piety, to his mind, consisted in trusting divine providence and justice, while emphasising the most terrifying truths about one's own depravity and the sinister holiness of God. He accordingly addressed himself, in his chief writings, to showing that all lives were parts of a single divine life in which all problems were solved and all evils justified.

It is characteristic of Royce that in his proof of something sublime, like the existence of God, his premiss should be something sad and troublesome, the existence of error. Error exists, he tells us, and common sense will readily agree, although the fact is not unquestionable, and pure mystics and pure sensualists deny it. But if error exists, Royce continues, there must be a truth from which it differs; and the existence of truth (according to the principle of idealism, that nothing can exist except for a mind that knows it) implies that some one knows the truth; but as to know the truth thoroughly, and supply the corrective to every possible error, involves omniscience, we have proved the existence of an omniscient mind or universal thought; and this is almost, if not quite, equivalent to the existence of God.

What carried Royce over the evident chasms and assumptions in this argument was his earnestness and passionate eloquence. He passed for an eminent logician, because he was dialectical and fearless in argument and delighted in the play of formal relations; he was devoted to chess, music, and mathematics; but all this show of logic was but a screen for his heart, and in his heart there was no clearness. His reasoning was not pure logic or pure observation; it was always secretly enthusiastic or malicious, and the result it arrived at had been presupposed. Here, for instance, no unprejudiced thinker, not to speak of a pure logician, would have dreamt of using the existence of error to found the being of truth upon. Error is a biological accident which may any day cease to exist, say at the extinction of the human race; whereas the being of truth or fact is involved indefeasibly and eternally in the existence of anything whatever, past, present, or future;

every event of itself renders true or false any proposition that refers to it. No one would conceive of such a thing as error or suspect its presence, unless he had already found or assumed many a truth; nor could anything be an error actually unless the truth was definite and real. All this Royce of course recognised, and it was in some sense the heart of what he meant to assert and to prove; but it does not need proving and hardly asserting. What needed proof was something else, of less logical importance but far greater romantic interest, namely, that the truth was hovering over us and about to descend into our hearts; and this Royce was not disinclined to confuse with the being of truth, so as to bring it within the range of logical argument. He was tormented by the suspicion that he might be himself in the toils of error, and fervently aspired to escape from it. Error to him was no natural, and in itself harmless, incident of finitude; it was a sort of sin, as finitude was too. It was a part of the problem of evil; a terrible and urgent problem when your first postulate or dogma is that moral distinctions and moral experience are the substance of the world, and not merely an incident in it. The mere being of truth, which is all a logician needs, would not help him in this wrestling for personal salvation; as he keenly felt and often said, the truth is like the stars, always laughing at us. Nothing would help him but *possession* of the truth, something eventual and terribly problematic. He longed to believe that all his troubles and questions, some day and somewhere, must find their solution and quietus; if not in his own mind, in some kindred spirit that he could, to that extent, identify with himself. There must be not only cold truth, not even cold truth personified, but victorious *knowledge* of the truth, breaking like a sun-burst through the clouds of error. The nerve of his argument was not logical at all; it was a confession of religious experience, in which the agonised consciousness of error led to a strong imaginative conviction that the truth would be found at last.

The truth, as here conceived, meant the whole truth about everything; and certainly, if any plausible evidence for such a conclusion could be adduced, it would be interesting to learn that we are destined to become omniscient, or are secretly omniscient already. Nevertheless, the aspiration of all religious minds does not run that way. Aristotle tells us that there are many things it is better not to know; and his sublime deity is happily ignorant of our errors and of our very existence; more emphatically so the even sublimer deities of Plotinus and the Indians. The omniscience which our religion attributes to God as the searcher of hearts and the judge of conduct has a moral function rather than a logical one; it prevents us from hiding our sins or being unrecognised in our merits; it is not conceived to be requisite in order that it may be true that those sins or merits have existed.

Atheists admit the facts, but they are content or perhaps relieved that they should pass unobserved. But here again Royce slipped into a romantic equivocation which a strict logician would not have tolerated. Knowledge of the truth, a passing psychological possession, was substituted for the truth known, and this at the cost of rather serious ultimate confusions. It is the truth itself, the facts in their actual relations, that honest opinion appeals to, not to another opinion or instance of knowledge; and if, in your dream of warm sympathy and public corroboration, you lay up your treasure in some instance of knowledge, which time and doubt might corrupt, you have not laid up your treasure in heaven. In striving to prove the being of truth, the young Royce absurdly treated it as doubtful, setting a bad example to the pragmatists; while in striving to lend a psychological quality to this truth and turning it into a problematical instance of knowledge, he unwittingly deprived it of all authority and sublimity. To personify the truth is to care less for truth than for the corroboration and sympathy which the truth, become human, might bring to our opinions. It is to set up another thinker, ourself enlarged, to vindicate us; without considering that this second thinker would be shut up, like us, in his own opinions, and would need to look to the truth beyond him as much as we do.

To the old problem of evil Royce could only give an old answer, although he rediscovered and repeated it for himself in many ways, since it was the core of his whole system. Good, he said, is essentially the struggle with evil and the victory over it; so that if evil did not exist, good would be impossible. I do not think this answer set him at rest; he could hardly help feeling that all goods are not of that bellicose description, and that not all evils produce a healthy reaction or are swallowed up in victory; yet the fact that the most specious solution to this problem of evil left it unsolved was in its way appropriate; for if the problem had been really solved, the struggle to find a solution and the faith that there was one would come to an end; yet perhaps this faith and this struggle are themselves the supreme good. Accordingly the true solution of this problem, which we may all accept, is that no solution can ever be found.

Here is an example of the difference between the being of truth and the ultimate solution of all our problems. There is certainly a truth about evil, and in this case not an unknown truth; yet it is no solution to the "problem" which laid the indomitable Royce on the rack. If a younger son asks why he was not born before his elder brother, that question may represent an intelligible state of his feelings; but there is no answer to it, because it is a childish question. So the question why it is right that there should be any evil is itself perverse and raised by false presumptions. To an unsophisticated mortal the existence of evil presents a task, never a problem. Evil, like error, is an incident of animal life, inevitable in a crowded and unsettled world, where one spontaneous movement is likely to thwart another, and all to run up against material impossibilities. While life lasts this task is recurrent, and every creature, in proportion to the vitality and integrity of his nature, strives to remove or abate those evils of which he is sensible. When the case is urgent and he is helpless, he will cry out for divine aid; and (if he does not perish first) he will soon see this aid coming to him through some shift in the circumstances that renders his situation endurable. Positive religion takes a naturalistic view of things, and requires it. It parts company with a scientific naturalism only in accepting the authority of instinct or revelation in deciding certain questions of fact, such as immortality or miracles. It rouses itself to crush evil, without asking why evil exists. What could be more intelligible than that a deity like Jehovah, a giant inhabitant of the natural world, should be confronted with rivals, enemies, and rebellious children? What could be more intelligible than that the inertia of matter, or pure chance, or some contrary purpose, should mar the expression of any platonic idea exercising its magic influence over the world? For the Greek as for the Jew the task of morals is the same: to subdue nature as far as possible to the uses of the soul, by whatever agencies material or spiritual may be at hand; and when a limit is reached in that direction, to harden and cauterise the heart in the face of inevitable evils, opening it wide at the same time to every sweet influence that may descend to it from heaven. Never for a moment was positive religion entangled in a sophistical optimism. Never did it conceive that the most complete final deliverance and triumph would *justify* the evils which they abolished. As William James put it, in his picturesque manner, if at the last day all creation was shouting hallelujah and there remained one cockroach with an unrequited love, *that* would spoil the universal harmony; it would spoil it, he meant, in truth and for the tender philosopher, but probably not for those excited saints. James was thinking chiefly of the present and future, but the same scrupulous charity has its application to the past. To remove an evil is not to remove the fact that it has existed. The tears that have been shed were shed in bitterness, even if a remorseful hand afterwards wipes them away. To be patted on the back and given a sugar-plum does not reconcile even a child to a past injustice. And the case is much worse if we are expected to make our heaven out of the foolish and cruel pleasures of contrast, or out of the pathetic offuscation produced by a great relief. Such a heaven would be a lie, like the sardonic heavens of Calvin and Hegel. The existence of any evil anywhere at any time absolutely ruins a total optimism.

Nevertheless philosophers have always had a royal road to complete satisfaction. One of the purest of pleasures, which they cultivate above all others, is the pleasure of understanding. Now, as playwrights and novelists know, the intellect is no less readily or agreeably employed in understanding evil than in understanding good — more so, in fact, if in the intellectual man, besides his intelligence, there is a strain of coarseness, irony, or desire to belittle the good things others possess and he himself has missed. Sometimes the philosopher, even when above all meanness, becomes so devoted a naturalist that he is ashamed to remain a moralist, although this is what he probably was in the beginning; and where all is one vast cataract of events, he feels it would be impertinent of him to divide them censoriously into things that ought to be and things that ought not to be. He may even go one step farther. Awestruck and humbled before the universe, he may insensibly transform his understanding and admiration of it into the assertion that the existence of evil is no evil at all, but that the order of the universe is in every detail necessary and perfect, so that the mere mention of the word evil is blind and blasphemous.

This sentiment, which as much as any other deserves the name of pantheism, is often expressed incoherently and with a false afflatus; but when rationally conceived, as it was by Spinoza, it amounts to this: that good and evil are relations which things bear to the living beings they affect. In itself nothing — much less this whole mixed universe — can be either good or bad; but the universe wears the aspect of a good in so far as it feeds, delights, or otherwise fosters any creature within it. If we define the intellect as the power to see things as they are, it is clear that in so far as the philosopher is a pure intellect the universe will be a pure good to the philosopher; everything in it will give play to his exclusive passion. Wisdom counsels us therefore to become philosophers and to concentrate our lives as much as possible in pure intelligence, that we may be led by it into the ways of peace. Not that the universe will be proved thereby to be intrinsically good (although in the heat of their intellectual egotism philosophers are sometimes betrayed into saying so), but that it will have become in that measure a good to us, and we shall be better able to live happily and freely in it. If intelligibility appears in things, it does so like beauty or use, because the mind of man, in so far as it is adapted to them, finds its just exercise in their society.

This is an ancient, shrewd, and inexpugnable position. If Royce had been able to adhere to it consistently, he would have avoided his gratuitous problem of evil without, I think, doing violence to the sanest element in his natural piety, which was joy in the hard truth, with a touch of humour and scorn in respect to mortal illusions. There was an observant and docile side to him; and as a child likes to see things work, he liked to see processions of facts marching on ironically, whatever we might say about it. This was his sense of the power of God. It attached him at first to Spinoza and later to mathematical logic. No small part of his life-long allegiance to the Absolute responded to this sentiment.

The outlook, however, was complicated and half reversed for him by the transcendental theory of knowledge which he had adopted. This theory regards all objects, including the universe, as merely terms posited by the will of the thinker, according to a definite grammar of thought native to his mind. In order that his thoughts may be addressed to any particular object, he must first choose and create it of his own accord; otherwise his opinions, not being directed upon any object in particular within his ken, cannot be either true or false, whatever picture they may frame. What anything external may happen to be, when we do not mean to speak of it, is irrelevant to our discourse. If, for instance, the real Royce were not a denizen and product of my mind — of my deeper self — I could not so much as have a wrong idea of him. The need of this initial relevance in our judgements seems to the transcendentalist to drive all possible objects into the fold of his secret thoughts, so that he has two minds, one that seeks the facts and another that already possesses or rather constitutes them.

Pantheism, when this new philosophy of knowledge is adopted, seems at first to lose its foundations. There is no longer an external universe to which to bow; no little corner left for us in the infinite where, after making the great sacrifice, we may build a safe nest. The intellect to which we had proudly reduced ourselves has lost its preeminence; it can no longer be called the faculty of seeing things as they are. It has become what psychological critics of intellectualism, such as William James, understand by it: a mass of human propensities to abstraction, construction, belief, or inference, by which imaginary things and truths are posited in the service of life. It is therefore on the same plane exactly as passion, music, or æsthetic taste: a mental complication which may be an index to other psychological facts connected with it genetically, but which has no valid intent, no ideal transcendence, no assertive or cognitive function. Intelligence so conceived understands nothing: it is a buzzing labour in the fancy which, by some obscure causation, helps us to live on.

To discredit the intellect, to throw off the incubus of an external reality or truth, was one of the boons which transcendentalism in its beginnings brought to the romantic soul. But although at first the sense of relief (to Fichte, for instance) was most exhilarating, the freedom achieved soon proved illusory: the terrible Absolute had been simply transplanted into the self. You were your own master, and omnipotent; but you were no less dark, hostile, and inexorable to yourself than the gods of Calvin or of Spinoza had been before. Since every detail of this mock world was your secret work, you were not only wiser but also more criminal than you knew. You were stifled, even more than formerly, in the arms of nature, in the toils of your own unaccountable character, which made your destiny. Royce never recoiled from paradox or from bitter fact; and he used to say that a mouse, when tormented and torn to pieces by a cat, was realising his own deepest will, since he had sub-consciously chosen to be a mouse in a world that should have cats in it. The mouse really, in his deeper self, wanted to be terrified, clawed, and devoured. Royce was superficially a rationalist, with no tenderness for superstition in detail and not much sympathy with civilised religions; but we see here that in his heart he was loyal to the aboriginal principle of all superstition: reverence for what hurts. He said to himself that in so far as God was the devil — as daily experience and Hegelian logic proved was largely the case — devil-worship was true religion.

A protest, however, arose in his own mind against this doctrine. Strong early bonds attached him to moralism — to the opinion of the Stoics and of Kant that virtue is the only good. Yet if virtue were conceived after their manner, as a heroic and sublimated attitude of the will, of which the world hardly afforded any example, how should the whole whirligig of life be good also? How should moralism, that frowns on this wicked world, be reconciled with pantheism and optimism, that hug it to their bosom? By the ingenious if rather melodramatic notion that we should hug it with a bear's hug, that virtue consisted (as Royce often put it) in holding evil by the throat; so that the world was good because it was a good world to strangle, and if we only managed to do so, the more it deserved strangling the better world it was. But this Herculean feat must not be considered as something to accomplish once for all; the labours of Hercules must be not twelve but infinite, since his virtue consisted in performing them, and if he ever rested or was received into Olympus he would have left virtue — the only good — behind. The wickedness of the world was no reason for quitting it; on the contrary, it invited us to plunge into all its depths and live through every phase of it; virtue was severe but not squeamish. It lived by endless effort, turbid vitality, and *Sturm und Drang*. Moralism and an apology for evil could thus be reconciled and merged in the praises of tragic experience.

This had been the burden of Hegel's philosophy of life, which Royce admired and adopted. Hegel and his followers seem to be fond of imagining that they are moving in a tragedy. But because Aeschylus and Sophocles were great poets, does it follow that life would be cheap if it did not resemble their fables? The life of tragic heroes is not good; it is misguided, unnecessary, and absurd. Yet that is what romantic philosophy would condemn us to; we must all strut and roar. We must lend ourselves to the partisan earnestness of persons and nations calling their rivals villains and themselves heroes; but this earnestness will be of the histrionic German sort, made to order and transferable at short notice from one object to another, since what truly matters is not that we should achieve our ostensible aim (which Hegel contemptuously called ideal) but that we should carry on perpetually, if possible with a *crescendo,* the strenuous experience of living in a gloriously bad world, and always working to reform it, with the comforting speculative assurance that we never can succeed. We never can succeed, I mean, in rendering reform less necessary or life happier; but of course in any specific reform we may succeed half the time, thereby sowing the seeds of new and higher evils, to keep the edge of virtue keen. And in reality we, or the Absolute in us, are succeeding all the time; the play is always going on, and the play's the thing.

It was inevitable that Royce should have been at home only in this circle of Protestant and German intuitions; a more refined existence would have seemed to him to elude moral experience. Although he was born in California he had never got used to the sunshine; he had never tasted peace. His spirit was that of courage and labour. He was tender in a bashful way, as if in tenderness there was something pathological, as indeed to his sense there was, since he conceived love and loyalty to be divine obsessions refusing to be rationalised; he saw their essence in the child who clings to an old battered doll rather than accept a new and better one. Following orthodox tradition in philosophy, he insisted on seeing reason at the bottom of things as well as at the top, so that he never could understand either the root or the flower of anything. He watched the movement of events as if they were mysterious music, and instead of their causes and potentialities he tried to divine their *motif.* On current affairs his judgements were highly seasoned and laboriously wise. If anything escaped him, it was only the simplicity of what is best. His reward was that he became a prophet to a whole class of earnest, troubled people who, having discarded doctrinal religion, wished to think their life worth living when, to look at what it contained, it might not have seemed so; it reassured them to learn that a strained and joyless existence was not their unlucky lot, or a consequence of their solemn folly, but was the necessary fate of all good men and angels. Royce had always experienced and seen about him a groping, burdened, mediocre life; he had observed how fortune is continually lying in ambush for us, in order to bring good out of evil and evil out of good. In his age and country all was change, preparation, hurry, material achievement; nothing was an old and sufficient possession; nowhere, or very much in the background, any leisure, simplicity, security, or harmony. The whole scene was filled with arts and virtues which were merely useful or remedial. The most pressing arts, like war and forced labour, presuppose evil, work immense havoc, and take the place of greater possible goods. The most indispensable virtues, like courage and industry, do likewise. But these seemed in Royce's world the only honourable things, and he took them to be typical of all art and virtue — a tremendous error. It is very true, however, that in the welter of material existence no concrete thing can be good or evil in every respect; and so long as our rough arts and virtues do more good than harm we give them honourable names, such as unselfishness, patriotism, or religion; and it remains a mark of good breeding among us to practise them instinctively. But an absolute love of such forced arts and impure virtues is itself a vice; it is, as the case may be, barbarous, vain, or fanatical. It mistakes something specific — some habit or emotion which may be or may have been good in some respect, or under some circumstances the lesser of two evils — for the very principle of excellence. But good and evil, like light and shade, are ethereal; all things, events, persons, and conventional virtues are in themselves utterly valueless, save as an immaterial harmony (of which mind is an expression) plays about them on occasion, when their natures meet propitiously, and bathes them in some tint of happiness or beauty. This immaterial harmony may be made more and more perfect; the difficulties in the way of perfection, either in man, in society, or in universal nature, are physical not logical. Worship of barbarous virtue is the blackest conservatism; it shuts the gate of heaven, and surrenders existence to perpetual follies and crimes. Moralism itself is a superstition. In its abstract form it is moral, too moral; it adores the conventional conscience, or perhaps a morbid one. In its romantic form, moralism becomes barbarous and actually immoral; it obstinately craves action and stress for their own sake, experience in the gross, and a good-and-bad way of living.

Royce sometimes conceded that there might be some pure goods, music, for instance, or mathematics; but the impure moral goods were better and could not be spared. Such a concession, however, if it had been taken to heart, would have ruined his whole moral philosophy. The romanticist must maintain that *only* what is painful can be noble and *only* what is lurid bright. A taste for turbid and contrasted values would soon seem perverse when once anything perfect had been seen and loved. Would it not have been better to leave out the worst of the crimes and plagues that have heightened the tragic value of the world? But if so, why stop before we had deleted them all? We should presently be horrified at the mere thought of passions that before had been found necessary by the barbarous tragedian to keep his audience awake; and the ear at the same time would become sensitive to a thousand harmonies that had been inaudible in the hurly-burly of romanticism. The romanticist thinks he has life by virtue of his confusion and torment, whereas in truth that torment and confusion are his incipient death, and it is only the modicum of harmony he has achieved in his separate faculties that keeps him alive at all. As Aristotle taught, unmixed harmony would be intensest life. The spheres might make a sweet and perpetual music, and a happy God is at least possible.

It was not in this direction, however, that Royce broke away on occasion from his Hegelian ethics; he did so in the direction of ethical dogmatism and downright sincerity. The deepest thing in him personally was conscience, firm recognition of duty, and the democratic and American spirit of service. He could not adopt a moral bias histrionically, after the manner of Hegel or Nietzsche. To those hardened professionals any rôle was acceptable, the more commanding the better; but the good Royce was like a sensitive amateur, refusing the rôle of villain, however brilliant and necessary to the play. In contempt of his own speculative insight, or in an obedience to it which forgot it for the time being, he lost himself in his part, and felt that it was infinitely important to be cast only for the most virtuous of characters. He retained inconsistently the Jewish allegiance to a God essentially the vindicator of only one of the combatants, not in this world often the victor; he could not stomach the providential scoundrels which the bad taste of Germany, and of Carlyle and Browning, was wont to glorify. The last notable act of his life was an illustration of this, when he uttered a ringing public denunciation of the sinking of the *Lusitania*. Orthodox Hegelians might well have urged that here, if anywhere, was a plain case of the providential function of what, from a finite merely moral point of view, was an evil in order to make a higher good possible — the virtue of German self-assertion and of American self-assertion in antithesis to it, synthesised in the concrete good of war and victory, or in the perhaps more blessed good of defeat. What could be more unphilosophical and *gedankenlos* than the intrusion of mere morality into the higher idea of world-development? Was not the Universal Spirit compelled to bifurcate into just such Germans and just such Americans, in order to attain self-consciousness by hating, fighting against, and vanquishing itself? Certainly it was American duty to be angry, as it was German duty to be ruthless. The Idea liked to see its fighting-cocks at it in earnest, since that was what it had bred them for; but both were good cocks. Villains, as Hegel had observed in describing Greek tragedy, were not less self-justified than heroes; they were simply the heroes of a lower stage of culture. America and England remained at the stage of individualism; Germany had advanced to the higher stage of organisation. Perhaps this necessary war was destined, through the apparent defeat of Germany, to bring England and America up to the German level. Of course; and yet somehow, on this occasion, Royce passed over these profound considerations, which life-long habit must have brought to his lips. A Socratic demon whispered No, No in his ear; it would have been better for such things never to be. The murder of those thousand passengers was not a providential act, requisite to spread abroad a vitalising war; it was a crime to execrate altogether. It would have been better for Hegel, or whoever was responsible for it, if a millstone had been hanged about his neck and he, and not those little ones, had been drowned at the bottom of the sea. Of this terrestrial cock-pit Royce was willing to accept the agony, but not the ignominy. The other cock was a wicked bird.

This honest lapse from his logic was habitual with him at the sight of sin, and sin in his eyes was a fearful reality. His conscience spoiled the pantheistic serenity of his system; and what was worse (for he was perfectly aware of the contradiction) it added a deep, almost remorseful unrest to his hard life. What calm could there be in the double assurance that it was really right that things should be wrong, but that it was really wrong not to strive to right them? There was no conflict, he once observed, between science and religion, but the real conflict was between religion and morality. There could indeed be no conflict in his mind between faith and science, because his faith began by accepting all facts and all scientific probabilities in order to face them religiously. But there was an invincible conflict between religion as he conceived it and morality, because morality takes sides and regards one sort of motive and one kind of result as better than another, whereas religion according to him gloried in everything, even in the evil, as fulfilling the will of God. Of course the practice of virtue was not excluded; it was just as needful as evil was in the scheme of the whole; but while the effort of morality was requisite, the judgements of morality were absurd. Now I think we may say that a man who finds himself in such a position has a divided mind, and that while he has wrestled with the deepest questions like a young giant, he has not won the fight. I mean, he has not seen his way to any one of the various possibilities about the nature of things, but has remained entangled, sincerely, nobly, and pathetically, in contrary traditions stronger than himself. In the goodly company of philosophers he is an intrepid martyr.

In metaphysics as in morals Royce perpetually laboured the same points, yet they never became clear; they covered a natural complexity in the facts which his idealism could not disentangle. There was a voluminous confusion in his thought; some clear principles and ultimate possibilities turned up in it, now presenting one face and now another, like chips carried down a swollen stream; but the most powerful currents were below the surface, and the whole movement was hard to trace. He had borrowed from Hegel a way of conceiving systems of philosophy, and also the elements of his own thought, which did not tend to clarify them. He did not think of correcting what incoherence there might remain in any view, and then holding it in reserve, as one of the possibilities, until facts should enable us to decide whether it was true or not. Instead he clung to the incoherence as if it had been the heart of the position, in order to be driven by it to some other position altogether, so that while every view seemed to be considered, criticised, and in a measure retained (since the argument continued on the same lines, however ill-chosen they might have been originally), yet justice was never done to it; it was never clarified, made consistent with itself, and then accepted or rejected in view of the evidence. Hence a vicious and perplexing suggestion that philosophies are bred out of philosophies, not out of men in the presence of things. Hence too a sophistical effort to find everything self-contradictory, and in some disquieting way both true and false, as if there were not an infinite number of perfectly consistent systems which the world might have illustrated.

Consider, for instance, his chief and most puzzling contention, that all minds are parts of one mind. It is easy, according to the meaning we give to the word mind, to render this assertion clear and true, or clear and false, or clear and doubtful (because touching unknown facts), or utterly absurd. It is obvious that all minds are parts of one flux or system of experiences, as all bodies are parts of one system of bodies. Again, if mind is identified with its objects, and people are said to be "of one mind" when they are thinking of the same thing, it is certain that many minds are often identical in part, and they would all be identical with portions of an omniscient mind that should perceive all that they severally experienced. The question becomes doubtful if what we mean by oneness of mind is unity of type; our information or plausible guesses cannot assure us how many sorts of experience may exist, or to what extent their development (when they develop) follows the same lines of evolution. The animals would have to be consulted, and the other planets, and the infinite recesses of time. The straitjacket which German idealism has provided is certainly far too narrow even for the varieties of human imagination. Finally, the assertion becomes absurd when it is understood to suggest that an actual instance of thinking, in which something, say the existence of America, is absent or denied, can be part of another actual instance of thinking in which it is present and asserted. But this whole method of treating the matter — and we might add anything that observation might warrant us in adding about multiple personalities — would leave out the problem that agitated Royce and that bewildered his readers. He wanted all minds to be one in some way which should be logically and morally necessary, and which yet, as he could not help feeling, was morally and logically impossible.

For pure transcendentalism, which was Royce's technical method, the question does not arise at all. Transcendentalism is an attitude or a point of view rather than a system. Its Absolute is thinking "as such," wherever thought may exert itself. The notion that there are separate instances of thought is excluded, because space, time, and number belong to the visionary world posited by thought, not to the function of thinking; individuals are figments of constructive fancy, as are material objects. The stress of moral being is the same wherever it may fall, and there are no finite selves, or relations between thinkers; also no infinite self, because on this principle the Absolute is not an existent being, a psychological monster, but a station or office; its essence is a task. Actual thinking is therefore never a part of the Absolute, but always the Absolute itself. Thinkers, finite or infinite, would be existing persons or masses of feelings; such things are dreamt of only. *Any* system of existences, *any* truth or matter of fact waiting to be recognised, contradicts the transcendental insight and stultifies it. The all-inclusive mind is my mind as I think, mind in its living function, and beyond that philosophy cannot go.

Royce, however, while often reasoning on this principle, was incapable of not going beyond it, or of always remembering it. He could not help believing that constructive fancy not only feigns individuals and instances of thought, but is actually seated in them. The Absolute, for instance, must be not merely the abstract subject or transcendental self in all of us (although it was that too), but an actual synthetic universal mind, the God of Aristotle and of Christian theology. Nor was it easy for Royce, a sincere soul and a friend of William James, not to be a social realist; I mean, not to admit that there are many collateral human minds, in temporal existential relations to one another, any of which may influence another, but never supplant it nor materially include it. Finite experience was not a mere element in infinite experience; it was a tragic totality in itself. I was not God looking at myself, I was myself looking for God. Yet this strain was utterly incompatible with the principles of transcendentalism; it turned philosophy into a simple anticipation of science, if not into an indulgence in literary psychology. Knowledge would then have been only faith leaping across the chasm of coexistence and guessing the presence and nature of what surrounds us by some hint of material influence or brotherly affinity. Both the credulity and the finality which such naturalism implies were offensive to Royce, and contrary to his sceptical and mystical instincts. Was there some middle course?

The audience in a theatre stand in a transcendental relation to the persons and events in the play. The performance may take place to-day and last one hour, while the fable transports us to some heroic epoch or to an age that never existed, and stretches through days and perhaps years of fancied time. Just so transcendental thinking, while actually timeless and not distributed among persons, might survey infinite time and rehearse the passions and thoughts of a thousand characters. Thought, after all, needs objects, however fictitious and ideal they may be; it could not think if it thought nothing. This indispensable world of appearance is far more interesting than the reality that evokes it; the qualities and divisions found in the appearance diversify the monotonous function of pure thinking and render it concrete. Instances of thought and particular minds may thus be introduced consistently into a transcendental system, provided they are distinguished not by their own times and places, but only by their themes. The transcendental mind would be a pure poet, with no earthly life, but living only in his works, and in the times and persons of his fable. This view, firmly and consistently held, would deserve the name of absolute idealism, which Royce liked to give to his own system. But he struggled to fuse it with social realism, with which it is radically incompatible. Particular minds and the whole process of time, for absolute idealism, are *ideas* only; they are thought of and surveyed, they never think or lapse actually. For this reason genuine idealists can speak so glibly of the mind of a nation or an age. It is just as real and unreal to them as the mind of an individual; for within the human individual they can trace unities that run through and beyond him, so that parts of him, identical with parts of other people, form units as living as himself; for it is all a web of themes, not a concourse of existences. This is the very essence and pride of idealism, that knowledge is not knowledge of the world but is the world itself, and that the units of discourse, which are interwoven and crossed units, are the only individuals in being. You may call them persons, because "person" means a mask; but you cannot call them souls. They are knots in the web of history. They are words in their context, and the only spirit in them is the sense they have for me.

Royce, however, in saying all this, also wished not to say it, and his two thick volumes on *The World and the Individual* leave their subject wrapped in utter obscurity. Perceiving the fact when he had finished, he very characteristically added a "Supplementary Essay" of a hundred more pages, in finer print, in which to come to the point. Imagine, he said, an absolutely exhaustive map of England spread out upon English soil. The map would be a part of England, yet would reproduce every feature of England, including itself; so that the map would reappear on a smaller scale within itself an infinite number of times, like a mirror reflected in a mirror. In this way we might be individuals within a larger individual, and no less actual and complete than he. Does this solve the problem? If we take the illustration as it stands, there is still only one individual in existence, the material England, all the maps being parts of its single surface; nor will it at all resemble the maps, since it will be washed by the sea and surrounded by foreign nations, and not, like the maps, by other Englands enveloping it. If, on the contrary, we equalise the status of all the members of the series, by making it infinite in both directions, then there would be no England at all, but only map within map of England. There would be no absolute mind inclusive but not included, and the Absolute would be the series as a whole, utterly different from any of its members. It would be a series while they were maps, a truth while they were minds; and if the Absolute from the beginning had been regarded as a truth only, there never would have been any difficulty in the existence of individuals under it. Moreover, if the individuals are all exactly alike, does not their exact similarity defeat the whole purpose of the speculation, which was to vindicate the equal reality of the whole and of its *limited* parts? And if each of us, living through infinite time, goes through precisely the same experiences as every one else, why this vain repetition? Is it not enough for this insatiable world to live its life once? Why not admit solipsism and be true to the transcendental method? Because of conscience and good sense? But then the infinite series of maps is useless, England is herself again, and the prospect opens before us of an infinite number of supplementary essays.

Royce sometimes felt that he might have turned his hand to other things than philosophy. He once wrote a novel, and its want of success was a silent disappointment to him. Perhaps he might have been a great musician. Complexity, repetitions, vagueness, endlessness are hardly virtues in writing or thinking, but in music they might have swelled and swelled into a real sublimity, all the more that he was patient, had a voluminous meandering memory, and loved technical devices. But rather than a musician — for he was no artist — he resembled some great-hearted mediæval peasant visited by mystical promptings, whom the monks should have adopted and allowed to browse among their theological folios; a Duns Scotus earnest and studious to a fault, not having the lightness of soul to despise those elaborate sophistries, yet minded to ferret out their secret for himself and walk by his inward light. His was a gothic and scholastic spirit, intent on devising and solving puzzles, and honouring God in systematic works, like the coral insect or the spider; eventually creating a fabric that in its homely intricacy and fulness arrested and moved the heart, the web of it was so vast, and so full of mystery and yearning.

CHAPTER V

LATER SPECULATIONS

A question which is curious in itself and may become important in the future is this: How has migration to the new world affected philosophical ideas? At first sight we might be tempted, perhaps, to dismiss this question altogether, on the ground that no such effect is discernible. For what do we find in America in the guise of philosophy? In the background, the same Protestant theology as in Europe and the same Catholic theology; on the surface, the same adoption of German idealism, the same vogue of evolution, the same psychology becoming metaphysics, and lately the same revival of a mathematical or logical realism. In no case has the first expression of these various tendencies appeared in America, and no original system that I know of has arisen there. It would seem, then, that in philosophy, as in letters generally, polite America has continued the common tradition of Christendom, in paths closely parallel to those followed in England; and that modern speculation, which is so very sensitive to changed times, is quite indifferent to distinctions of place.

Perhaps; but I say advisedly *polite* America, for without this qualification what I have been suggesting would hardly be true. Polite America carried over its household gods from puritan England in a spirit of consecration, and it has always wished to remain in communion with whatever its conscience might value in the rest of the world. Yet it has been cut off by distance and by revolutionary prejudice against things ancient or foreign; and it has been disconcerted at the same time by the insensible shifting of the ground under its feet: it has suffered from in-breeding and anæmia. On the other hand, a crude but vital America has sprung up from the soil, undermining, feeding, and transforming the America of tradition.

This young America was originally composed of all the prodigals, truants, and adventurous spirits that the colonial families produced: it was fed continually by the younger generation, born in a spacious, half-empty world, tending to forget the old straitened morality and to replace it by another, quite jovially human. This truly native America was reinforced by the miscellany of Europe arriving later, not in the hope of founding a godly commonwealth, but only of prospering in an untrammelled one. The horde of immigrants eagerly accepts the external arrangements and social spirit of American life, but never hears of its original austere principles, or relegates them to the same willing oblivion as it does the constraints which it has just escaped — Jewish, Irish, German, Italian, or whatever they may be. We should be seriously deceived if we overlooked for a moment the curious and complex relation between these two Americas.

Let me give one illustration. Professor Norton, the friend of Carlyle, of Burne-Jones, and of Matthew Arnold, and, for the matter of that, the friend of everybody, a most urbane, learned, and exquisite spirit, was descended from a long line of typical New England divines: yet he was loudly accused, in public and in private, of being un-American. On the other hand, a Frenchman of ripe judgement, who knew him perfectly, once said to me: "Norton wouldn't like to hear it, but he is a terrible Yankee." Both judgements were well grounded. Professor Norton's mind was deeply moralised, discriminating, and sad; and these qualities rightly seemed American to the French observer of New England, but they rightly seemed un-American to the politician from Washington.

Philosophical opinion in America is of course rooted in the genteel tradition. It is either inspired by religious faith, and designed to defend it, or else it is created somewhat artificially in the larger universities, by deliberately proposing problems which, without being very pressing to most Americans, are supposed to be necessary problems of thought. Yet if you expected academic philosophers in America, because the background of their minds seems perfunctory, to resemble academic philosophers elsewhere, you would be often mistaken. There is no prig's paradise in those regions. Many of the younger professors of philosophy are no longer the sort of persons that might as well have been clergymen or schoolmasters: they have rather the type of mind of a doctor, an engineer, or a social reformer; the wide-awake young man who can do most things better than old people, and who knows it. He is less eloquent and apostolic than the older generation of philosophers, very professional in tone and conscious of his *Fach*; not that he would deny for a moment the many-sided ignorance to which nowadays we are all reduced, but that he thinks he can get on very well without the things he ignores. His education has been more pretentious than thorough; his style is deplorable; social pressure and his own great eagerness have condemned him to over-work, committee meetings, early marriage, premature authorship, and lecturing two or three times a day under forced draught. He has no peace in himself, no window open to a calm horizon, and in his heart perhaps little taste for mere scholarship or pure speculation. Yet, like the plain soldier staggering under his clumsy equipment, he is cheerful; he keeps his faith in himself and in his allotted work, puts up with being toasted only on one side, remains open-minded, whole-hearted, appreciative, helpful, confident of the future of goodness and of science. In a word, he is a cell in that teeming democratic body; he draws from its warm, contagious activities the sanctions of his own life and, less consciously, the spirit of his philosophy.

It is evident that such minds will have but a loose hold on tradition, even on the genteel tradition in American philosophy. Not that in general they oppose or dislike it; their alienation from it is more radical; they forget it. Religion was the backbone of that tradition, and towards religion, in so far as it is a private sentiment or presumption, they feel a tender respect; but in so far as religion is a political institution, seeking to coerce the mind and the conscience, one would think they had never heard of it. They feel it is as much every one's right to choose and cherish a religion as to choose and cherish a wife, without having his choice rudely commented upon in public. Hitherto America has been the land of universal good-will, confidence in life, inexperience of poisons. Until yesterday it believed itself immune from the hereditary plagues of mankind. It could not credit the danger of being suffocated or infected by any sinister principle. The more errors and passions were thrown into the melting-pot, the more certainly would they neutralise one another and would truth come to the top. Every system was met with a frank gaze. "Come on," people seemed to say to it, "show us what you are good for. We accept no claims; we ask for no credentials; we just give you a chance. Plato, the Pope, and Mrs. Eddy shall have one vote each." After all, I am not sure that this toleration without deference is not a cruel test for systematic delusions: it lets the daylight into the stage.

Philosophic tradition in America has merged almost completely in German idealism. In a certain sense this system did not need to be adopted: something very like it had grown up spontaneously in New England in the form of transcendentalism and unitarian theology. Even the most emancipated and positivistic of the latest thinkers — pragmatists, new realists, pure empiricists — have been bred in the atmosphere of German idealism; and this fact should not be forgotten in approaching their views. The element of this philosophy which has sunk deepest, and which is reinforced by the influence of psychology, is the critical attitude towards knowledge, subjectivism, withdrawal into experience, on the assumption that experience is something substantial. Experience was regarded by earlier empiricists as a method for making real discoveries, a safer witness than reasoning to what might exist in nature; but now experience is taken to be in itself the only real existence, the ultimate object that all thought and theory must regard. This empiricism does not look to the building up of science, but rather to a more thorough criticism and disintegration of conventional beliefs, those of empirical science included. It is in the intrepid prosecution of this criticism and disintegration that American philosophy has won its wings.

It may seem a strange Nemesis that a critical philosophy, which on principle reduces everything to the consciousness of it, should end by reducing consciousness itself to other things; yet the path of this boomerang is not hard to trace. The word consciousness originally meant what Descartes called thought or cogitation — the faculty which attention has of viewing together objects which may belong together neither in their logical essence nor in their natural existence. It colours events with memories and facts with emotions, and adds images to words. This synthetic and transitive function of consciousness is a positive fact about it, to be discovered by study, like any other somewhat recondite fact. You will discover it if you institute a careful comparison and contrast between the way things hang together in thought and the way they hang together in nature. To have discerned the wonderful perspectives both of imagination and of will seems to me the chief service done to philosophy by Kant and his followers. It is the positive, the non-malicious element in their speculation; and in the midst of their psychologism in logic and their egotism about nature and history, consciousness seems to be the one province of being which they have thrown true light upon. But just because this is a positive province of being, an actual existence to be discovered and dogmatically believed in, it is not what a malicious criticism of knowledge can end with. Not the nature of consciousness, but the data of consciousness, are what the critic must fall back upon in the last resort; and Hume had been in this respect a more penetrating critic than Kant. One cannot, by inspecting consciousness, find consciousness itself as a passive datum, because consciousness is cogitation; one can only take note of the immediate objects of consciousness, in such private perspective as sense or imagination may present.

Philosophy seems to be richer in theories than in words to express them in; and much confusion results from the necessity of using old terms in new meanings. In this way, when consciousness is disregarded, in the proper sense of cogitation, the name of consciousness can be transferred to the stream of objects immediately present to consciousness; so that consciousness comes to signify the evolving field of appearances unrolled before any person.

This equivocation is favoured by the allied ambiguity of an even commoner term, idea. It is plausible to say that consciousness is a stream of ideas, because an idea may mean an opinion, a cogitation, a view taken of some object. And it is also plausible to say that ideas are objects of consciousness, because an idea may mean an image, a passive datum. Passive data may be of any sort you like — things, qualities, relations, propositions — but they are never cogitations; and to call *them* consciousness or components of consciousness is false and inexcusable. The ideas that may be so called are not these passive objects, but active thoughts. Indeed, when the psychological critic has made this false step, he is not able to halt: his method will carry him presently from this position to one even more paradoxical.

Is memory knowledge of a past that is itself absent and dead, or is it a present experience? A complete philosophy would doubtless reply that it is both; but psychological criticism can take cognisance of memory only as a mass of present images and presumptions. The experience remembered may indeed be exactly recovered and be present again; but the fact that it was present before cannot possibly be given now; it can only be suggested and believed.

It is evident, therefore, that the historical order in which data flow is not contained bodily in any one of them. This order is conceived; the hypothesis is framed instinctively and instinctively credited, but it is only an hypothesis. And it is often wrong, as is proved by all the constitutional errors of memory and legend. Belief in the order of our personal experiences is accordingly just as dogmatic, daring, and realistic as the parallel belief in a material world. The psychological critic must attribute both beliefs to a mere tendency to feign; and if he is true to his method he must discard the notion that the objects of consciousness are arranged in psychological sequences, making up separate minds. In other words, he must discard the notion of consciousness, not only in the sense of thought or cogitation, but in the sense he himself had given it of a stream of ideas. Actual objects, he will now admit, not without a certain surprise, are not ideas at all: they do not lie in the mind (for there is no mind to be found) but in the medium that observably surrounds them. Things are just what they seem to be, and to say they are consciousness or compose a consciousness is absurd. The so-called appearances, according to a perfected criticism of knowledge, are nothing private or internal; they are merely those portions of external objects which from time to time impress themselves on somebody's organs of sense and are responded to by his nervous system.

Such is the doctrine of the new American realists, in whose devoted persons the logic of idealism has worked itself out and appropriately turned idealism itself into its opposite. Consciousness, they began by saying, is merely a stream of ideas; but then ideas are merely the parts of objects which happen to appear to a given person; but again, a person (for all you or he can discover) is nothing but his body and those parts of other objects which appear to him; and, finally, to appear, in any discoverable sense, cannot be to have a ghostly sort of mental existence, but merely to be reacted upon by an animal body. Thus we come to the conclusion that objects alone exist, and that consciousness is a name for certain segments or groups of these objects.

I think we may conjecture why this startling conclusion, that consciousness does not exist, a conclusion suggested somewhat hurriedly by William James, has found a considerable echo in America, and why the system of Avenarius, which makes in the same direction, has been studied there sympathetically. To deny consciousness is to deny a pre-requisite to the obvious, and to leave the obvious standing alone. That is a relief to an overtaxed and self-impeded generation; it seems a blessed simplification. It gets rid of the undemocratic notion that by being very reflective, circumspect, and subtle you might discover something that most people do not see. They can go on more merrily with their work if they believe that by being so subtle, circumspect, and reflective you would only discover a mare's nest. The elimination of consciousness not only restores the obvious, but proves all parts of the obvious to be equally real. Not only colours, beauties, and passions, but all things formerly suspected of being creatures of thought, such as laws, relations, and abstract qualities, now become components of the existing object, since there is no longer any mental vehicle by which they might have been created and interposed. The young American is thus reassured: his joy in living and learning is no longer chilled by the contempt which idealism used to cast on nature for being imaginary and on science for being intellectual. All fictions and all abstractions are now declared to be parcels of the objective world; it will suffice to live on, to live forward, in order to see everything as it really is.

If we look now at these matters from a slightly different angle, we shall find psychological criticism transforming the notion of truth much as it has transformed the notion of consciousness. In the first place, there is a similar ambiguity in the term. The truth properly means the sum of all true propositions, what omniscience would assert, the whole ideal system of qualities and relations which the world has exemplified or will exemplify. The truth is all things seen under the form of eternity. In this sense, a psychological criticism cannot be pertinent to the truth at all, the truth not being anything psychological or human. It is an ideal realm of being properly enough not discussed by psychologists; yet so far as I know it is denied by nobody, not even by Protagoras or the pragmatists. If Protagoras said that whatever appears to any man at any moment is true, he doubtless meant true on that subject, true of that appearance: because for a sensualist objects do not extend beyond what he sees of them, so that each of his perceptions defines its whole object and is infallible. But in that case the truth about the universe is evidently that it is composed of these various sensations, each carrying an opinion impossible for it to abandon or to revise, since to revise the opinion would simply be to bring a fresh object into view. The truth would further be that these sensations and opinions stand to one another in certain definite relations of diversity, succession, duration, *et cætera,* whether any of them happens to assert these relations or not. In the same way, I cannot find that our contemporary pragmatists, in giving their account of what truth is (in a different and quite abstract sense of the word truth), have ever doubted, or so much as noticed, what in all their thinking they evidently assume to be the actual and concrete truth: namely, that there are many states of mind, many labouring opinions more or less useful and good, which actually lead to others, more or less expected and satisfactory. Surely every pragmatist, like every thinking man, always assumes the reality of an actual truth, comprehensive and largely undiscovered, of which he claims to be reporting a portion. What he rather confusingly calls truth, and wishes to reduce to a pragmatic function, is not this underlying truth, the sum of all true propositions, but merely the abstract quality which all true propositions must have in common, to be called true. By truth he means only correctness. The possibility of correctness in an idea is a great puzzle to him, on account of his idealism, which identifies ideas with their objects; and he asks himself how an idea can ever come to be correct or incorrect, as if it referred to something beyond itself.

The fact is, of course, that an idea can be correct or incorrect only if by the word idea we mean not a datum but an opinion; and the abstract relation of correctness, by virtue of which any opinion is true, is easily stated. An opinion is true if what it is talking about is constituted as the opinion asserts it to be constituted. To test this correctness may be difficult or even impossible in particular cases; in the end we may be reduced to believing on instinct that our fundamental opinions are true; for instance, that we are living through time, and that the past and future are not, as a consistent idealism would assert, mere notions in the present. But what renders such instinctive opinions true, if they are true, is the fact affirmed being as it is affirmed to be. It is not a question of similarity or derivation between a passive datum and a hidden object; it is a question of identity between the fact asserted and the fact existing. If an opinion could not freely leap to its object, no matter how distant or hypothetical, and assert something of that chosen object, an opinion could not be so much as wrong; for it would not be an opinion about anything.

Psychologists, however, are not concerned with what an opinion asserts logically, but only with what it is existentially; they are asking what existential relations surround an idea when it is called true which are absent when it is called false. Their problem is frankly insoluble; for it requires us to discover what makes up the indicative force of an idea which by hypothesis is a passive datum; as if a grammarian should inquire how a noun in the accusative case could be a verb in the indicative mood.

It was not idly that William James dedicated his book on Pragmatism to the memory of John Stuart Mill. The principle of psychological empiricism is to look for the elements employed in thinking, and to conclude that thought is nothing but those elements arranged in a certain order. It is true that since the days of Mill analysis has somewhat extended the inventory of these elements, so as to include among simples, besides the data of the five senses, such things as feelings of relation, sensations of movement, vague ill-focused images, and perhaps even telepathic and instinctive intuitions. But some series or group of these immediate data, kept in their crude immediacy, must according to this method furnish the whole answer to our question: the supposed power of an idea to have an object beyond itself, or to be true of any other fact, must be merely a name for a certain position which the given element occupies in relation to other elements in the routine of experience. Knowledge and truth must be forms of contiguity and succession.

We must not be surprised, under these circumstances, if the problem is shifted, and another somewhat akin to it takes its place, with which the chosen method can really cope. This subterfuge is not voluntary; it is an instinctive effect of fidelity to a point of view which has its special validity, though naturally not applicable in every sphere. We do not observe that politicians abandon their party when it happens to have brought trouble upon the country; their destiny as politicians is precisely to make effective all the consequences, good or evil, which their party policy may involve. So it would be too much to expect a school of philosophers to abandon their method because there are problems it cannot solve; their business is rather to apply their method to everything to which it can possibly be applied; and when they have reached that limit, the very most we can ask, if they are superhumanly modest and wise, is that they should make way gracefully for another school of philosophers.

Now there is a problem, not impossible to confuse with the problem of correctness in ideas, with which psychological criticism can really deal; it is the question of the relation between a sign and the thing signified. Of this relation a genuinely empirical account can be given; both terms are objects of experience, present or eventual, and the passage between them is made in time by an experienced transition. Nor need the signs which lead to a particular object be always the same, or of one sort; an object may be designated and announced unequivocally by a verbal description, without any direct image, or by images now of one sense and now of another, or by some external relation, such as its place, or by its proper name, if it possesses one; and these designations all convey knowledge of it and may be true signs, if in yielding to their suggestion we are brought eventually to the object meant.

Here, if I am not mistaken, is the genuine application of what the pragmatists call their theory of truth. It concerns merely what links a sign to the thing signified, and renders it a practical substitute for the same. But this empirical analysis of signification has been entangled with more or less hazardous views about truth, such as that an idea is true so long as it is believed to be true, or that it is true if it is good and useful, or that it is not true until it is verified. This last suggestion shows what strange reversals a wayward personal philosophy may be subject to. Empiricism used to mean reliance on the past; now apparently all empirical truth regards only the future, since truth is said to arise by the verification of some presumption. Presumptions about the past can evidently never be verified; at best they may be corroborated by fresh presumptions about the past, equally dependent for their truth on a verification which in the nature of the case is impossible. At this point the truly courageous empiricist will perhaps say that the real past only means the ideas of the past which we shall form in the future. Consistency is a jewel; and, as in the case of other jewels, we may marvel at the price that some people will pay for it. In any case, we are led to this curious result: that radical empiricism ought to deny that any idea of the past can be true at all.

Such dissolving views, really somewhat like those attributed to Protagoras, do not rest on sober psychological analysis: they express rather a certain impatience and a certain despairing democracy in the field of opinion. Great are the joys of haste and of radicalism, and young philosophers must not be deprived of them. We may the more justly pass over these small scandals of pragmatism in that William James and his American disciples have hardly cared to defend them, but have turned decidedly in the direction of a universal objectivism.

The spirit of these radical views is not at all negative: it is hopeful, revolutionary, inspired entirely by love of certitude and clearness. It is very sympathetic to science, in so far as science is a personal pursuit and a personal experience, rather than a body of doctrine with moral implications. It is very close to nature, as the lover of nature understands the word. If it denies the existence of the cognitive energy and the colouring medium of mind, it does so only in a formal sense; all the colours with which that medium endows the world remain painted upon it; and all the perspectives and ideal objects of thought are woven into the texture of things. Not, I think, intelligibly or in a coherent fashion; for this new realism is still immature, and if it is ever rendered adequate it will doubtless seem much less original. My point is that in its denial of mind it has no bias against things intellectual, and if it refuses to admit ideas or even sensations, it does not blink the sensible or ideal objects which ideas and sensations reveal, but rather tries to find a new and (as it perhaps thinks) a more honourable place for them; they are not regarded as spiritual radiations from the natural world, but as parts of its substance.

This may have the ring of materialism; but the temper and faith of these schools are not materialistic. Systematic materialism is one of the philosophies of old age. It is a conviction that may overtake a few shrewd and speculative cynics, who have long observed their own irrationality and that of the world, and have divined its cause; by such men materialism may be embraced without reserve, in all its rigour and pungency. But the materialism of youth is part of a simple faith in sense and in science; it is not exclusive; it admits the co-operation of any other forces — divine, magical, formal, or vital — if appearances anywhere seem to manifest them. The more we interpret the ambiguities or crudites of American writers in this sense, the less we shall misunderstand them.

It seems, then, that the atmosphere of the new world has already affected philosophy in two ways. In the first place, it has accelerated and rendered fearless the disintegration of conventional categories; a disintegration on which modern philosophy has always been at work, and which has precipitated its successive phases. In the second place, the younger cosmopolitan America has favoured the impartial assemblage and mutual confrontation of all sorts of ideas. It has produced, in intellectual matters, a sort of happy watchfulness and insecurity. Never was the human mind master of so many facts and sure of so few principles. Will this suspense and fluidity of thought crystallise into some great new system? Positive gifts of imagination and moral heroism are requisite to make a great philosopher, gifts which must come from the gods and not from circumstances. But if the genius should arise, this vast collection of suggestions and this radical analysis of presumptions which he will find in America may keep him from going astray. Nietzsche said that the earth has been a mad-house long enough. Without contradicting him we might perhaps soften the expression, and say that philosophy has been long enough an asylum for enthusiasts. It is time for it to become less solemn and more serious. We may be frightened at first to learn on what thin ice we have been skating, in speculation as in government; but we shall not be in a worse plight for knowing it, only wiser to-day and perhaps safer to-morrow.

CHAPTER VI

MATERIALISM AND IDEALISM IN AMERICAN LIFE

The language and traditions common to England and America are like other family bonds: they draw kindred together at the greater crises in life, but they also occasion at times a little friction and fault-finding. The groundwork of the two societies is so similar, that each nation, feeling almost at home with the other, and almost able to understand its speech, may instinctively resent what hinders it from feeling at home altogether. Differences will tend to seem anomalies that have slipped in by mistake and through somebody's fault. Each will judge the other by his own standards, not feeling, as in the presence of complete foreigners, that he must make an effort of imagination and put himself in another man's shoes.

In matters of morals, manners, and art, the danger of comparisons is not merely that they may prove invidious, by ranging qualities in an order of merit which might wound somebody's vanity; the danger is rather that comparisons may distort comprehension, because in truth good qualities are all different in kind, and free lives are different in spirit. Comparison is the expedient of those who cannot reach the heart of the things compared; and no philosophy is more external and egotistical than that which places the essence of a thing in its relation to something else. In reality, at the centre of every natural being there is something individual and incommensurable, a seed with its native impulses and aspirations, shaping themselves as best they can in their given environment. Variation is a consequence of freedom, and the slight but radical diversity of souls in turn makes freedom requisite. Instead of instituting in his mind any comparisons between the United States and other nations, I would accordingly urge the reader to forget himself and, in so far as such a thing may be possible for him or for me, to transport himself ideally with me into the outer circumstances of American life, the better to feel its inner temper, and to see how inevitably the American shapes his feelings and judgements, honestly reporting all things as they appear from his new and unobstructed station.

I speak of the American in the singular, as if there were not millions of them, north and south, east and west, of both sexes, of all ages, and of various races, professions, and religions. Of course the one American I speak of is mythical; but to speak in parables is inevitable in such a subject, and it is perhaps as well to do so frankly. There is a sort of poetic ineptitude in all human discourse when it tries to deal with natural and existing things. Practical men may not notice it, but in fact human discourse is intrinsically addressed not to natural existing things but to ideal essences, poetic or logical terms which thought may define and play with. When fortune or necessity diverts our attention from this congenial ideal sport to crude facts and pressing issues, we turn our frail poetic ideas into symbols for those terrible irruptive things. In that paper money of our own stamping, the legal tender of the mind, we are obliged to reckon all the movements and values of the world. The universal American I speak of is one of these symbols; and I should be still speaking in symbols and creating moral units and a false simplicity, if I spoke of classes pedantically subdivided, or individuals ideally integrated and defined. As it happens, the symbolic American can be made largely adequate to the facts; because, if there are immense differences between individual Americans — for some Americans are black — yet there is a great uniformity in their environment, customs, temper, and thoughts. They have all been uprooted from their several soils and ancestries and plunged together into one vortex, whirling irresistibly in a space otherwise quite empty. To be an American is of itself almost a moral condition, an education, and a career. Hence a single ideal figment can cover a large part of what each American is in his character, and almost the whole of what most Americans are in their social outlook and political judgements.

The discovery of the new world exercised a sort of selection among the inhabitants of Europe. All the colonists, except the negroes, were voluntary exiles. The fortunate, the deeply rooted, and the lazy remained at home; the wilder instincts or dissatisfaction of others tempted them beyond the horizon. The American is accordingly the most adventurous, or the descendant of the most adventurous, of Europeans. It is in his blood to be socially a radical, though perhaps not intellectually. What has existed in the past, especially in the remote past, seems to him not only not authoritative, but irrelevant, inferior, and outworn. He finds it rather a sorry waste of time to think about the past at all. But his enthusiasm for the future is profound; he can conceive of no more decisive way of recommending an opinion or a practice than to say that it is what everybody is coming to adopt. This expectation of what he approves, or approval of what he expects, makes up his optimism. It is the necessary faith of the pioneer.

Such a temperament is, of course, not maintained in the nation merely by inheritance. Inheritance notoriously tends to restore the average of a race, and plays incidentally many a trick of atavism. What maintains this temperament and makes it national is social contagion or pressure — something immensely strong in democracies. The luckless American who is born a conservative, or who is drawn to poetic subtlety, pious retreats, or gay passions, nevertheless has the categorical excellence of work, growth, enterprise, reform, and prosperity dinned into his ears: every door is open in this direction and shut in the other; so that he either folds up his heart and withers in a corner — in remote places you sometimes find such a solitary gaunt idealist — or else he flies to Oxford or Florence or Montmartre to save his soul — or perhaps not to save it.

The optimism of the pioneer is not limited to his view of himself and his own future: it starts from that; but feeling assured, safe, and cheery within, he looks with smiling and most kindly eyes on everything and everybody about him. Individualism, roughness, and self-trust are supposed to go with selfishness and a cold heart; but I suspect that is a prejudice. It is rather dependence, insecurity, and mutual jostling that poison our placid gregarious brotherhood; and fanciful passionate demands upon people's affections, when they are disappointed, as they soon must be, breed ill-will and a final meanness. The milk of human kindness is less apt to turn sour if the vessel that holds it stands steady, cool, and separate, and is not too often uncorked. In his affections the American is seldom passionate, often deep, and always kindly. If it were given me to look into the depths of a man's heart, and I did not find good-will at the bottom, I should say without any hesitation, You are not an American. But as the American is an individualist his good-will is not officious. His instinct is to think well of everybody, and to wish everybody well, but in a spirit of rough comradeship, expecting every man to stand on his own legs and to be helpful in his turn. When he has given his neighbour a chance he thinks he has done enough for him; but he feels it is an absolute duty to do that. It will take some hammering to drive a coddling socialism into America.

As self-trust may pass into self-sufficiency, so optimism, kindness, and good-will may grow into a habit of doting on everything. To the good American many subjects are sacred: sex is sacred, women are sacred, children are sacred, business is sacred, America is sacred, Masonic lodges and college clubs are sacred. This feeling grows out of the good opinion he wishes to have of these things, and serves to maintain it. If he did not regard all these things as sacred he might come to doubt sometimes if they were wholly good. Of this kind, too, is the idealism of single ladies in reduced circumstances who can see the soul of beauty in ugly things, and are perfectly happy because their old dog has such pathetic eyes, their minister is so eloquent, their garden with its three sunflowers is so pleasant, their dead friends were so devoted, and their distant relations are so rich.

Consider now the great emptiness of America: not merely the primitive physical emptiness, surviving in some regions, and the continental spacing of the chief natural features, but also the moral emptiness of a settlement where men and even houses are easily moved about, and no one, almost, lives where he was born or believes what he has been taught. Not that the American has jettisoned these impedimenta in anger; they have simply slipped from him as he moves. Great empty spaces bring a sort of freedom to both soul and body. You may pitch your tent where you will; or if ever you decide to build anything, it can be in a style of your own devising. You have room, fresh materials, few models, and no critics. You trust your own experience, not only because you must, but because you find you may do so safely and prosperously; the forces that determine fortune are not yet too complicated for one man to explore. Your detachable condition makes you lavish with money and cheerfully experimental; you lose little if you lose all, since you remain completely yourself. At the same time your absolute initiative gives you practice in coping with novel situations, and in being original; it teaches you shrewd management. Your life and mind will become dry and direct, with few decorative flourishes. In your works everything will be stark and pragmatic; you will not understand why anybody should make those little sacrifices to instinct or custom which we call grace. The fine arts will seem to you academic luxuries, fit to amuse the ladies, like Greek and Sanskrit; for while you will perfectly appreciate generosity in men's purposes, you will not admit that the execution of these purposes can be anything but business. Unfortunately the essence of the fine arts is that the execution should be generous too, and delightful in itself; therefore the fine arts will suffer, not so much in their express professional pursuit — for then they become practical tasks and a kind of business — as in that diffused charm which qualifies all human action when men are artists by nature. Elaboration, which is something to accomplish, will be preferred to simplicity, which is something to rest in; manners will suffer somewhat; speech will suffer horribly. For the American the urgency of his novel attack upon matter, his zeal in gathering its fruits, precludes meanderings in primrose paths; devices must be short cuts, and symbols must be mere symbols. If his wife wants luxuries, of course she may have them; and if he has vices, that can be provided for too; but they must all be set down under those headings in his ledgers.

At the same time, the American is imaginative; for where life is intense, imagination is intense also. Were he not imaginative he would not live so much in the future. But his imagination is practical, and the future it forecasts is immediate; it works with the clearest and least ambiguous terms known to his experience, in terms of number, measure, contrivance, economy, and speed. He is an idealist working on matter. Understanding as he does the material potentialities of things, he is successful in invention, conservative in reform, and quick in emergencies. All his life he jumps into the train after it has started and jumps out before it has stopped; and he never once gets left behind, or breaks a leg. There is an enthusiasm in his sympathetic handling of material forces which goes far to cancel the illiberal character which it might otherwise assume. The good workman hardly distinguishes his artistic intention from the potency in himself and in things which is about to realise that intention. Accordingly his ideals fall into the form of premonitions and prophecies; and his studious prophecies often come true. So do the happy workmanlike ideals of the American. When a poor boy, perhaps, he dreams of an education, and presently he gets an education, or at least a degree; he dreams of growing rich, and he grows rich — only more slowly and modestly, perhaps, than he expected; he dreams of marrying his Rebecca and, even if he marries a Leah instead, he ultimately finds in Leah his Rebecca after all. He dreams of helping to carry on and to accelerate the movement of a vast, seething, progressive society, and he actually does so. Ideals clinging so close to nature are almost sure of fulfilment; the American beams with a certain self-confidence and sense of mastery; he feels that God and nature are working with him.

Idealism in the American accordingly goes hand in hand with present contentment and with foresight of what the future very likely will actually bring. He is not a revolutionist; he believes he is already on the right track and moving towards an excellent destiny. In revolutionists, on the contrary, idealism is founded on dissatisfaction and expresses it. What exists seems to them an absurd jumble of irrational accidents and bad habits, and they want the future to be based on reason and to be the pellucid embodiment of all their maxims. All their zeal is for something radically different from the actual and (if they only knew it) from the possible; it is ideally simple, and they love it and believe in it because their nature craves it. They think life would be set free by the destruction of all its organs. They are therefore extreme idealists in the region of hope, but not at all, as poets and artists are, in the region of perception and memory. In the atmosphere of civilised life they miss all the refraction and all the fragrance; so that in their conception of actual things they are apt to be crude realists; and their ignorance and inexperience of the moral world, unless it comes of ill-luck, indicates their incapacity for education. Now incapacity for education, when united with great inner vitality, is one root of idealism. It is what condemns us all, in the region of sense, to substitute perpetually what we are capable of imagining for what things may be in themselves; it is what condemns us, wherever it extends, to think *a priori*; it is what keeps us bravely and incorrigibly pursuing what we call the good — that is, what would fulfil the demands of our nature — however little provision the fates may have made for it. But the want of insight on the part of revolutionists touching the past and the present infects in an important particular their idealism about the future; it renders their dreams of the future unrealisable. For in human beings — this may not be true of other animals, more perfectly preformed — experience is necessary to pertinent and concrete thinking; even our primitive instincts are blind until they stumble upon some occasion that solicits them; and they can be much transformed or deranged by their first partial satisfactions. Therefore a man who does not idealise his experience, but idealises *a priori,* is incapable of true prophecy; when he dreams he raves, and the more he criticises the less he helps. American idealism, on the contrary, is nothing if not helpful, nothing if not pertinent to practicable transformations; and when the American frets, it is because whatever is useless and impertinent, be it idealism or inertia, irritates him; for it frustrates the good results which he sees might so easily have been obtained.

The American is wonderfully alive; and his vitality, not having often found a suitable outlet, makes him appear agitated on the surface; he is always letting off an unnecessarily loud blast of incidental steam. Yet his vitality is not superficial; it is inwardly prompted, and as sensitive and quick as a magnetic needle. He is inquisitive, and ready with an answer to any question that he may put to himself of his own accord; but if you try to pour instruction into him, on matters that do not touch his own spontaneous life, he shows the most extraordinary powers of resistance and oblivescence; so that he often is remarkably expert in some directions and surprisingly obtuse in others. He seems to bear lightly the sorrowful burden of human knowledge. In a word, he is young.

What sense is there in this feeling, which we all have, that the American is young? His country is blessed with as many elderly people as any other, and his descent from Adam, or from the Darwinian rival of Adam, cannot be shorter than that of his European cousins. Nor are his ideas always very fresh. Trite and rigid bits of morality and religion, with much seemly and antique political lore, remain axiomatic in him, as in the mind of a child; he may carry all this about with an unquestioning familiarity which does not comport understanding. To keep traditional sentiments in this way insulated and uncriticised is itself a sign of youth. A good young man is naturally conservative and loyal on all those subjects which his experience has not brought to a test; advanced opinions on politics, marriage, or literature are comparatively rare in America; they are left for the ladies to discuss, and usually to condemn, while the men get on with their work. In spite of what is old-fashioned in his more general ideas, the American is unmistakably young; and this, I should say, for two reasons: one, that he is chiefly occupied with his immediate environment, and the other, that his reactions upon it are inwardly prompted, spontaneous, and full of vivacity and self-trust. His views are not yet lengthened; his will is not yet broken or transformed. The present moment, however, in this, as in other things, may mark a great change in him; he is perhaps now reaching his majority, and all I say may hardly apply to-day, and may not apply at all to-morrow. I speak of him as I have known him; and whatever moral strength may accrue to him later, I am not sorry to have known him in his youth. The charm of youth, even when it is a little boisterous, lies in nearness to the impulses of nature, in a quicker and more obvious obedience to that pure, seminal principle which, having formed the body and its organs, always directs their movements, unless it is forced by vice or necessity to make them crooked, or to suspend them. Even under the inevitable crust of age the soul remains young, and, wherever it is able to break through, sprouts into something green and tender. We are all as young at heart as the most youthful American, but the seed in his case has fallen upon virgin soil, where it may spring up more bravely and with less respect for the giants of the wood. Peoples seem older when their perennial natural youth is encumbered with more possessions and prepossessions, and they are mindful of the many things they have lost or missed. The American is not mindful of them.

In America there is a tacit optimistic assumption about existence, to the effect that the more existence the better. The soulless critic might urge that quantity is only a physical category, implying no excellence, but at best an abundance of opportunities both for good and for evil. Yet the young soul, being curious and hungry, views existence *a priori* under the form of the good; its instinct to live implies a faith that most things it can become or see or do will be worth while. Respect for quantity is accordingly something more than the childish joy and wonder at bigness; it is the fisherman's joy in a big haul, the good uses of which he can take for granted. Such optimism is amiable. Nature cannot afford that we should begin by being too calculating or wise, and she encourages us by the pleasure she attaches to our functions in advance of their fruits, and often in excess of them; as the angler enjoys catching his fish more than eating it, and often, waiting patiently for the fish to bite, misses his own supper. The pioneer must devote himself to preparations; he must work for the future, and it is healthy and dutiful of him to love his work for its own sake. At the same time, unless reference to an ultimate purpose is at least virtual in all his activities, he runs the danger of becoming a living automaton, vain and ignominious in its mechanical constancy. Idealism about work can hide an intense materialism about life. Man, if he is a rational being, cannot live by bread alone nor be a labourer merely; he must eat and work in view of an ideal harmony which overarches all his days, and which is realised in the way they hang together, or in some ideal issue which they have in common. Otherwise, though his technical philosophy may call itself idealism, he is a materialist in morals; he esteems things, and esteems himself, for mechanical uses and energies. Even sensualists, artists, and pleasure-lovers are wiser than that, for though their idealism may be desultory or corrupt, they attain something ideal, and prize things only for their living effects, moral though perhaps fugitive. Sensation, when we do not take it as a signal for action, but arrest and peruse what it positively brings before us, reveals something ideal — a colour, shape, or sound; and to dwell on these presences, with no thought of their material significance, is an æsthetic or dreamful idealism. To pass from this idealism to the knowledge of matter is a great intellectual advance, and goes with dominion over the world; for in the practical arts the mind is adjusted to a larger object, with more depth and potentiality in it; which is what makes people feel that the material world is real, as they call it, and that the ideal world is not. Certainly the material world is real; for the philosophers who deny the existence of matter are like the critics who deny the existence of Homer. If there was never any Homer, there must have been a lot of other poets no less Homeric than he; and if matter does not exist, a combination of other things exists which is just as material. But the intense reality of the material world would not prevent it from being a dreary waste in our eyes, or even an abyss of horror, if it brought forth no spiritual fruits. In fact, it does bring forth spiritual fruits, for otherwise we should not be here to find fault with it, and to set up our ideals over against it. Nature is material, but not materialistic; it issues in life, and breeds all sorts of warm passions and idle beauties. And just as sympathy with the mechanical travail and turmoil of nature, apart from its spiritual fruits, is moral materialism, so the continual perception and love of these fruits is moral idealism — happiness in the presence of immaterial objects and harmonies, such as we envisage in affection, speculation, religion, and all the forms of the beautiful.

The circumstances of his life hitherto have necessarily driven the American into moral materialism; for in his dealings with material things he can hardly stop to enjoy their sensible aspects, which are ideal, nor proceed at once to their ultimate uses, which are ideal too. He is practical as against the poet, and worldly as against the clear philosopher or the saint. The most striking expression of this materialism is usually supposed to be his love of the almighty dollar; but that is a foreign and unintelligent view. The American talks about money, because that is the symbol and measure he has at hand for success, intelligence, and power; but as to money itself he makes, loses, spends, and gives it away with a very light heart. To my mind the most striking expression of his materialism is his singular preoccupation with quantity. If, for instance, you visit Niagara Falls, you may expect to hear how many cubic feet or metric tons of water are precipitated per second over the cataract; how many cities and towns (with the number of their inhabitants) derive light and motive power from it; and the annual value of the further industries that might very well be carried on by the same means, without visibly depleting the world's greatest wonder or injuring the tourist trade. That is what I confidently expected to hear on arriving at the adjoining town of Buffalo; but I was deceived. The first thing I heard instead was that there are more miles of asphalt pavement in Buffalo than in any city in the world. Nor is this insistence on quantity confined to men of business. The President of Harvard College, seeing me once by chance soon after the beginning of a term, inquired how my classes were getting on; and when I replied that I thought they were getting on well, that my men seemed to be keen and intelligent, he stopped me as if I was about to waste his time. "I meant," said he, "*what is the number* of students in your classes."

Here I think we may perceive that this love of quantity often has a silent partner, which is diffidence as to quality. The democratic conscience recoils before anything that savours of privilege; and lest it should concede an unmerited privilege to any pursuit or person, it reduces all things as far as possible to the common denominator of quantity. Numbers cannot lie: but if it came to comparing the ideal beauties of philosophy with those of Anglo-Saxon, who should decide? All studies are good — why else have universities? — but those must be most encouraged which attract the greatest number of students. Hence the President's question. Democratic faith, in its diffidence about quality, throws the reins of education upon the pupil's neck, as Don Quixote threw the reins on the neck of Rocinante, and bids his divine instinct choose its own way.

The American has never yet had to face the trials of Job. Great crises, like the Civil War, he has known how to surmount victoriously; and now that he has surmounted a second great crisis victoriously, it is possible that he may relapse, as he did in the other case, into an apparently complete

absorption in material enterprise and prosperity. But if serious and irreme-
diable tribulation ever overtook him, what would his attitude be? It is then
that we should be able to discover whether materialism or idealism lies at
the base of his character. Meantime his working mind is not without its
holiday. He spreads humour pretty thick and even over the surface of conversation, and humour is one form of moral emancipation. He loves landscape, he loves mankind, and he loves knowledge; and in music at least
he finds an art which he unfeignedly enjoys. In music and landscape, in
humour and kindness, he touches the ideal more truly, perhaps, than in his
ponderous academic idealisms and busy religions; for it is astonishing how
much even religion in America (can it possibly be so in England?) is a
matter of meetings, building-funds, schools, charities, clubs, and picnics.
To be poor in order to be simple, to produce less in order that the product
may be more choice and beautiful, and may leave us less burdened with
unnecessary duties and useless possessions — that is an ideal not articulate
in the American mind; yet here and there I seem to have heard a sigh after it,
a groan at the perpetual incubus of business and shrill society. Significant
witness to such aspirations is borne by those new forms of popular religion,
not mere variations on tradition, which have sprung up from the soil —
revivalism, spiritualism, Christian Science, the New Thought. Whether or
no we can tap, through these or other channels, some cosmic or inner
energy not hitherto at the disposal of man (and there is nothing incredible in
that), we certainly may try to remove friction and waste in the mere process
of living; we may relax morbid strains, loosen suppressed instincts, iron out
the creases of the soul, discipline ourselves into simplicity, sweetness, and
peace. These religious movements are efforts toward such physiological
economy and hygiene; and while they are thoroughly plebeian, with no
great lights, and no idea of raising men from the most vulgar and humdrum
worldly existence, yet they see the possibility of physical and moral health
on that common plane, and pursue it. That is true morality. The dignities of
various types of life or mind, like the gifts of various animals, are relative.
The snob adores one type only, and the creatures supposed by him to
illustrate it perfectly; or envies and hates them, which is just as snobbish.
Veritable lovers of life, on the contrary, like Saint Francis or like Dickens,
know that in every tenement of clay, with no matter what endowment or
station, happiness and perfection are possible to the soul. There must be no
brow-beating, with shouts of work or progress or revolution, any more than
with threats of hell-fire. What does it profit a man to free the whole world if
his soul is not free? Moral freedom is not an artificial condition, because the
ideal is the mother tongue of both the heart and the senses. All that is

requisite is that we should pause in living to enjoy life, and should lift up our hearts to things that are pure goods in themselves, so that once to have found and loved them, whatever else may betide, may remain a happiness that nothing can sully. This natural idealism does not imply that we are immaterial, but only that we are animate and truly alive. When the senses are sharp, as they are in the American, they are already half liberated, already a joy in themselves; and when the heart is warm, like his, and eager to be just, its ideal destiny can hardly be doubtful. It will not be always merely pumping and working; time and its own pulses will lend it wings.

CHAPTER VII

ENGLISH LIBERTY IN AMERICA

The straits of Dover, which one may sometimes see across, have sufficed so to isolate England that it has never moved quite in step with the rest of Europe in politics, morals, or art. No wonder that the Atlantic Ocean, although it has favoured a mixed emigration and cheap intercourse, should have cut off America so effectually that all the people there, even those of Latin origin, have become curiously different from any kind of European. In vain are they reputed to have the same religions or to speak the same languages as their cousins in the old world; everything has changed its accent, spirit, and value. Flora and fauna have been intoxicated by that untouched soil and fresh tonic air, and by those vast spaces; in spite of their hereditary differences of species they have all acquired the same crude savour and defiant aspect. In comparison with their European prototypes they seem tough, meagre, bold, and ugly. In the United States, apart from the fact that most of the early colonists belonged to an exceptional type of Englishman, the scale and speed of life have made everything strangely un-English. There is cheeriness instead of doggedness, confidence instead of circumspection; there is a desire to quizz and to dazzle rather than a fear of being mistaken or of being shocked; there is a pervasive cordiality, exaggeration, and farcical humour; and in the presence of the Englishman, when by chance he turns up or is thought of, there is an invincible impatience and irritation that his point of view should be so fixed, his mind so literal, and the freight he carries so excessive (when you are sailing in ballast yourself), and that he should seem to take so little notice of changes in the wind to which you are nervously sensitive.

Nevertheless there is one gift or habit, native to England, that has not only been preserved in America unchanged, but has found there a more favourable atmosphere in which to manifest its true nature — I mean the spirit of free co-operation. The root of it is free individuality, which is deeply seated in the English inner man; there is an indomitable instinct or mind in him which he perpetually consults and reveres, slow and embarrassed as his expression of it may be. But this free individuality in the

Englishman is crossed and biased by a large residue of social servitude. The church and the aristocracy, entanglement in custom and privilege, mistrust and bitterness about particular grievances, warp the inner man and enlist him against his interests in alien causes; the straits of Dover were too narrow, the shadow of a hostile continent was too oppressive, the English sod was soaked with too many dews and cut by too many hedges, for each individual, being quite master of himself, to confront every other individual without fear or prejudice, and to unite with him in the free pursuit of whatever aims they might find that they had in common. Yet this slow co-operation of free men, this liberty in democracy — the only sort that America possesses or believes in — is wholly English in its personal basis, its reserve, its tenacity, its empiricism, its public spirit, and its assurance of its own rightness; and it deserves to be called English always, to whatever countries it may spread.

The omnipresence in America of this spirit of co-operation, responsibility, and growth is very remarkable. Far from being neutralised by American dash and bravura, or lost in the opposite instincts of so many alien races, it seems to be adopted at once in the most mixed circles and in the most novel predicaments. In America social servitude is reduced to a minimum; in fact we may almost say that it is reduced to subjecting children to their mothers and to a common public education, agencies that are absolutely indispensable to produce the individual and enable him to exercise his personal initiative effectually; for after all, whatever metaphysical egotism may say, one cannot vote to be created. But once created, weaned, and taught to read and write, the young American can easily shoulder his knapsack and choose his own way in the world. He is as yet very little trammelled by want of opportunity, and he has no roots to speak of in place, class, or religion. Where individuality is so free, co-operation, when it is justified, can be all the more quick and hearty. Everywhere co-operation is taken for granted, as something that no one would be so mean or so short-sighted as to refuse. Together with the will to work and to prosper, it is of the essence of Americanism, and is accepted as such by all the unkempt polyglot peoples that turn to the new world with the pathetic but manly purpose of beginning life on a new principle. Every political body, every public meeting, every club, or college, or athletic team, is full of it. Out it comes whenever there is an accident in the street or a division in a church, or a great unexpected emergency like the late war. The general instinct is to run and help, to assume direction, to pull through somehow by mutual adaptation, and by seizing on the readiest practical measures and working compromises. Each man joins in and gives a helping hand, without a preconceived plan or a prior motive. Even the leader, when he is a natural leader and not a professional, has nothing up his sleeve to force on the rest, in their obvious good-will and mental blankness. All meet in a genuine spirit of consultation, eager to persuade but ready to be persuaded, with a cheery confidence in their average ability, when a point comes up and is clearly put before them, to decide it for the time being, and to move on. It is implicitly agreed, in every case, that disputed questions shall be put to a vote, and that the minority will loyally acquiesce in the decision of the majority and build henceforth upon it, without a thought of ever retracting it.

Such a way of proceeding seems in America a matter of course, because it is bred in the bone, or imposed by that permeating social contagion which is so irresistible in a natural democracy. But if we consider human nature at large and the practice of most nations, we shall see that it is a very rare, wonderful, and unstable convention. It implies a rather unimaginative optimistic assumption that at bottom all men's interests are similar and compatible, and a rather heroic public spirit — such that no special interest, in so far as it has to be overruled, shall rebel and try to maintain itself absolutely. In America hitherto these conditions happen to have been actually fulfilled in an unusual measure. Interests have been very similar — to exploit business opportunities and organise public services useful to all; and these similar interests have been also compatible and harmonious. A neighbour, even a competitor, where the field is so large and so little pre-empted, has more often proved a resource than a danger. The rich have helped the public more than they have fleeced it, and they have been emulated more than hated or served by the enterprising poor. To abolish millionaires would have been to dash one's own hopes. The most opposite systems of religion and education could look smilingly upon one another's prosperity, because the country could afford these superficial luxuries, having a constitutional religion and education of its own, which everybody drank in unconsciously and which assured the moral cohesion of the people. Impulses of reason and kindness, which are potential in all men, under such circumstances can become effective; people can help one another with no great sacrifice to themselves, and minorities can dismiss their special plans without sorrow, and cheerfully follow the crowd down another road. It was because life in America was naturally more co-operative and more plastic than in England that the spirit of English liberty, which demands co-operation and plasticity, could appear there more boldly and universally than it ever did at home.

English liberty is a method, not a goal. It is related to the value of human life very much as the police are related to public morals or commerce to wealth; and it is no accident that the Anglo-Saxon race excels in commerce and in the commercial as distinguished from the artistic side of industry, and that having policed itself successfully it is beginning to police the world at large. It is all an eminence in temper, good-will, reliability, accommodation. Probably some other races, such as the Jews and Arabs, make individually better merchants, more shrewd, patient, and loving of their art. Englishmen and Americans often seem to miss or force opportunities, to play for quick returns, or to settle down into ponderous corporations; for successful men they are not particularly observant, constant, or economical. But the superiority of the Oriental is confined to his private craft; he has not the spirit of partnership. In English civilisation the individual is neutralised; it does not matter so much even in high places if he is rather stupid or rather cheap; public spirit sustains him, and he becomes its instrument all the more readily, perhaps, for not being very distinguished or clear-headed in himself. The community prospers; comfort and science, good manners and generous feelings are diffused among the people, without the aid of that foresight and cunning direction which sometimes give a temporary advantage to a rival system like the German. In the end, adaptation to the world at large, where so much is hidden and unintelligible, is only possible piecemeal, by groping with a genuine indetermination in one's aims. Its very looseness gives the English method its lien on the future. To dominate the world co-operation is better than policy, and empiricism safer than inspiration. Anglo-Saxon imperialism is unintended; military conquests are incidental to it and often not maintained; it subsists by a mechanical equilibrium of habits and interests, in which every colony, province, or protectorate has a different status. It has a commercial and missionary quality, and is essentially an invitation to pull together — an invitation which many nations may be incapable of accepting or even of understanding, or which they may deeply scorn, because it involves a surrender of absolute liberty on their part; but whether accepted or rejected, it is an offer of co-operation, a project for a limited partnership, not a complete plan of life to be imposed on anybody.

It is a wise instinct, in dealing with foreigners or with material things (which are foreigners to the mind), to limit oneself in this way to establishing external relations, partial mutual adjustments, with a great residuum of independence and reserve; if you attempt more you will achieve less; your interpretations will become chimerical and your regimen odious. So deepseated is this prudent instinct in the English nature that it appears even at home; most of the concrete things which English genius has produced are expedients. Its spiritual treasures are hardly possessions, except as character is a possession; they are rather a standard of life, a promise, an insurance. English poetry and fiction form an exception; the very incoherence and artlessness which they share with so much else that is English lend them an absolute value as an expression. They are the mirror and prattle of the inner man — a boyish spirit astray in the green earth it loves, rich in wonder, perplexity, valour, and faith, given to opinionated little prejudices, but withal sensitive and candid, and often laden, as in *Hamlet,* with exquisite music, tender humour, and tragic self-knowledge. But apart from the literature that simply utters the inner man, no one considering the English language, the English church, or English philosophy, or considering the common law and parliamentary government, would take them for perfect realisations of art or truth or an ideal polity. Institutions so jumbled and limping could never have been planned; they can never be transferred to another setting, or adopted bodily; but special circumstances and contrary currents have given them birth, and they are accepted and prized, where they are native, for keeping the door open to a great volume and variety of goods, at a moderate cost of danger and absurdity.

Of course no product of mind is *merely* an expedient; all are concomitantly expressions of temperament; there is something in their manner of being practical which is poetical and catches the rhythm of the heart. In this way anything foreign — and almost all the elements of civilisation in England and America are foreign — when it is adopted and acclimatised, takes on a native accent, especially on English lips; like the Latin words in the language, it becomes thoroughly English in texture. The English Bible, again, with its archaic homeliness and majesty, sets the mind brooding, not less than the old ballad most redolent of the native past and the native imagination; it fills the memory with solemn and pungent phrases; and this incidental spirit of poetry in which it comes to be clothed is a self-revelation perhaps more pertinent and welcome to the people than the alien revelations it professes to transmit. English law and parliaments, too, would be very unjustly judged if judged as practical contrivances only; they satisfy at the same time the moral interest people have in uttering and enforcing their feelings. These institutions are ceremonious, almost sacramental; they are instinct with a dramatic spirit deeper and more vital than their utility. Englishmen and Americans love debate; they love sitting round a table as if in consultation, even when the chairman has pulled the wires and settled everything beforehand, and when each of the participants listens only to his own remarks and votes according to his party. They love committees and commissions; they love public dinners with after-dinner speeches, those stammering compounds of facetiousness, platitude, and business. How distressing such speeches usually are, and how helplessly prolonged, does not escape anybody; yet every one demands them notwithstanding, because in pumping them up or sitting through them he feels he is leading the political life. A public man must show himself in public, even if not to advantage. The moral expressiveness of such institutions also helps to redeem their clumsy procedure; they would not be useful, nor work at all as they should, if people did not smack their lips over them and feel a profound pleasure in carrying them out. Without the English spirit, without the faculty of making themselves believe in public what they never feel in private, without the habit of clubbing together and facing facts, and feeling duty in a cautious, consultative, experimental way, English liberties forfeit their practical value; as we see when they are extended to a volatile histrionic people like the Irish, or when a jury in France, instead of pronouncing simply on matters of fact and the credibility of witnesses, rushes in the heat of its patriotism to carry out, by its verdict, some political policy.

The practice of English liberty presupposes two things: that all concerned are fundamentally unanimous, and that each has a plastic nature, which he is willing to modify. If fundamental unanimity is lacking and all are not making in the same general direction, there can be no honest co-operation, no satisfying compromise. Every concession, under such circumstances, would be a temporary one, to be retracted at the first favourable moment; it would amount to a mutilation of one's essential nature, a partial surrender of life, liberty, and happiness, tolerable for a time, perhaps, as the lesser of two evils, but involving a perpetual sullen opposition and hatred. To put things to a vote, and to accept unreservedly the decision of the majority, are points essential to the English system; but they would be absurd if fundamental agreement were not presupposed. Every decision that the majority could conceivably arrive at must leave it still possible for the minority to live and prosper, even if not exactly in the way they wished. Were this not the case, a decision by vote would be as alien a fatality to any minority as the decree of a foreign tyrant, and at every election the right of rebellion would come into play. In a hearty and sound democracy all questions at issue must be minor matters; fundamentals must have been silently agreed upon and taken for granted when the democracy arose. To leave a decision to the majority is like leaving it to chance — a fatal procedure unless one is willing to have it either way. You must be able to risk losing the toss; and if you do you will acquiesce all the more readily in the result, because, unless the winners cheated at the game, they had no more influence on it than yourself — namely none, or very little. You acquiesce in democracy on the same conditions and for the same reasons, and perhaps a little more cheerfully, because there is an infinitesimally better chance of winning on the average; but even then the enormity of the risk involved would be intolerable if anything of vital importance was at stake. It is therefore actually required that juries, whose decisions may really be of moment, should be unanimous; and parliaments and elections are never more satisfactory than when a wave of national feeling runs through them and there is no longer any minority nor any need of voting.

Free government works well in proportion as government is superfluous. That most parliamentary measures should be trivial or technical, and really devised and debated only in government offices, and that government in America should so long have been carried on in the shade, by persons of no name or dignity, is no anomaly. On the contrary, like the good fortune of those who never hear of the police, it is all a sign that co-operative liberty is working well and rendering overt government unnecessary. Sometimes kinship and opportunity carry a whole nation before the wind; but this happy unison belongs rather to the dawn of national life, when similar tasks absorb all individual energies. If it is to be maintained after lines of moral cleavage appear, and is to be compatible with variety and distinction of character, all further developments must be democratically controlled and must remain, as it were, in a state of fusion. Variety and distinction must not become arbitrary and irresponsible. They must take directions that will not mar the general harmony, and no interest must be carried so far as to lose sight of the rest. Science and art, in such a vital democracy, should remain popular, helpful, bracing; religion should be broadly national and in the spirit of the times. The variety and distinction allowed must be only variety and distinction of service. If they ever became a real distinction and variety of life, if they arrogated to themselves an absolute liberty, they would shatter the unity of the democratic spirit and destroy its moral authority.

The levelling tendency of English liberty (inevitable if plastic natures are to co-operate and to make permanent concessions to one another's instincts) comes out more clearly in America than in England itself. In England there are still castles and rural retreats, there are still social islands within the Island, where special classes may nurse particular allegiances. America is all one prairie, swept by a universal tornado. Although it has always thought itself in an eminent sense the land of freedom, even when it was covered with slaves, there is no country in which people live under more overpowering compulsions. The prohibitions, although important and growing, are not yet, perhaps, so many or so blatant as in some other countries; but prohibitions are less galling than compulsions. What can be forbidden specifically — bigamy, for instance, or heresy — may be avoided by a prudent man without renouncing the whole movement of life and mind which, if carried beyond a certain point, would end in those trespasses against convention. He can indulge in hypothesis or gallantry without falling foul of the positive law, which indeed may even stimulate his interest and ingenuity by suggesting some indirect means of satisfaction. On the other hand, what is exacted cuts deeper; it creates habits which overlay nature, and every faculty is atrophied that does not conform with them. If, for instance, I am compelled to be in an office (and up to business, too) from early morning to late afternoon, with long journeys in thundering and sweltering trains before and after and a flying shot at a quick lunch between, I am caught and held both in soul and body; and except for the freedom to work and to rise by that work — which may be very interesting in itself — I am not suffered to exist morally at all. My evenings will be drowsy, my Sundays tedious, and after a few days' holiday I shall be wishing to get back to business. Here is as narrow a path left open to freedom as is left open in a monastic establishment, where bell and book keep your attention fixed at all hours upon the hard work of salvation — an infinite vista, certainly, if your soul was not made to look another way. Those, too, who may escape this crushing routine — the invalids, the ladies, the fops — are none the less prevented by it from doing anything else with success or with a good conscience; the bubbles also must swim with the stream. Even what is best in American life is compulsory — the idealism, the zeal, the beautiful happy unison of its great moments. You must wave, you must cheer, you must push with the irresistible crowd; otherwise you will feel like a traitor, a soulless outcast, a deserted ship high and dry on the shore. In America there is but one way of being saved, though it is not peculiar to any of the official religions, which themselves must silently conform to the national orthodoxy, or else become impotent and merely ornamental. This national faith and morality are vague in idea, but inexorable in spirit; they are the gospel of work and the belief in progress. By them, in a country where all men are free, every man finds that what most matters has been settled for him beforehand.

Nevertheless, American life *is* free as a whole, because it is mobile, because every atom that swims in it has a momentum of its own which is felt and respected throughout the mass, like the weight of an atom in the solar system, even if the deflection it may cause is infinitesimal. In temper America is docile and not at all tyrannical; it has not predetermined its career, and its merciless momentum is a passive resultant. Like some Mississippi or Niagara, it rolls its myriad drops gently onward, being but the suction and pressure which they exercise on one another. Any tremulous thought or playful experiment anywhere may be a first symptom of great changes, and may seem to precipitate the cataract in a new direction. Any snowflake in a boy's sky may become the centre for his *boule de neige,* his prodigious fortune; but the monster will melt as easily as it grew, and leaves nobody poorer for having existed. In America there is duty everywhere, but everywhere also there is light. I do not mean superior understanding or even moderately wide knowledge, but openness to light, an evident joy in seeing things clearly and doing them briskly, which would amount to a veritable triumph of art and reason if the affairs in which it came into play were central and important. The American may give an exorbitant value to subsidiary things, but his error comes of haste in praising what he possesses, and trusting the first praises he hears. He can detect sharp practices, because he is capable of them, but vanity or wickedness in the ultimate aims of a man, including himself, he cannot detect, because he is ingenuous in that sphere. He thinks like splendid and blameless, without stopping to consider how far folly and malice may be inherent in it. He feels that he himself has nothing to dread, nothing to hide or apologise for; and if he is arrogant in his ignorance, there is often a twinkle in his eye when he is most boastful. Perhaps he suspects that he is making a fool of himself, and he challenges the world to prove it; and his innocence is quickly gone when he is once convinced that it exists. Accordingly the American orthodoxy, though imperious, is not unyielding. It has a keener sense for destiny than for policy. It is confident of a happy and triumphant future, which it would be shameful in any man to refuse to work for and to share; but it cannot prefigure what that bright future is to be. While it works feverishly in outward matters, inwardly it only watches and waits; and it feels tenderly towards the unexpressed impulses in its bosom, like a mother towards her unborn young.

There is a mystical conviction, expressed in Anglo-Saxon life and philosophy, that our labours, even when they end in failure, contribute to some ulterior achievement in which it is well they should be submerged. This Anglo-Saxon piety, in the form of trust and adaptability, reaches somewhat the same insight that more speculative religions have reached through asceticism, the insight that we must renounce our wills and deny ourselves. But to have a will remains essential to animals, and having a will we must kick against the pricks, even if philosophy thinks it foolish of us. The spirit in which parties and nations beyond the pale of English liberty confront one another is not motherly nor brotherly nor Christian. Their valorousness and morality consist in their indomitable egotism. The liberty they want is absolute liberty, a desire which is quite primitive. It may be identified with the love of life which animates all creation, or with the pursuit of happiness which all men would be engaged in if they were rational. Indeed, it might even be identified with the first law of motion, that all bodies, if left free, persevere in that state of rest, or of motion in a straight line, in which they happen to find themselves. The enemies of this primitive freedom are all such external forces as make it deviate from the course it is in the habit of taking or is inclined to take; and when people begin to reflect upon their condition, they protest against this alien tyranny, and contrast in fancy what they would do if they were free with what under duress they are actually doing. All human struggles are inspired by what, in this sense, is the love of freedom. Even craving for power and possessions may be regarded as the love of a free life on a larger scale, for which more instruments and re-sources are needed. The apologists of absolute will are not slow, for in-stance, to tell us that Germany in her laborious ambitions has been pursuing the highest form of freedom, which can be attained only by organising all the resources of the world, and the souls of all subsidiary nations, around one luminous centre of direction and self-consciousness, such as the Prus-sian government was eminently fitted to furnish. Freedom to exercise abso-lute will methodically seems to them much better than English liberty, because it knows what it wants, pursues it intelligently, and does not rely for success on some measure of goodness in mankind at large. English liberty is so trustful! It moves by a series of checks, mutual concessions, and limited satisfactions; it counts on chivalry, sportsmanship, brotherly love, and on that rarest and least lucrative of virtues, fair-mindedness: it is a broad-based, stupid, blind adventure, groping towards an unknown goal. Who but an Englishman would think of such a thing! A fanatic, a poet, a doctrinaire, a dilettante — any one who has a fixed aim and clear passions — will not relish English liberty. It will seem bitter irony to him to give the name of liberty to something so muffled, exacting, and oppressive. In fact English liberty is a positive infringement and surrender of the freedom most fought for and most praised in the past. It makes impossible the sort of liberty for which the Spartans died at Thermopylæ, or the Christian martyrs in the arena, or the Protestant reformers at the stake; for these people all died because they would not co-operate, because they were not plastic and would never consent to lead the life dear or at least customary to other men. They insisted on being utterly different and independent and inflexible in their chosen systems, and aspired either to destroy the society round them or at least to insulate themselves in the midst of it, and live a jealous, private, unstained life of their own within their city walls or mystical con-claves. Any one who passionately loves his particular country or passion-ately believes in this particular region cannot be content with less liberty or more democracy than that; he must be free to live absolutely according to his ideal, and no hostile votes, no alien interests, must call on him to deviate from it by one iota. Such was the claim to religious liberty which has played so large a part in the revolutions and divisions of the western world. Every new heresy professed to be orthodoxy itself, purified and restored; and woe to all backsliders from the reformed faith! Even the popes, without thinking to be ironical, have often raised a wail for liberty. Such too was the aspiration of those mediæval cities and barons who fought for their liberties and rights. Such was the aspiration even of the American declaration of independence and the American constitution: cast-iron documents, if only the spirit of co-operative English liberty had not been there to expand, embosom, soften, or transform them. So the French revolution and the Russian one of to-day have aimed at establishing society once for all on some eternally just principle, and at abolishing all traditions, interests, faiths, and even words that did not belong to their system. Liberty, for all these pensive or rabid apostles of liberty, meant liberty for themselves to be just so, and to remain just so for ever, together with the most vehement defiance of anybody who might ask them, for the sake of harmony, to be a little different. They summoned every man to become free in exactly their own fashion, or have his head cut off.

Of course, to many an individual, life even in any such free city or free church, fiercely jealous of its political independence and moral purity, would prove to be a grievous servitude; and there has always been a sprinkling of rebels and martyrs and scornful philosophers protesting and fuming against their ultra-independent and nothing-if-not-protesting sects. To co-operate with anybody seems to these *esprits forts* contamination, so sensitive are they to any deviation from the true north which their compass might suffer through the neighbourhood of any human magnet. If it is a weakness to be subject to influence, it is an imprudence to expose oneself to it; and to be subject to influence seems ignominious to any one whose inward monitor is perfectly articulate and determined. A certain vagueness of soul, together with a great gregariousness and tendency to be moulded by example and by prevalent opinion, is requisite for feeling free under English liberty. You must find the majority right enough to live with; you must give up lost causes; you must be willing to put your favourite notions to sleep in the family cradle of convention. Enthusiasts for democracy, peace, and a league of nations should not deceive themselves; they are not everybody's friends; they are the enemies of what is deepest and most primitive in everybody. They inspire undying hatred in every untamable people and every absolute soul.

It is in the nature of wild animal life to be ferocious or patient, and in either case heroic and uncompromising. It is inevitable, in the beginning, that each person or faction should come into the lists to serve some express interest, which in itself may be perfectly noble and generous. But these interests are posited alone and in all their ultimate consequences. The parties meet, however diplomatic their procedure, as buyers and sellers bargain in primitive markets. Each has a fixed programme or, as he perhaps calls it, an ideal; and when he has got as much as he can get to-day, he will return to the charge to-morrow, with absolutely unchanged purpose. All opposed parties he regards as sheer enemies to be beaten down, driven off, and ultimately converted or destroyed. Meantime he practises political craft, of which the climax is war; a craft not confined to priests, though they are good at it, but common to every missionary, agitator, and philosophical politician who operates in view of some vested interest or inflexible plan, in the very un-English spirit of intrigue, cajolery, eloquence, and dissimulation. His art is to worm his way forward, using people's passions to further his own ends, carrying them off their feet in a wave of enthusiasm, when that is feasible, and when it is not, recommending his cause by insidious half-measures, flattery of private interests, confidence-tricks, and amiable suggestions, until he has put his entangled victims in his pocket; or when he feels strong enough, brow-beating and intimidating them into silence. Such is the inevitable practice of every prophet who heralds an absolute system, political or religious, and who pursues the unqualified domination of principles which he thinks right in themselves and of a will which is self-justified and irresponsible.

Why, we may ask, are people so ready to set up absolute claims, when their resources are obviously so limited that permanent success is impossible, and their will itself, in reality, is so fragile that it abandons each of its dreams even before it learns that it cannot be realised? The reason is that the feebler, more ignorant, and more childlike an impulse is, the less it can restrain itself or surrender a part of its desire in order the better to attain the rest. In most nations and most philosophies the intellect is rushed; it is swept forward and enamoured by the first glimpses it gets of anything good. The dogmas thus precipitated seem to relieve the will of all risks and to guarantee its enterprises; whereas in fact they are rendering every peril tragic by blinding us to it, and every vain hope incorrigible. A happy shyness in the English mind, a certain torpor and lateness in its utterance, have largely saved it from this calamity, and just because it is not brilliant it is safe. Being reticent, it remains fertile; being vague in its destination, it can turn at each corner down the most inviting road. In this race the intellect has chosen the part of prudence, leaving courage to the will, where courage is indispensable. How much more becoming and fortunate is this balance of faculties for an earthly being than an intellect that scales the heavens, refuting and proving everything, while the will dares to attempt and to reform nothing, but fritters itself away in sloth, petty malice, and irony! In the English character modesty and boldness appear in the right places and in a just measure. Manliness ventures to act without pretending to be sure of the issue; it does not cry that all is sure, in order to cover up the mortal perils of finitude; and manliness has its reward in the joys of exploration and comradeship.

It is this massive malleable character, this vigorous moral youth, that renders co-operation possible and progressive. When interests are fully articulate and fixed, co-operation is a sort of mathematical problem; up to a certain precise limit, people can obviously help one another by summing their efforts, like sailors pulling at a rope, or by a division of labour; they can obviously help one another when thereby they are helping themselves. But beyond that, there can be nothing but mutual indifference or eternal hostility. This is the old way of the world. Most of the lower animals, although they run through surprising transformations during their growth, seem to reach maturity by a predetermined method and in a predetermined form. Nature does everything for them and experience nothing, and they live or die, as the case may be, true to their innate character. Mankind, on the contrary, and especially the English races, seem to reach physical maturity still morally immature; they need to be finished by education, experience, external influences. What so often spoils other creatures improves them. If left to themselves and untrained, they remain all their lives stupid and coarse, with no natural joy but drunkenness; but nurseries and schools and churches and social conventions can turn them into the most refined and exquisite of men, and admirably intelligent too, in a cautious and special fashion. They may never become, for all their pains, so agile, graceful, and sure as many an animal or *a priori* man is without trouble, but they acquire more representative minds and a greater range of material knowledge. Such completion, in the open air, of characters only half-formed in the womb may go on in some chance direction, or it may go on in the direction of a greater social harmony, that is, in whatever direction is suggested to each man by the suasion of his neighbours. Society is a second mother to these souls; and the instincts of many animals would remain inchoate if the great instinct of imitation did not intervene and enable them to learn by example. Development in this case involves assimilation; characters are moulded by contagion and educated by democracy. The sphere of unanimity tends to grow larger, and to reduce the margin of diversity to insignificance. The result is an ever-increasing moral unison, which is the simplest form of moral harmony and emotionally the most coercive.

Democracy is often mentioned in the same breath with liberty, as if they meant the same thing; and both are sometimes identified with the sort of elective government that prevails in Great Britain and the United States. But just as English liberty seems servitude to some people because it requires them to co-operate, to submit to the majority, and to grow like them, so English democracy seems tyranny to the wayward masses, because it is constitutional, historical, and sacred, narrowing down the power of any group of people at any time to voting for one of two or three candidates for office, or to saying yes or no to some specific proposal — both the proposals and the candidates being set before them by an invisible agency; and fate was never more inexorable or blinder than is the grinding of this ponderous political mill, where routine, nepotism, pique, and swagger, with love of office and money, turn all the wheels. And the worst of it is that the revolutionary parties that oppose this historical machine repeat all its abuses, or even aggravate them. It would be well if people in England and America woke up to the fact that it is in the name of natural liberty and direct democracy that enemies both within and without are already rising up against their democracy and their liberty. Just as the Papacy once threatened English liberties, because it would maintain one inflexible international religion over all men, so now an international democracy of the disinherited many, led by the disinherited few, threatens English liberties again, since it would abolish those private interests which are the factors in any co-operation, and would reduce everybody to forced membership and forced service in one universal flock, without property, family, country, or religion. That life under such a system might have its comforts, its arts, and its atomic liberties, is certain, just as under the Catholic system it had its virtues and consolations; but both systems presuppose the universality of a type of human nature which is not English, and perhaps not human.

The great advantage of English liberty is that it is in harmony with the nature of things; and when living beings have managed to adapt their habits to the nature of things, they have entered the path of health and wisdom. No doubt the living will is essentially absolute, both at the top and at the bottom, in the ferocious animal and in the rapt spirit; but it is absolute even then only in its deliverance, in what it asserts or demands; nothing can be less absolute or more precarious than the living will in its existence. A living will is the flexible voice of a thousand submerged impulses, of which now one and now another comes to the surface; it is responsive, without knowing it, to a complex forgotten past and a changing, unexplored environment. The will is a mass of passions; when it sets up absolute claims it is both tragic and ridiculous. It may be ready to be a martyr, but it will have to be one. Martyrs are heroic; but unless they have the nature of things on their side and their cause can be victorious, their heroism is like that of criminals and madmen, interesting dramatically but morally detestable. Madmen and criminals, like other martyrs, appeal to the popular imagination, because in each of us there is a little absolute will, or a colony of little absolute wills, aching to be criminal, mad, and heroic. Yet the equilibrium by which we exist if we are sane, and which we call reason, keeps these rebellious dreams under; if they run wild, we are lost. Reason is a harmony; and it has been reputed by egotistical philosophers to rule the world (in which unreason of every sort is fundamental and rampant), because when harmony between men and nature supervenes at any place or in any measure, the world becomes intelligible and safe, and philosophers are able to live in it. The passions, even in a rational society, remain the elements of life, but under mutual control, and the life of reason, like English liberty, is a perpetual compromise. Absolute liberty, on the contrary, is impracticable; it is a foolish challenge thrown by a new-born insect buzzing against the universe; it is incompatible with more than one pulse of life. All the declarations of independence in the world will not render anybody really independent. You may disregard your environment, you cannot escape it; and your disregard of it will bring you moral empoverishment and some day unpleasant surprises. Even Robinson Crusoe — whom offended America once tried to imitate — lived on what he had saved from the wreck, on footprints and distant hopes. Liberty to be left alone, not interfered with and not helped, is not English liberty. It is the primeval desire of every wild animal or barbarous tribe or jealous city or religion, claiming to live and to tramp through the world in its own sweet way. These combative organisms, however, have only such strength as the opposite principle of co-operation lends them inwardly; and the more liberty they assume in foreign affairs the less liberty their members can enjoy at home. At home they must then have organisation at all costs, like ancient Sparta and modern Germany; and even if the restraints so imposed are not irksome and there is spontaneous unison and enthusiasm in the people, the basis of such a local harmony will soon prove too narrow. Nations and religions will run up against one another, against change, against science, against all the realities they had never reckoned with; and more or less painfully they will dissolve. And it will not be a normal and fruitful dissolution, like that of a man who leaves children and heirs. It will be the end of that evolution, the choking of that ideal in the sand.

This collapse of fierce liberty is no ordinary mutation, such as time brings sooner or later to everything that exists, when the circumstances that sustained it in being no longer prevail. It is a deep tragedy, because the narrower passions and swifter harmonies are more beautiful and perfect than the chaos or the dull broad equilibrium that may take their place. Co-operative life is reasonable and long-winded; but it always remains imperfect itself, while it somewhat smothers the impulses that enter into it. Absolute liberty created these elements; inspiration, free intelligence, uncompromising conviction, a particular home and breeding-ground, were requisite to give them birth. Nothing good could arise for co-operation to diffuse or to qualify unless first there had been complete liberty for the artist and an uncontaminated perfection in his work. Reason and the principle of English liberty have no creative afflatus; they presuppose spontaneity and yet they half stifle it; and they can rest in no form of perfection, because they must remain plastic and continually invite amendments, in order to continue broadly adjusted to an infinite moving world. Their work is accordingly like those cathedrals at which many successive ages have laboured, each in its own style. We may regret, sometimes, that some one design could not have been carried out in its purity, and yet all these secular accretions have a wonderful eloquence; a common piety and love of beauty have inspired them; age has fused them and softened their incongruities; and an inexpressible magic seems to hang about the composite pile, as if God and man breathed deeply within it. It is a harmony woven out of accidents, like every work of time and nature, and all the more profound and fertile because no mind could ever have designed it. Some such natural structure, formed and reformed by circumstances, is the requisite matrix and home for every moral being.

Accordingly there seems to have been sober sense and even severe thought behind the rant of Webster when he cried, "Liberty *and* Union, now and for ever, one and inseparable!" because if for the sake of liberty you abandon union and resist a mutual adaptation of purposes which might cripple each of them, your liberty loses its massiveness, its plasticity, its power to survive change; it ceases to be tentative and human in order to become animal and absolute. Nature must always produce little irresponsible passions that will try to rule her, but she can never crown any one of them with more than a theatrical success; the wrecks of absolute empires, communisms, and religions are there to prove it. But English liberty, because it is co-operative, because it calls only for a partial and shifting unanimity among living men, may last indefinitely, and can enlist every reasonable man and nation in its service. This is the best heritage of America, richer than its virgin continents, which it draws from the temperate and manly spirit of England. Certainly absolute freedom would be more beautiful if we were birds or poets; but co-operation and a loving sacrifice of a part of ourselves — or even of the whole, save the love in us — are beautiful too, if we are men living together. Absolute liberty and English liberty are incompatible, and mankind must make a painful and a brave choice between them. The necessity of rejecting and destroying some things that are beautiful is the deepest curse of existence.

Essays

The Unclaimed Legacy
of George Santayana

WILFRED M. McCLAY

The first difficulty in writing about George Santayana, the one that points toward all the others, arises out of the question of style. Clearly the fact that Santayana is such an elegant and deliciously entertaining writer is a large part of what makes him so worth writing about. But there are few philosophical writers for whom medium and message are more closely entwined, and that fact presents one with a problem. How does a mere scholar do justice to a subtle and intriguing philosopher who was also a prose stylist of the first order — particularly when the philosophical substance of his work is so closely bound up in the luminous style in which it was expressed?

There are two obvious ways to address this difficulty, and each is unsatisfactory. One can try, in the time-honored manner of assiduous, well-trained academics, to stand back from one's subject, extract what is essential and distinctive in the oeuvre, and then work to formulate and restate it in as crisp, precise, and systematic a way as possible, perhaps providing scraps of historical, literary, and biographical context along the way. In so doing, one at least avoids the self-destructive folly of competing with the master himself. But the price paid in understanding will be very high indeed, as it always is when the warm fluidity of ongoing thought is intercepted, diverted into the inert molds of textbook prose, and then made to emerge as cold, hard stone. Just like those nineteenth-century academics who thought they were doing Plato a favor by imposing a tidy little system of "Platonism" upon those tricky and unsystematic "dialogues" in which he had quite unaccountably chosen to present his ideas, so do present-day writers who take such an approach to Santayana also run the risk of violating the man's thought in the very process of celebrating it.

Careful and attentive readers of *Character and Opinion in the United States* will find it very hard to reduce its contents to anything approaching a system; and to the extent that they spend their time trying to do so, it is time wasted, time that could have been better spent contemplating, say, Santayana's astonishing facility in tapping the revelatory power of metaphor and simile. In that sense, his work is best seen as itself a form of reflective literature, a genre all its own which cannot be converted into something radically different from itself without the whole effect being lost or trivialized. When read in close and appreciative detail, rather than with a view to extracting summarizing abstractions, Santayana's prose is itself a civilizing agent, which promotes the very forms of sensibility that it extols.

So perhaps this is a case in which an object of study can only be approached by means that are broadly congruent with and sympathetic to its own nature; a case, so to speak, of like calling unto like, where one must be content to come alongside a book and engage it in its own terms, entering into its spirit rather than analyzing it primly with clean and well-starched categories drawn from elsewhere. "Only an American," declares Santayana, "can speak for the heart of America"; and perhaps something of the same principle can be taken to apply to the full appreciation of a thinker as literary as Santayana.[1] But if Santayana's claim were really to be taken at face value, one could hardly make much of a case for the signal importance to Americans of his book, which is after all the work of a self-declared outsider. Perhaps speaking for the heart is a different thing from knowing it.

Besides, the embrace of such a principle leaves us with an even more daunting alternative in approaching the challenge of Santayana. If we are to conclude that one can only represent Santayana's thinking by, in some way, following its own pattern, seeking to respect the windings of its disciplined but essayistic structure, paying mimetic homage to the finely spun texture of his mind, and attending to the ways in which his writing style conveyed that texture, then we may be setting ourselves up for abject failure. To be sure, it is an imposition upon the reader to do nothing more than quote Santayana again and again, tempting as that may be (and I hope I have not yielded too much to that temptation in what follows). But one will be faced with an impossible task, if in order to write adequately about Santayana one has no choice but to write just as brilliantly and wittily as he does. If that is taken as the standard, then honesty and prudence would require me (and most other writers) to give up at the very outset and leave the master to speak for himself, in his own books.

Still, the effort must be made, if for no other reason than that one is obliged to do what one can to resist the terrible neglect of this rare and indispensable thinker, who was not only a philosopher of richness, range, and distinction but a peerless critic of American culture, providing the kind of broad-brush account of the American mind that Americans have never quite been able to muster for themselves. In addition, *Character and Opinion* is particularly deserving of preservation, not only because of its relative neglect, but because it offers a compact but quite accessible précis of the chief themes inhabiting Santayana's mature mind, sounding nearly all the characteristic notes in his always penetrating, occasionally cranky, and consistently vivid and thought-provoking analyses of the United States, and of the possibilities and liabilities of modernity itself. Even those readers who have never read a word of Santayana before will be able to experience the full range and flavor of him in *Character and Opinion,* including the distinctive cut of his philosophical writing. It is a great service to have brought this book back before the public eye, along with Santayana's famous reflections on "the genteel tradition," and particularly appropriate to do so at a time when Americans seem to have launched into a fresh installment of their perpetual quest to figure out who they are.

Santayana always cut a somewhat peculiar figure in the American milieu. In it, yes, for many years; but never of it. One can see it plainly as early as the group photos from his 1886 Harvard graduating class, where, with his unmistakably Spanish facial features, he seems an exotic compared to his Yankee classmates: "a ripe mango," quipped his biographer John McCormick, "among Jonathan apples."[2] But even so, he was for much of the twentieth century a public figure to reckon with in America, and *Character and Opinion,* from the moment of its first appearance in 1920, would be a book to conjure with, one of that handful of works about America (along with "The Genteel Tradition in American Philosophy") that serious students were expected to read and digest. It is indicative that David Riesman's immensely influential book *The Lonely Crowd* (1950) includes a lengthy quotation from *Character and Opinion* as an epigraph, a sure testimony to its contemporary importance.

"I speak of the American," Riesman quotes Santayana, "as if there were not millions of them, north and south, east and west, of both sexes, of all ages, and of various races, professions, and religions."[3] But that very sentence hints at a reason why, in an age in which all the emphasis is on the diversity of American cultures and subcultures, Santayana's cultural criticism is no longer much pondered. In any event, we can guess that Santayana himself would be neither surprised nor greatly troubled to know of his neglect over a half-century after his death, even if he might not have been able to predict all the proximate causes. Indeed, he fully expected such things. By all accounts, he regarded the world with serene detachment, savoring the tart ironies and bittersweet paradoxes that pervade our existence, and he cheerfully faced up to the futility of much human striving.

Nor did he anticipate that the capacity for such stoical detachment would be very widely distributed in the world. "Reason," as he says in these pages, "is a later comer into this world, and weak"; it can only do so much when pitted against "the mighty resistance of habit and of moral presumption."[4] One even suspects he would be mildly amused, rather than angered or wounded, to know how he is chiefly remembered today: for his association with a portentous, wise-sounding (though nearly always misquoted) epigram taken from midparagraph in one of his philosophical works: "Those who cannot remember the past are condemned to repeat it."[5]

So memorable has this adage proved that we seem condemned to hear it repeated again and again, in sober op-ed pieces, earnest letters to the editor, high-school valedictory addresses, and other such pulpits. But the quote does not do him justice. Santayana meant something rather different by these words than what the platitudinarians take them to have meant, as becomes readily apparent when it is read in its full context, in his *Reason in Common Sense:* "Progress, far from consisting in change, depends on retentiveness. When change is absolute there remains no being to improve and no direction is set for possible improvement: and when experience is not retained, as among savages, infancy is perpetual. Those who cannot remember the past are condemned to repeat it. In the first stage of life the mind is frivolous and easily distracted, it misses progress by failing in consecutiveness and persistence. This is the condition of children and barbarians, in which instinct has learned nothing from experience."[6]

Clearly Santayana was concerned here not with the putative "lessons of history" — about whose precise contents he was in any event always extraordinarily skeptical and circumspect — but with the basic preconditions for an adult, civilized way of life, a subject about which he knew a great deal. It is a quotation that, rightly understood, challenges both those "conservatives" who believe that their ideology requires unyielding opposition to change, and those "progressives" who believe that their ideology requires relentless opposition to stasis, showing the utter fatuousness of the supposed opposition between them.

It may seem preposterous to argue that Santayana is unknown, given how often he is quoted, even if the quote is always the same. But what if those who quote him do not understand what they are quoting? What if it never occurs to them that they have taken Santayana's sentence out of context and altered its meaning? What if, irony of ironies, these eleven anodyne words praising the practical utility of historical knowledge are taken to express a view that Santayana himself would have been unlikely to put forward? It would be as if Abraham Lincoln were remembered by history for nothing more than the contents of an apocryphal joke told to his Cabinet. Such hardly seems a just fate for one of the most subtle and interesting minds in American history. It is not, after all, as if there have been so many thinkers of Santayana's caliber that we can afford to let even one go unnoticed.

To be sure, we Americans have often revealed ourselves to be a wasteful people, in tending to our cultural legacies no less than to our natural resources. This careless prodigality, which also ensures that the wheel is reinvented with discouraging regularity in our thinking, is something of a national disease, albeit not a fatal one. Those who cannot remember the critiques of the past may be condemned to recycle them unknowingly. To say this is not to deny the benefit in working through a problem freshly for oneself, a benefit that Santayana himself recognized. But still, the neglect suffered by Santayana today stands in such stark contrast to his achievements, not to mention his reputation at the height of his long and productive career, that one is led to wonder whether part of the explanation lies in the unwelcomeness of the messages he sought to convey.

The scope of that achievement is beyond dispute. Not only was he the author of a shelf-long array of distinguished philosophical tomes, but he also wrote volumes of poetry, general and occasional essays, literary and cultural criticism (such as the present work), political and social thought, a superb novel called *The Last Puritan* (a Book of the Month Club selection in 1935), and a classic autobiography, *Persons and Places,* which equals in many respects *The Education of Henry Adams.*[7] In short, he was a complete man of letters, par excellence, and what he wrote was written to last.

It has, at least for those who have cared to read it. Only the formal poetry falls short of greatness, perhaps because "reason," as his admirer Wallace Stevens once observed, "is a jealous mistress," who insists that "a man whose whole life is thought" not stray too far from his calling.[8] But the prose writings are another matter, and they are where Santayana's poetic gifts find their most congenial setting. All of them, even hastily tossed off journalistic pieces, bear the signs of Santayana's mastery. His was a style of power and suppleness, exemplary in its elegance, lucidity, spareness, and directness; filled with wry and understated humor; made wonderfully vivid by ingenious but unforced metaphors; and molded throughout into beautifully turned, lapidary sentences. In matters of style, Santayana's writings left those of his contemporary philosophical competitors (except, perhaps, for his Harvard colleague and friendly rival William James) far behind; indeed, the best of Santayana's prose deserves comparison with the finest such achievements in the English language — something that can be said of precious few philosophical writings.

And, although his detractors dismissed him as a belletristic dilettante, the charge is false. Santayana did not needlessly scatter his energies by venturing into such a wide range of prose genres. Instead, he broadened his range and clarified his thinking through the use of such a various palette. His creations turn out to have been remarkably of a piece, despite their formal differences, since each served as a subtly different way of organizing and expressing the same philosophical vision. For him, literature and cultural criticism were merely forms of philosophy pursued by other means. Nothing irked him more than the gap that so often existed between what thinkers philosophized about and what they actually believed, or more generally between the activity of the parlor and the motives of the street. Whatever his other failings, such inconsistency did not bedevil him. All the works in his oeuvre support and interpenetrate one another, like the warp and woof of a single fabric. The poet and the philosopher are never far from one another.

The neglect of so substantial a writer, then, cries out for an explanation; and possible explanations are not hard to find. If his present fate is unjust, it was not entirely unforeseeable. For Santayana's thoughts were thoughts out of season, both in his time and in our own; and obscurity is one of the prices paid for unseasonableness. Historians of American thought tend to ignore him because they find it so hard to "place" him; his thought's unusual blend of unflinching materialism and unswerving devotion to the life of the spirit did not have much in common with German idealism, or pragmatism, or the Social Gospel, or any other current of thought then prevailing or emerging in the United States. He did not fit their textbook narratives, and he still doesn't.

Nor was this the only way his timing was unfortunate. He began to carve out a niche for himself as a philosophically inclined man of letters at the very moment, in the late 1880s, that philosophy began its transformation into a professionalized discipline, the exclusive intellectual domain of specialists and technicians.[9] Along with William James, Santayana fought a brave rearguard action against this development, not only by abstract arguments, but more importantly, by the very way he chose to write — clearly, elegantly, and engagingly, in a manner accessible to an educated "lay" audience. Such indiscretion did no lasting harm to James's reputation, but for Santayana, it only helped seal his fate.

Finding himself a misfit, however, was hardly an unfamiliar feeling for Santayana. He lived for four decades in Boston and Cambridge, from the time he was transplanted there at the age of eight until the day he left his Harvard professorship for good; but his stubbornly independent spirit could never take root in that stolid Protestant soil. Instead, his imagination was irresistibly drawn back to the Spanish Catholic world of his birth, with its rich storehouse of mythological imagery and poetic resonances. Under these circumstances it became his responsibility, as he once put it, to "say plausibly in English as many un-English things as possible": a statement that would arguably be even more accurate if the word "un-American" were substituted for "un-English."[10] Such was hardly the way to court fame and immortality. We love to mock the conventional wisdom, so long as it is yesterday's, not today's; we love eccentricity in theory but dislike it in practice, and Santayana was nothing if not eccentric to American conventional wisdom.

Yet his extraordinary circumstances were precisely what made him so valuable an observer of American civilization, for these gave him the detachment necessary to see American life without first accepting its premises. It was as if he were bred for the role by the tangled circumstances of his birth and personal history. More than that of many philosophers, Santayana's thought emerged in a very direct way out of his struggle to give shape to his experience.

Born in Madrid in 1863, he was the offspring of an unlikely marriage, whose contours already suggest an interplay between the "English" and "un-English."[11] To begin with, his mother Josefina Borrás, despite her name and her Catalonian parents, had actually been born in Glasgow and was brought up both there and in Winchester, Virginia. When she moved to the Philippines in the company of her diplomat father, the first of several tragedies struck her: her father unexpectedly died. The eighteen-year-old Josefina suddenly had to fend for herself, an orphan in a strange land. Eventually she met and married the tall blond Yankee merchant George Sturgis, scion of a solid Bostonian family. But that marriage too was touched by tragedy. Although she bore Sturgis five children, only three grew to maturity, and the death of her first child at the age of two seems to have stricken her with crippling grief; by all accounts she was never the same person again. "She regarded [her later born children] as inferior," wrote George Santayana, himself one of their number, "entirely inadequate to console her for what she had lost"; as a consequence she became a "cold, determined" mother absorbed in her "separateness."[12]

When George Sturgis died in 1857 at the age of forty, Josefina found it necessary to come to Boston in order to raise her children under the protective wing of the Sturgises. But on a visit to Madrid in 1861 she reencountered Agustín Ruiz de Santayana, a retired Spanish diplomat in his fifties, whom she had met years before in the Philippines. She married him in 1861, and a son named George Santayana was born two years later: Josefina's sixth, and last, child. He was named, revealingly enough, after the deceased George Sturgis.

It was a strange, unpromising marriage. For one thing, Josefina was committed to bring up her Sturgis children in Boston, while Agustín was irrevocably bound to Spain and to Spanish ways. By 1869, Josefina decided to leave George in the care of his father, and she returned to Boston to raise her Sturgis children there. Three years later, when George was eight, Agustín and George joined the family in Boston; but Agustín returned to Spain a year later, having found he could not adjust to American ways. George was left behind, alone in an alien world, one that he would never learn to love. For the next decade he would know his father chiefly through letters, in which Agustín addressed his beloved son as "Jorge," and kept alive in his son's mind the remembrance of a world of humane warmth and poetry that he had known in Spain. Those memories proved a valued resource that he frequently drew upon, in the midst of a Yankee "pettiness and practicality of outlook and ambition" that he quickly came to despise, as he came to terms with the cold unresponsiveness of his mother. The wrenching away from Spain, and from his father, ensured that all his future loyalties, whether national or personal, would be highly provisional and susceptible to change. He had been compelled to learn the hard lessons of detachment very early in life.

But if there was great pain in Santayana's unusual situation, he made the most of it. Like any immigrant, he had a complex perspective on American society, defined by multiple frames of reference. He grew up in close connection with an old and distinguished Bostonian family, but his own home was bilingual, drawn by inevitable and living ties to an Old World that his father still inhabited. From that other world George received a steady stream of epistolary advice and support, in which a distinctly non-American philosophy of life and language was on offer, a philosophy that very much included Agustín's anticlerical and freethinking agnosticism. It was likely from Agustín that Santayana first got the idea that the objects of religious faith might be creations of man himself, like poems; it was a lesson he took very much to heart. The move from his father's ancient Castilian town of Avila to the cold impersonality of the Sturgis home at 302 Beacon Street must have represented a dizzying change for the boy, making a deep impression on his character. Exposed at a relatively young age to such radically different perspectives upon the world, Santayana absorbed the lesson that one should not rely upon any one of them. This may help explain why he had the ability to thrive for so many years within the Puritan-Protestant milieu of Cambridge and Boston without either being driven crazy by it or being driven to accept it. From a very early age Santayana learned to ask little of the world and keep what was precious to him safe behind walls of reticence. That was how he made his peace with things.

Evidence of how successfully he managed that peace can be found in his academic record, for Santayana was very much a success, both in the classroom and in his social activities. In the latter category, one has to be impressed by the fact that this Spanish boy was, in his final year as a student at the Boston Latin School, made both Major and Lieutenant Colonel of the Latin School Battalion. It was also during his eight years at the Latin School that Santayana discovered a knack for poetry, filling the *Latin School Register* (of which he was the first editor) with his fluent and clever verses. At Harvard, he was of course an outstanding student, graduating summa cum laude; he also had a very full and satisfying social life, managing despite the relative modesty of his financial means to be active in some eleven organizations, including the *Lampoon,* the *Harvard Monthly,* the O.K. Society, and the Hasty Pudding. He was no gloomy recluse, in short, and the good-natured jollity of those days is reflected in a lovely passage in *Character and Opinion* in which he speaks with evident affection of the "droll incidents and broad farce" that made up so much of life at Harvard College and places like it: American college life provided one with an "idyllic, haphazard, humoristic existence," and there was much to like about it.[13]

Yet mingled with the affection was detached honesty, even asperity. Santayana was never one to let nostalgia cloud his thinking, and he takes care to remark, in reflecting upon these same years, that they were "without fine imagination . . . a flutter of intelligence in a void, flying into trivial play, in order to drop back, as soon as college days were over, into the drudgery of affairs," years that were by any sensible reckoning "trivial and wasted."[14] Despite his seeming absorption in the Harvard scene, his Spanish connections continued to loom large, and his mind gradually became capable of moving comfortably on two tracks at once. The steady flow of correspondence from his father in Avila kept him informed of events there and refreshed his Spanish sympathies. And at the close of a week caught up in the round of Cambridge life, he would repair to his mother's house for the weekend, and there would speak Spanish with her and his half-sister. After finishing his freshman year of college, he spent part of the summer with his father in Avila; it was the first time he had seen Agustín in a decade. He would make such visits frequently in the years to come. In shuttling between old Avila, with its medieval walls and its static way of life, and the drab industrial modernity of cold, practical, progress-minded Anglo-Saxon

Boston, Santayana became a shuttler between worlds, a practical relativist. This oddly dichotomous existence would continue as long as he remained in the United States.

After graduation, Santayana spent time abroad studying in Berlin; he then returned to Harvard and applied himself to graduate studies, dutifully producing a dissertation on the philosophy of Hermann Lotze. The dissertation was accepted, and Santayana (who was, they told him, "the most normal doctor of philosophy that they had ever created") was offered an instructorship.[15] Despite his growing reservations about American academic life, especially as it was evolving under the direction of such educational entrepreneurs as Harvard president Charles W. Eliot (whom he loathed — see his gibe[16] against him in *Character and Opinion*), he was now becoming a part of it. Eventually he would rise to the rank of full professor, becoming a fixture in the department of philosophy during its Golden Age, a historical moment that is also very much a part of the subject matter in *Character and Opinion*.

But once Santayana joined the faculty at Harvard, his annoyances with that institution, kept at bay during his student years, began to build. The problems were partly rooted in clashes of taste, personality, and temperament; but as was always the case for Santayana, such clashes ultimately correlated with disagreements on the level of ideas. It may have been a Golden Age, but Santayana found his colleagues — who included William James, Josiah Royce, Hugo Munsterberg, and George H. Palmer — to be insufferably narrow and moralistic, their minds filled with an unwarranted sense of Anglo-Saxon cultural superiority and their hearts still reflexively bound by archaic Protestant pieties that had no basis in reason or nature. The latter two, Munsterberg and Palmer, were so egregious that they did not even rate treatment in *Character and Opinion*.

But even James, whose pragmatism and openness to experience Santayana admired and whose antinomies are examined here in penetrating detail in Chapter III, fell victim to this harsh verdict. "I wonder if you realize," Santayana complained in a letter to James written in 1900, "the years of suppressed irritation which I have passed in the midst of an unintelligible sanctimonious and often disingenuous Protestantism, which is thoroughly alien and repulsive to me, and the need I have of joining hands with something far away from it and far above it."[17] It was a view that never changed. Santayana's aversion to compulsory Protestant uplift and his reverence for pagan thinkers like Lucretius and for the rich symbolic pageant of Spanish Catholicism were bound to set him at odds with the others; and they returned much of the disdain. Even the hypertolerant James, who could lend a sympathetic ear to almost any doctrine, no matter how eccentric, derided Santayana's thought as "a perfection of rottenness . . . representative of moribund Latinity."[18]

What, then, was this system of perfect rottenness? Although, as I have already suggested, Santayana is unusually difficult to summarize with fairness and accuracy, the basic elements of his thought can be easily grasped. First of all, Santayana was a convinced materialist, and that conviction was never absent for long from anything he wrote. He did not grant any separate existence to the soul; consciousness, he held, was merely a special outgrowth of matter, the result of a chain of complex chemical interactions. All gods and theologies were products of the human imagination. He accepted, without any difficulty, Darwin's conclusions about the origin and development of species and the implications of these conclusions for humankind's status in the universe. He entertained no illusions about man's significance in the ultimate scheme of things.

But Santayana was no garden-variety mechanistic philosopher, for he was equally devoted to the life of the spirit; this was a residue, in part, of the Catholicism in his makeup. The spirit, to be sure, was in the end nothing more than a byproduct of matter, and the characteristic American sin of anthropocentrism, of believing man and the will of man to be the center of all things, was completely without foundation. But the realm of the spirit was all the more to be cherished, he believed, as the only truly human consolation within the immense sprawling indifference of nature. The sphere of the spirit encompassed poetry as well as religion, as Santayana argued at length in his *Interpretations of Poetry and Religion*, for the two were different expressions of the same thing. "I am not myself a believer in the ordinary sense," he admitted, "yet my feeling on this subject is like that of believers, and not at all like that of my fellow materialists." The enduring value of religion lay not in its pretension to deal with matters of fact, but in "its ideal adequacy, in its fit rendering of the meanings and values of life, in its anticipation of perfection."[19] In his later and more technical philosophical work, Santayana would devote much energy to an elaborate doctrine of "essences," meant to define with more precision the realm in which such meanings and anticipations had their being.

Small wonder, then, that Santayana objected so violently to liberal Protestantism's attempts to demythologize Christianity, by eliminating from it all the beliefs that could no longer pass scientific muster. This was exactly what religions should not do. Liberalism, he complained, "subtracts from faith that imagination by which faith becomes an interpretation and idealization of human life" and leaves behind only "a stale and superfluous principle of superstition."[20] Nor did he have a higher opinion of those who gave themselves over entirely to materialism and the natural sciences, for they neglected the noblest and most precious capacities of man. Naturalistic philosophers, he found, generally had "cursory and wretched notions of the inner life of the mind," a defect that he could not possibly let pass.[21] And so once again he found himself in an unusual position, as a kind of materialistic idealist or atheistic Catholic, able to appreciate the virtues of both camps, insistent upon the errors of each, and in the end a party to neither.

Yet at bottom Santayana's thought was an attempt to reconcile just these opposites. Like the romantics, Santayana reserved his deepest reverence for the products of the imagination; and like the faithful, he valued religion for the glimpses of eternity it promised. But at the same time he always insisted that these creations of the mind had no ground in nature. It was a paradoxical stance, guaranteed to confound the literal-minded.

It may also have been his attempt to have it both ways at once. The seductive dance of Santayana's mind moves between an easygoing subjectivism ("it is only my mind that I speak for at bottom, or wish to speak for") along with a tender love for the realm of ideas, and a vehement rejection of any romantic subjectivism that seats reality in the ego and deprives nature of the hard and inhuman ultimacy that he demanded for it.[22] One is entitled to ask whether this whirl of insights and contrarities can actually hold together, or instead only can be made to seem to do so, thanks to the legerdemain of Santayana's magical prose and the easy, composed confidence of his diction. Perhaps that is why one cannot step away for long from Santayana's prose itself without running the risk of losing him entirely. Perhaps it holds together only when gathered by that golden thread.

However odd his ideas may have been in the context of his time, he was very well liked by the Harvard students he taught; and the feelings were warmly reciprocated, for Santayana preferred the company of students to that of his colleagues. For him, the honest and energetic crudeness of young American men was always to be preferred to the artificial and feeble moralism of their elders. It is astonishing how many intellectual figures of the twentieth century can be counted among his former charges: a short list would have to include T. S. Eliot, Walter Lippmann, Gilbert Seldes, Max Eastman, Van Wyck Brooks, Horace Kallen, Conrad Aiken, Wallace Stevens, Samuel Eliot Morison, Felix Frankfurter, and James B. Conant, among others.

Many of them remembered Santayana with awed reverence, as a quiet, reserved, and gently aristocratic presence. He dressed with impeccable care and attention to detail; he liked to wear a military cape instead of an over-coat, swinging it off in a single dramatic sweep as he entered his classroom. His lectures, too, were models of precision, clarity, and eloquence. Capti-vated by his powerful dark eyes and exotic Spanish features, not to mention his exotic ideas, many of the students spun elaborate fantasies around his person. Conrad Aiken compared him to Merlin or Prospero, "with his wizard's mantle from Spain." Another saw in his "poise, with the fine domed forehead, the brilliant myopic brown eyes, the fine dark moustache, and the smiling detachment . . . something akin to the presence of a Chinese sage or a Mongolian Buddhist." Fanciful as these descriptions are, they give us some sense of how striking a figure he cut.[23]

But the pleasure he took from his students' admiration and affection only went so far. It was not enough to compensate for his ever growing discomfort in Harvard Yard and in the United States. Despite his success, Santayana never felt comfortable as a professor of philosophy, for he felt that truly being a philosopher was different from the work of explicating other people's philosophies in front of young people. "Free reflection about everything is a habit to be imitated," he observed in *Character and Opin-ion,* "but not a subject to expound." The genuine philosopher is not a team player but instead is one who "wanders alone like the rhinoceros," con-fident in his idiosyncrasy and free from the institutional requirement to look after the moral formation of the young.[24]

Such freedom, though, was simply not possible at Harvard, where the American habit of compulsory moralizing seemed to him to burden the life of the entire faculty, even disfiguring the otherwise exemplary and promis-ing thought of a man like William James. One could see that a break was likely to come. In 1905, he wrote James from Europe, exhilarated by the experience of giving a series of lectures at the Sorbonne. There, he exulted, "You can say what is really true," without having always to "remember that you are in Cambridge . . . addressing the youth entrusted to your personal charge."[25] By 1911, he would finally come to the conclusion that the circumstances of American intellectual life would always be unpro-pitious for a thinker like him, and he began plotting ways to make his escape. Finally, in 1912, after his mother's death had freed him of family obligation, Santayana left the United States, and Harvard, never to return again. He would spend the next forty years in a second career as a peripa-tetic scholar, living in rooms and hotels all over Europe and finally settling in Rome in 1941 at the Clinica della Piccola Compagna di Maria, also known as the Blue Nuns for the color of the habit worn by its residents. There he remained secluded for his final eleven years — his final act, as it were, of withdrawal.

Character and Opinion was then, if considered in a strictly personal sense, his valedictory gesture to the America he had so gladly departed. But it was far more than a personal statement or apologia. It was also a rich and fully rounded portrait of a land he knew very well, containing a perceptive analysis that he had been pondering and burnishing for many years. The summer before he left America, he delivered a lecture at the University of California at Berkeley, in which he made clear some of his reasons for leaving. In "The Genteel Tradition in American Philosophy," Santayana bequeathed to subsequent observers not only an indispensable term of analysis — "the genteel tradition" — but an enduring diagnosis of what he perceived to be a fault line in American culture. The American mind was divided, he asserted, between what was inherited and what was native born — or, as he expressed it, between "the belief and standards of the fathers" and "the instincts, practices, and discoveries of the younger generations."[26]

The contrast suggests the contrast between his colleagues and his students. The latter represented the burgeoning, if somewhat callow, vitality of a young, prosperous, and enterprising industrial America; it was this America that Santayana found to be most admirable and healthy, even if its coarseness was not entirely to his own taste. But the former represented the artificial, derivative, moralistic, and disconnected world of genteel "culture," what passed for intellectual and artistic achievement in the American strand. That was the world he had known for many years in Boston and Cambridge; and that world was hopeless. As he wrote in a mischievous letter to Van Wyck Brooks, "art, etc. has a better soil in the ferocious 100% America than in the Intelligentsia of New York," for it was "veneer, rouge, aestheticism, art museums, new theatres, etc. that make America impotent. The good things are football, kindness, and jazz bands."[27]

The becalmed artificiality of the American intellect, he concluded, resulted from its continuing enslavement to a moralistic Protestant tradition. That tradition continued to be rigidly upheld, even though its basis in reality had disappeared; but the strain of supporting beliefs that ran contrary to nature made the production of a vibrant culture next to impossible. Unless Americans abandoned the genteel tradition, he argued, the outmoded premise that "man, or human reason, or the human distinction between good and evil, is the center and pivot of the universe," there would continue to be a disjunction between their intellectual life and their actual life, with neither doing much to inform the other.[28]

Better, he argued, to remember how infinitesimal was one's place in the vastness and impersonality of nature: "What you can do avails little materially, and in the end nothing." Better to dispense with the genteel tradition and instead "learn what you are really fitted to do, and where lie your natural dignity and joy, namely, in representing many things, without being them, and in letting your imagination, through sympathy, celebrate and echo their life." It is the "interest and beauty of this inward landscape, rather than any fortunes that may await [man's] body in the outer world, [that] constitute his proper happiness." The conquest of nature and perfection of material life were not goals worthy of our human nature. "Let us therefore be frankly human. Let us be content to live in the mind."[29] Like a strange hybrid, a cross between Lucretius and Teresa of Avila or between his fellow Spaniards Don Quixote and Sancho Panza, Santayana could hardly have projected a more puzzling image to Americans.

His willingness to "live in the mind" certainly bespeaks the aspect of him that preferred to withdraw and detach. To some, it also bespeaks a cold and isolated man, one who delights more in the inner music of unheard rhymes and rhythms or the daydreams of intellect and night thoughts of morbid imagination than in the hearty and passionate engagement with his world. It is an impression many have had of Santayana, but it is not entirely fair, for it presumes he was without passion, and that would be wrong. Consider, for example, the following passage from his autobiography, a passage that also serves as a splendid sample of his style: "The passion of love, sublimated, does not become bloodless, or free from bodily trepidation, as charity and philanthropy are. It is essentially the spiritual flame of a carnal fire that has turned all its fuel into light. The psyche is not thereby atrophied; on the contrary, the range of its reactions has been enlarged. It has learned to vibrate harmoniously to many things at once in a peace which is an orchestra of transcended sorrows."[30] These words bespeak not affectlessness, but an intense interior drama, an endless series of internal battles, renunciations, and transformations, all leading to the augmentation of an ever-growing, ever-deepening sense of inner capacity. It reflects a kind of stoicism, for a stoic learns not to join battles he cannot win, since the will is most free when it reaches only for what it can grasp: the realm of essence, not the realm of nature. But it also reflects something far more than stoicism, or Buddhism, or any garden-variety renunciation, for it affirms the emotional life — not on its own terms, but as refined and reworked by intelligence and experience. As usual, Santayana himself put it best, in his autobiography: "It lay in my nature to foresee disappointment, and never to bet on the issue of any event. Yet without experience of the world, this programmatic distrust remained itself empty and insecure. Genuine detachment presupposes attachment. What can it signify for you to say that you renounce everything, if as yet you have loved nothing?"[31]

The passivity in Santayana's makeup, his willingness to dwell in the mind at the expense of the world, may strike Americans as a strange combination of dreaminess and asceticism, alien to their temperament. So, too, might Santayana's disdain for the idea of progress, which he derided as a destructive superstition, a force that seems beneficial but that actually undermines the possibility of independent life. Nor did he have much respect for modern liberalism, the political handmaiden of progress, for he considered that it denied the very existence of an intractable human nature, and Santayana's first philosophical loyalty was always to nature.

Liberalism's genius lay in the provision and extension of individual freedom, goals that Santayana generally did not disdain. But the English liberty that he praises so highly in these pages was a limited and culturally specific thing, built up patiently and unconsciously over many years through discrete and concrete actions taken, thereby taking on a modest and skeptical and empirical cast. The abstractions of absolute liberty that had been hatched by philosophes were an entirely different matter, particularly when, precisely because of liberalism's dogma of tolerance, they offered no directions as to how liberalism's freedoms ought to be used. As Santayana argued in *The Genteel Tradition at Bay,* "a universal culture always tolerant, always fluid, smiling on everything exotic and on everything new, sins against the principle of life itself. We exist by distinction, by integration round a specific nucleus according to a particular pattern. Life demands a great insensibility, as well as a great sensibility. If the humanist could really live up to his ancient maxim, *humani nil a me alienum puto,* he would sink into moral anarchy and artistic impotence — the very things from which our liberal, romantic world is so greatly suffering."[32]

In addition to serving as a thoughtful challenge to liberalism, these assertions also tell us something about the author. For Santayana himself possessed both a great sensibility and a great insensibility, and it is impossible to separate the two. The preternatural serenity with which he contemplated the human condition made him a most penetrating observer; but that same detachment led him into a quietism bordering on fatalism. Such is a danger facing any serious and deeply considered conservatism, for a premature acceptance of existing evils may shrink too soon from those evils that can be altered. There was a strain of irresponsibility in Santayana's natural-ism — not a recklessness, but in the strict sense that he never regarded his insights as categorical imperatives, laying down the rules by which we all should live. On the contrary, his philosophy was an exquisitely wrought image of his own highly individual condition. It was rather like one of his custom-tailored European suits: cut from fine material, artfully tailored, beautifully appointed, elegantly turned out but perhaps too much designed to fit but one body.

Like any number of other modern philosophers, too, Santayana could make political judgments that were less than acute, and sometimes down-right appalling. When William James objected to American annexation of the Philippines, on the ground that such imperialism violated the principles of the Declaration of Independence, the Spaniard brushed such moral reser-vations aside. The Declaration was a piece of literature, he sniffed, and a salad of illusions. James was lapsing into the genteel tradition, imposing universalistic Protestant morals on the amoral workings of history, in which ripeness of material capacity was all. Santayana also had surprisingly be-nign feelings about the Mussolini regime in Italy, and on a number of occa-sions he expressed a preference for the focused energy of authoritarian re-gimes, whether fascist, communist, or theocratic, as opposed to the "moral anarchy" and centrifugal impotence of liberal ones.

Perhaps least attractive of all were Santayana's anti-Semitic thoughts and sentiments, which were never systematically propounded, but rather pop up disturbingly in various letters and occasional obiter dicta. Such sentiments become far more prominent as he entered old age, during his post-American years, but they are certainly detectable early on in his writ-ings. In general they reflect the automatic prejudices characteristic of his Avila upbringing and his fin de siècle Harvard milieu — although, some-what more ominously, we also know that in the 1930s he frequently read the virulent anti-Semitic writings of Louis Ferdinand Celine. Little of this shows in any public way; Santayana was certainly no Ezra Pound. But it is hard nevertheless to reconcile such tastes with the equipoise and fineness of mind Santayana shows elsewhere. According to John McCormick, the most judicious and knowledgeable of Santayana's critics, his anti-Semitism was the exception rather than the rule; but McCormick also insists that such failure of moral imagination not be airbrushed out of the picture. It was an example of Santayana's insensibility, the shadow side of his sensibility.

Perhaps his self-protective detachment helped make him prone to such lapses; it is not given to us to face the world with such absolute compo-sure and closure without also sacrificing some of our very humanity. And indeed, there is something about the spectacle of Santayana's wartime years with the Blue Nuns in Rome that captures both the strengths and the weaknesses of his example. Recall the historical circumstances: By the time General Mark Clark and his Fifth Army had recaptured Rome on June 4, 1944, the Eternal City had gone through nine months of German occupation, and the country had experienced all the horrors of modern warfare — the pounding of Allied bombing raids, fierce guerrilla clashes between Germans and partisans, forced labor roundups of Roman men, mass deportations of Italian Jews to German death camps, grisly executions culminating in the Italian partisans' spectacular hanging of Mussolini and his mistress in Milan's Piazzale Loreto, and roving packs of the hungry scouring the countryside in desperate search of food.

But amid the darkness and chaos of this dragon-ridden time, the secluded and aging Santayana (by now into his eighties) continued to work placidly and industriously on his many projects, reflecting upon the highest things as he had all his life. There is something awesome in such a picture; but there also is something disturbing in it. Great genius often contains an element of the monstrous, and even the godly single-mindedness of saints can sometimes manifest itself as an icy hardness of the heart.

His war years became a form of benign imprisonment, in which travel was unthinkable and communications with America and the rest of Europe increasingly difficult. This perhaps reinforced Santayana's predisposition to "live in the mind," but it did not mean any diminution of his literary presence in America, as successive volumes of his memoirs were published to considerable attention and impressive sales. Soon after the liberation of Rome, a steady stream of admirers began to appear at the Blue Nuns, pilgrims bent on seeing this mysterious sage in the flesh. After the years of isolation he was now, he remarked amusedly, "visited by dozens of strangers, as if I were one of the ruins of Rome."[33] First came a flock of U.S. military men and war correspondents, such as Herbert Matthews of the *New York Times;* then the French philosopher Jacques Maritain, the Spanish poet Jose Maria Alonso Gamo, the American poet Robert Lowell, Richard Lyon, Cyril Clemens, and Edmund Wilson, whose word portrait of Santayana served as the basis for Wallace Stevens's magnificent poem of homage, "To an Old Philosopher in Rome." It was, of course, both ironic and fitting that Santayana chose to spend his last days in the company of nuns — ironic, in that, to all indications, he remained a firmly convinced materialist to the very end; fitting, given the profound Catholicism in his temperament and his unyielding devotion to religion as poetic truth and an "anticipation of perfection."

But this flurry of attention proved, to use one of Santayana's favorite bittersweet metaphors, a kind of Indian summer for his reputation and influence. After his death in 1952, interest in his work fell off widely and rapidly, and by the 1970s he was well on his way to permanent obscurity. But the signs are growing that this decline is reversing and that a modest revival of interest has been underway for the past two decades. The appearance and respectful reception of McCormick's magisterial biography, a finalist for the 1987 Pulitzer Prize, was one encouraging sign, as has been the steady progress of the MIT Santayana Edition project. There has also been a sharp increase in the serious attention devoted to such American thinkers as Ralph Waldo Emerson and William James, in part due to those thinkers' insistence that philosophical writing ought not become the province of specialists; such an insistence will be bound to cast Santayana's even more masterly and evocative prose in a more favorable light.

But one wonders whether Santayana's writings can ever grow to be more than a minority taste in the United States. Certainly his thought will never be as widely cherished as that of Emerson and James, who perform for Americans something of the role of national philosophers. That is a role Santayana certainly would not have relished, to put it mildly, and for which he is unlikely ever to be proposed. For his thoughts ran doggedly against the American grain, and especially against its modern, Protestant, democratic, liberal, progressive, technological, and quantitative propensities — although, to be sure, he had no desire to counter-evangelize the American people or transform their institutions in his image. The principal task of Santayana's philosophy is the task of cultivating the riches of interior life. That, in the end, is its weakness. But that is also its strength. If it is not all sufficient — and, as he would be likely to add himself, what philosophy is? — it offers a corrective precisely where one is most needed. It presents, by the richness of its example, a bracing challenge to a civilization that tends to dote on the external, the perishable, and the quantifiable.

Like Alexis de Tocqueville — another European observer of American society, to whom he bears some resemblance — Santayana fully accepted the demise of the world of the ancien regime and the rise of egalitarian liberal democracy. He was not a reactionary, dreaming of neo-medieval utopias or Bourbon restorations. Indeed, one sees running through his pages, both here and elsewhere, a sense that much of the old order richly deserved to go. His naturalism made him, in an odd sense, into a kind of cosmic

optimist, who, while insisting upon the decentering of man and while pre-
dicting that our current civilization is likely to perish, nevertheless exulted
in the fact that "the elasticity of life is wonderful," that nature is endlessly
fertile, and that "even if the world lost its memory it could not lose its
youth."[34] And, like Tocqueville, he believed that some part of the coming changes could already be glimpsed in America, the world's vanguard,
where "this destruction and this restoration have already occurred." (24)
Although Santayana was often snobbish and dismissive toward many aspects of American culture, he could also be surprisingly dismissive of that
very same snobbery when it emanated from others, precisely because he
distinguished between his tastes and the tectonic movements of an era. He
understood and accepted the fact that the fresh possibilities of a democratic
age would not come clothed in the same drapery as in the past.

There is, then, nearly as much praise for America in these pages, and
nearly as much hope for its future, as there is carping and criticism. He
worried, though, that Americans' fervent and one-sided faith in progress,
especially material and technological progress, might lead them thought-
lessly to despoil all the spiritual fruits that had given life meaning in the
past, just as, in a very different way, the effects of the genteel tradition had
continued to estrange them from the sustaining vitality of nature. Contrary
to the usual pattern, Santayana was a conservative precisely because of his
materialism. He had no doubt that the realm of essences rested upon the
fragility of civilizations; and that civilizations in turn were answerable to
the ineluctable force of nature. But Santayana also cherished the ideal realm
above all else; it alone can make our lives worth living, by giving shape to
our peculiar human need for beauty, love, speculation, and ultimate meaning. The aim of perfecting material existence is doomed to inadequacy:
"Man, if he is a rational being, cannot live by bread alone, nor be a labourer
merely: he must eat and work in view of an ideal harmony which overarches all his days, and which is realized in the way they hang together or in
some ideal issue which they have in common. Otherwise, though his technical philosophy may call itself idealism, he is a materialist in morals; he
esteems things, and esteems himself, for mechanical uses and energies."[35]

Such words deserve a hearing in any age, but perhaps especially in our
own. Hence, it was with good reason that Charles Frankel remarked, in
1956, that "what happens to Santayana's reputation will be a touchstone of
the quality of our culture, and of our growth in maturity and wisdom."[36]
This does not mean that we ought to turn Santayana into the new Emerson,
demanding that his every dictum become a star to which we can confidently
hitch our wagons. It means that his vision and his example have much in

them by which our present civilization, and especially our present intellectual life, could be made saner, richer, more modest, and more sustaining. Moreover, we ought not deprive ourselves of a voice so independent, a presence so singular, a life so devoted; his like has been too rare in our history for that. Notwithstanding Santayana to the contrary, those who cannot remember the past are condemned, not to repeat it, but to lose it entirely. This we cannot afford.

But it is not enough to say this, since a question remains, and it is a question that Santayana himself insists upon raising. Why should it matter? Why not let it go? If a new order is coming, why should we not be content to let the dead bury their dead and leave the past clearly and cleanly behind us, preferring instead to cast our lot with the endless flood of nature's onrushing, inexorable fertility? Santayana's own testimony is ambivalent on this point, but perhaps the answer closest to his heart may be gleaned from one last quotation, taken from his autobiography. It is an example, perhaps, of the insensibility of his Roman years, and of his swirling dance between the poles of subjectivity and nature. But it is also an example of words that deserve to ring through all time, vibrant as they are with an intimation of a fully human form of completion, of an experience of release into the fullness of conscious being, and a corresponding release from the burden of human self-importance, that a relentlessly dynamic and youth-obsessed American culture (and the modernity and postmodernity it exemplifies) has yet to experience:

> In Rome, in the eternal city, I feel nearer to my own past, and to the whole past and future of the world, than I should in any cemetery or in any museum of relics. Old places and old persons in their turn, when spirit dwells in them, have an intrinsic vitality of which youth is incapable; precisely the balance and wisdom that come from long perspectives and broad foundations. Everything shines then for the spirit by its own light in its own place and time; but not as it shone in its own restless eyes. For in its own eyes each person and each place was the centre of a universe full of threatening and tempting things; but old age, having less intensity at the centre has more clearness at the circumference, and knows that just because spirit, at each point, is a private centre for all things, no one point, no one phase of spirit, is materially a public centre for all the rest."[37]

Of course, America has no Romes of its own; and besides, there were (and are) many other Romes extant, each quite different from the one that Santayana chose to inhabit mentally, though occupying the same space. But that is not the point. What Santayana instead here indicates, once again, is the fact that the deepest meaning of a thing is never entirely conveyed or contained in its certified self-revelation, and is never entirely intelligible to the conscious will by which that thing has been brought into being. Its self-understanding is never the center of its actual world, and its meaning can never be controlled or brought into line with a foreordained intention or conclusion. Instead, the most durable meanings unfold themselves by and through the mixing of elements in the due course of time, emerging like the flowering of a plant — or, better, like the beauty of weather-beaten wood, or the lines of an aged human face. The spirit comes to dwell happily and abundantly only in those places that, thanks to time's taming vicissitudes and the remission of the will, have developed the right kind of space to accommodate it, and the generosity and liberality to invite it in.

It may seem mildly self-subverting to invoke such a spirit of *Gelassenheit* as a form of cultural self-improvement; and to be sure, one does not want, perversely, to turn Santayana into the new guru of moral uplift and self-help, who should be embraced because he is so good for us. To will to abolish the will is still a form of willfulness, as Santayana's critiques of romanticism amply demonstrated; and while the hypertrophy of the will, as expressed in our anthropocentrism, was for Santayana the root of the American problem, resisting its pressures is easier said than done. But at the same time, one does want to appreciate his legacy for what it is and what it could mean to us. The latter dimension, especially, is still entirely up for grabs. Like all legacies, it cannot be defined or specified with precision for all time by the will of the benefactor, and so we should feel free to accept it and appropriate it on whatever terms make sense to us. A genuine and sustaining tradition, as Jaroslav Pelikan has observed, is the living faith of the dead, not the dead faith of the living — a formulation that Santayana would have surely embraced.[38]

And so we should accept his legacy with alacrity and gratitude. Santayana can offer us, at a bare minimum, a keener awareness of precisely this "intrinsic vitality" to be found in attending to the things that are old and weather-beaten and time-tamed — in attending, that is, to the intense and unrepeatable beauty and truth to be found in the things that have been gnarled and pitted and faded by the batterings of experience, only to be redeemed into something of radiance and depth in the alchemy of history, memory, and imagination. Even in a largely man-made world, the fashioning of enduring beauty and truth remains something largely out of our hands, a thing that happens to the world while we are busy making other plans for it, a process that regularly manages to spite our will. The beauty that Santayana saw in Rome is precisely of this order. No one planned it. No one ever could have. Instead, it has come about because of the haphazard survival of so many ancient places and things that are no longer what they were made to be, but that live on, not only as familiar objects of everyday life, but as ghostly presences and angelic harbingers, unspeaking couriers of time who bear messages of a nearly unfathomable and unutterable scope, such as only the passage of many centuries could ever have bestowed upon them.

At the same time, Santayana teaches us to attend to the essences, whatever we believe to be their source, which also are presences and perhaps even harbingers, which help us rise above passing things and console us for their decay and loss — though he teaches us to do so without ever asking that we cease to love and cherish the passing things and intensely feel their loss. To achieve such a complex awareness, and learn to attend to such things closely and carefully and persistently and courageously, would itself be the beginning of a greater and more sustainable balance in our lives, and a greater and deeper humanity in us. It would be the greatest of Santayana's gifts, if we are willing and able to receive it.

NOTES

1. George Santayana, *Character and Opinion in the United States,* p. 23 above.

2. John McCormick, *George Santayana: A Biography* (New York: Alfred A. Knopf, 1987), 32.

3. David Riesman, with Nathan Glazer and Reuel Denny, *The Lonely Crowd: A Study of the Changing American Character* ([1950] abridged edition New Haven: Yale University Press, 1969), 3. The Santayana passage quoted appears in this volume on page 92–93 above.

4. Santayana, *Character and Opinion,* 31.

5. George Santayana, *Reason in Common Sense,* Volume 1 of *The Life of Reason or The Phases of Human Progress* (New York: Charles Scribner's Sons, 1905), 218.

6. Ibid.

7. *Persons and Places, The Last Puritan,* and much else in Santayana's oeuvre, including an exhaustive edition of his correspondence, is now available in the definitive MIT Press edition edited by William G. Holzberger and Herman J. Saatkamp, Jr. For further information on this worthy project, see http://www.iupui .edu/~santedit/edition.html.

8. Stevens to Mrs. Church, Hartford, Connecticut, September 29, 1952. By

permission The Huntington Library, San Marino, California, cited in McCormick, *George Santayana*, 505.

9. The classic study on this is still Bruce Kuklick, *The Rise of American Philosophy: Cambridge, Massachusetts, 1860–1930* (New Haven: Yale University Press, 1977). In its pages, Kuklick rightly observes that "Of all the philosophers of the Golden Age of American philosophy, none has suffered more than Santayana. . . . Posterity has ignored his philosophy and, to that extent, missed a complete understanding of the man" (649).

10. George Santayana, "A Brief History of My Opinions," from George P. Adams and William Pepperell Montague, eds., *Contemporary American Philosophy* (London: Allen & Unwin, 1930), 242.

11. Biographical details are drawn from McCormick, *George Santayana*, and from Santayana's own account of his early life in *Persons and Places*.

12. Memorandum, "To George Sturgis," cited in McCormick, *George Santayana*, 15. The quotation in the next paragraph, "pettiness and practicality of outlook and ambition," is cited in McCormick, *George Santayana*, 17, from Santayana, *Persons and Places: Fragments of Autobiography* (Cambridge: MIT Press, 1986), 10.

13. Santayana, *Character and Opinion*, 45.

14. Ibid., 45–46.

15. Santayana, *Persons and Places*, 390.

16. "The President of Harvard College, seeing me once by chance soon after the beginning of a term, inquired how my classes were getting on; and when I replied that I thought they were getting on well, that my men seemed to be keen and intelligent, he stopped me as if I was about to waste his time. 'I meant,' said he, '*what is the number* of students in your classes' " (100).

17. Daniel Cory, ed., *The Letters of George Santayana* (New York: Scribner's, 1955), 62.

18. *The Letters of William James: Edited by His Son, Henry James,* Volume 2 (Boston: Atlantic Monthly Press, 1920), 122–23.

19. George Santayana, *Interpretations of Poetry and Religion* (New York: Scribner's, 1911), 4.

20. Santayana, "A Brief History," 244; *Interpretations of Poetry and Religion*, ix.

21. Santayana, *Character and Opinion*, 37.

22. Ibid., 23.

23. Descriptions and quotations come from McCormick, *George Santayana*, 98–103.

24. Santayana, *Character and Opinion*, 39.

25. *Letters*, 80.

26. George Santayana, "The Genteel Tradition in American Philosophy," 4.

27. *Letters,* 225–26.

28. Santayana, "The Genteel Tradition," 19.

29. Ibid., 19, 20.

30. Santayana, *Persons and Places,* 429.

31. Santayana, *Persons and Places,* 421.

32. There are several editions of *The Genteel Tradition at Bay,* but the one perhaps most readily available is included in Douglas L. Wilson's extraordinarily valuable book *The Genteel Tradition: Nine Essays by George Santayana* (Cambridge: Harvard University Press, 1967), 153–96. The quotation above appears on 157.

33. McCormick, *George Santayana,* 436.

34. Santayana, *Character and Opinion,* 24.

35. Ibid., 99.

36. Cited in McCormick, *George Santayana,* 508.

37. Santayana, *Persons and Places,* 536.

38. Jaroslav Pelikan, *The Vindication of Tradition* (New Haven: Yale University Press, 1986).

Understanding America

JOHN LACHS

There is a striking difference between how members of certain nationalities and religions behave in the Old World and how they relate to each other in the New. The changes may be situational or due to some deeper valuational transformation that accompanies immigration. In either case, this difference sheds light on the nature and practices of American society. It also illuminates the extent to which Santayana understood the soul of America.

Members of some nations, ethnic groups, and religions are mortal enemies in the parts of the world that are their native homes. There are historical reasons for the enmity between Pakistanis and Indians, Hutus and Tutsis, and Serbs and Bosnians. The reasons, typically taking the form of memories of ancient oppression, persecution, and murder, exercise a momentous hold on interactions among these people. The embers of enduring hatred create conflagrations of violence again and again, and each side to the conflict takes delight in waging war or at least inflicting retaliatory cruelties on people who belong to the other.

Rival groups experience much more than distaste for each other: they seek the destruction of their opponents. The struggles between Muslims and Christians, Germans and the French, and Greeks and Turks display a vicious stridency that is difficult to lay to rest. From time to time, people show themselves prepared to undergo all manners of hardship to be able to cause permanent grief to their enemies. The idea of leaving others be seems not to occur; on the contrary, periodically they perceive a duty to exterminate those who belong to the wrong side. Hegel's depiction of the encounter of the bondsman and the lord is a good example of this conceptual frame: seeing each other is enough for them to prepare for a struggle to the death.

By comparison with this fury, the relation in America of Old World antagonists is surprisingly tame. Traditional enemies live at peace with each other, in many cases on the same street or in the same apartment building. Genocidal tendencies remain in check and instead of laboring to make others miserable, people endeavor to make themselves happy. Acts of violence directed at people on account of their nationality, ethnic origin, or religion are rare. Aggression is controlled to such an extent that there is hardly an attempt to deface the buildings and stores of antagonists.

I do not mean to suggest that America is free of prejudice and of racial, religious, and ethnic tensions. Members of some groups view individuals who belong to other groups with suspicion and quiet hostility. But it is worth remarking that much of the nastiness tends to remain attitudinal, with minimal behavioral outcomes. And the bulk of the ill-feeling flows from long-standing residents of the country toward newcomers, whatever their religion or ethnic background, who do not understand the local language and customs. Traditional Old World enemies live in relative peace with each other.

What accounts for this striking change of attitude and action attendant on moving from Asia and Europe to North America? A number of explanations may be proposed. Probably, there are multiple causal factors at work, at least some of which are obvious and relatively easy to identify. But I suspect that there are also some more interesting and perhaps even surprising influences to uncover.

Much of the violence and destruction of organized hatred occurs through mob action. Crowds are easily mobilized in countries where there are large numbers of people with similar beliefs and emotional triggers. Demagogues can manipulate such masses, although fancied slights and ancient grievances are enough by themselves to precipitate disastrous consequences. Might the reason for peace in America be that members of ethnic groups and aggressive religions lack the critical mass necessary for violence?

This explanation is likely to be attractive to anyone who knows how anger feeds on itself in crowds and how the mood of the mob can make even sensible people act without concern for decency. In fact, however, it does not stand scrutiny. As to religions, there are, for example, enough Muslims and Hindus in the United States to create deadly clashes over their differences. Members of ethnic groups tend to live concentrated in areas where they vastly outnumber their antagonists. Since their traditional enemies usually live only a block or two away, it would be easy for them to start fights or at least to create significant nuisance. In any case, even one individual or a small number of people is enough to stir up a great deal of trouble. The striking fact is that in the United States, at least on the whole and in a systematic way, no such trouble is created.

Is it possible, then, that peace is due to effective peacekeeping efforts? There is no denying that police in the Old World sometimes look the other way when ethnic or religious violence breaks out. Although America has experienced severe racial inequities in law enforcement, violence against ethnic and religious minorities is, on the whole, approached with a strong and even hand. The police in major American cities would certainly not sit back while bands fired by anger roughed up people and bombed churches, mosques, or synagogues. And timely, severe measures would undoubtedly nip disturbances in the bud.

The interesting fact, however, is that large-scale police action just does not seem to be needed. Apart from the hapless tough full of threats and boasts or the occasional thug who tries to set fire to a Catholic church or a synagogue, one sees no attempt to incite ethnic or religious violence. And, interestingly, the young or deranged perpetrators of such isolated attacks tend to be native-born Americans rather than members of some immigrant minority. The police do not have much in the way of ethnic or religious mob action to control.

Large-scale violence in other regions tends to be evoked or supported by politicians and the press. Can the absence of these catalysts of conflict account for relative ethnic and religious peace in America? This is a plausible line of thought because politicians in the United States rarely get elected on a platform of narrow ethnic or religious concerns. From time to time, legislators are put in office at least in part because they are members of a race, a gender, an ethnic group, or a religion, but the scope of their interests tends to transcend such narrowing influences. And, indeed, there is no concentration of media in the United States that is a match for the nationalist publications bombarding the citizens of Old World countries. Without continuing agitation and demagoguery, people tend to turn their attention to pursuits other than harming their neighbors.

The last point rings true and surely constitutes one of the reasons for peace among previously feuding people when they move to America. But we live in a world of instant communication: telephones and the Internet provide access for immigrants to their native lands, and in fact many of them are in close contact with sentiments "at home." Some immigrant communities print their own newspapers, and many of the religious leaders and senior opinion-makers who set the tone of these enclaves are exclusivists or nationalists. So there is certainly enough leadership and communication to whip immigrants into a fury. The remarkable fact is that what would have been incendiary in the Old World falls on deaf ears in the New; that Palestinians and Israelis kill each other in the Middle East seems not to be a good enough reason for murderous clashes between them in the United States.

This suggests another possible line of explanation. In some human affairs, context is all. We know that turning out the lights is conducive to sleep and thrusting a young man into a fraternity makes it probable that he will drink. Living in a new country may well exercise the same sort of influence on immigrants. It takes a while for them to learn the language and the customs of their new society, but they quickly catch on to what is clearly unacceptable. Systematic hate-mongering is just not a part of the culture of America as it exists today: both the legal system and the ordinary consciousness of people reject it as offensive. Newcomers might therefore shelve their ethnic or religious aggressions to fall in line with what their new home expects of them.

That some such process contributes to peace in America is difficult to deny. The adoption of local customs occurs as a natural consequence of immigration. But it does not happen everywhere. Pakistanis in Britain and Algerians in France have failed to adopt some vital customs of the larger culture. That raises the question of what there is about American society that renders compliance with local values attractive and likely. And that, in turn, points to the need for a more substantive look at what America teaches its immigrants and makes available to them. The current explanation accounts, therefore, for very little if viewed in isolation from broader issues.

What about the possibility that immigrants to the United States are selected, or self-selected, for their non-violent tendencies? The Immigration and Naturalization Service certainly does all it can to deny entry to people who engage in ideologically motivated mayhem. Legal immigrants tend to be professionals or at least somewhat educated people who can be expected to know better than to create trouble. The political refugees among them have experienced persecution, so they are at least unlikely to want to visit it on others. The rest of them, entrepreneurs and merchants, normally focus on making money, not on achieving national or racial purity.

The events of 9/11 showed, however, that government screening is not very successful. It cannot readily measure nationalist or religious fervor, and it is ill-equipped to unmask well-constructed lies. Professionals are by no means free of ideological commitments, and many a person persecuted for political beliefs can hardly wait to return the favor. There is ample evidence that even business people, if brought up to hate a group of others, can be whipped into violent action. Selectivity in immigration may account for a little of the differential in tension between the New and the Old Worlds, but not for very much.

This is a good place to turn to Santayana's *Character and Opinion in the United States* to see if his vision might provide the explanation we seek. And, indeed, his account of English liberty goes a long way toward helping us understand the change immigrants undergo when they arrive in the New

World. Many of them come from nations devoted to what he calls "absolute liberty," which is the single-minded effort to follow one's will, however arbitrary. This absolute liberty is the freedom for persons and nations "to be just so" (113), to follow a master passion even in the teeth of nature and resistance. Many of the cultures from which immigrants hail display an unconditional commitment to the values and practices that have structured their past; they are convinced that there is only one right way to live and it is theirs. Santayana characterizes such convictions as natural to animals that are unbending in what they want and unyielding in their pursuit of it (113–14).

Absolute liberty allows no compromise. The distinction it sees between right and wrong is infinite, and it is ready to bring the house down on all the traitors and infidels that surround it. It tends to use force to overwhelm its enemies, which are many, and is ever ready to take on all comers in its uncompromising quest to be itself. It is a newborn insect prepared to fight the world to maintain its nature and attain its purposes. Such liberty may be heroic and beautiful, but it is neither wise nor reflective; it will certainly fail because it misreads reality. It does not understand that its energy and its values are contingent, passing phases in the life of nature, and that all its victories are temporary.

This description of absolute liberty is a splendid frame in which to situate all the despotisms that have made life awful throughout history and all the empires founded on religion and ideology. Nationalist fervor, racial exclusiveness, and ethnic strife are varied expressions of absolute liberty, which is the unyielding, egotistical drive to remake the world according to one's own ideas. The philosophical observer in Santayana sees the drive as natural though tragic, but he finds it difficult to sympathize with the inflated, absurd goals of little people and little nations. There is much about animal life that is understandable and natural, yet malodorous.

English liberty, by contrast, thrives on the spirit of compromise. It presupposes broad agreement about the goals and methods of life along with a readiness to adjust one's nature sufficiently to get along with others (108). It is the freedom that comes of cooperative endeavors, of trusting each other and entrusting to others what one cannot do alone. Faith in the decency of people and the conviction that in the end everyone will be accommodated ground majority rule as the proper way to make social decisions. But such choices never touch fundamental issues: the values on the basis of which the society operates command the unspoken consent of all.

The underlying tone of English liberty is tolerant and optimistic. Ready collaboration promises a future that is "happy and triumphant" (111). The triumph is not meant to be military; conquest that requires the application of physical force is incidental and serves mainly to protect commercial life. Contrary to countries that seek absolute liberty, the motivating force of American society is not the desire to rule over others, but "the gospel of work and the belief in progress" (110), ideas that evoke sustained and occasionally stunning exertions. Zealous idealism permeates all facets of American life; one cannot claim to be an American so long as one lacks the spirit of cooperation and a hearty appreciation of one's friends and neighbors.

Caring for each other and uniting in pursuit of a common end come into view most clearly on the occasion of great national emergencies, such as the tragedy of 9/11. At such times, strangers from far away become friends in need of help and service. The consequent outpouring of supportive sentiment and material aid can make one believe that human nature has been transformed to answer the demands of its harshest critics. But even under ordinary circumstances, Americans tend to be wide-ranging in their sympathies and generous with their resources. They feel fortunate in their possessions and think it appropriate to share them with those in need. The munificence is spontaneous and personal: they are not satisfied to shift the task of aid to government but go to the scene of disaster themselves to lend a helping hand.

Admittedly, English liberty is of a very odd sort, for Santayana claims that generous social-mindedness is compulsory in America (110). I suspect he thinks it is a form of liberty because people embrace its elements voluntarily. "Compulsory" does not mean forced; good humor and trust are contagious attitudes supported by expectation and temperament. No one could evoke these traits in people with rifle butts or by threatening their loved ones. They grow naturally among individuals who are confident and successful, and acquire hallowed standing as the right alignment to life and to each other because everyone seems to approve them. English liberty is the ethos of American society; it is difficult to escape even though no laws mandate it and the violation of its spirit does not land one in jail.

Immigrants to America enter this energetic benign world, seeking the benefits it can provide. The English liberty that structures and permeates American society goes a long distance toward explaining the changes in their attitudes and values. They see the helpfulness and accommodating spirit of people around them and do what they can to enter the life of the community. To speed their assimilation, they begin to act like their new neighbors and to entertain, perhaps for the first time in their lives, the possibility that the habits and commitments with which they grew up are not uniquely and exclusively right. They move, in Santayana's language, from the absolute liberty of insisting on the rightness of their ways to the open and tolerant practices of the American landscape.

Promising as this explanation appears, it cannot constitute the whole story. Why would immigrants find embracing the ethos of English liberty attractive? When they first arrive in America, they settle in enclaves inhabited primarily by people from their Old World homes; they continue to speak the language of their childhood, eat the food their mothers used to cook, and cling to the comfortable traditions of their native culture. Change comes slowly and not without pain. Giving up the conviction that one's habits and values are absolutely right is to endanger one's identity; no one does this lightly and voluntarily. By itself, the spirit of English liberty is not powerful enough to reach into the Iraqi, Korean, and Pakistani ghettos in the hearts of many larger American cities. What moves the inhabitants of these subcultures into the mainstream of American life?

To answer this question, we must look more closely at what immigration to America involves. To those who come to settle here, the change is momentous and in some ways excruciating. The involutions of the English language, strange customs, and the need to communicate with people who, though superficially friendly, seem deeply alien make the first few months, even years, of life in the new land painful and baffling. English liberty does not seem liberating to recent immigrants; toleration appears to them as lack of principle, and in cooperating with others they worry that their partners take advantage of them. Suspicion and fear die slowly and would never be swept away were it not necessary for new immigrants to move into mainstream American culture.

The necessity derives not from government edict but from natural need. Immigrants, along with nearly everybody else, have to work in order to eat. The language of work is English and its habits are dictated by a tolerant but hard-driving postindustrial society. The pressure to hold down jobs and earn advancement exercises a profound influence on the human soul: one cannot spend the bulk of one's waking hours at work and shake off its lessons and demands the moment one gets home. Work teaches docility and cooperation, introducing newcomers to practices needed for success and acquainting them with the living values of the culture. Observation and informal talk at work reveal to immigrants how Americans relate to their spouses, their children, and their futures. The ever-present formal requirements of continued employment keep before their minds the opportunities and the vast costs of establishing their place in a commercial culture.

The economic system of the United States is a mighty engine of persuasion. It attracts and engulfs people, making them do what they would otherwise never imagine, in return for fulfilling their dreams. It promises rich returns on labor and champions the ideal of a carefree life. The rewards it heaps on intelligence and hard work make successful business people the envy of all; even if one cannot do as well, there is reason to wait for the next raise or bonus or promotion. People assent to the old adage that money isn't all, but they believe even more deeply that there isn't much it will not buy and that lack of it makes even an idealist's life miserable. Admittedly, the economic system focuses on material values, but these are the rewards that motivate people to give up the best hours of their days and that ground their hopes for a better future.

Material values receive poor press from the guardians of high culture. They are said to be inferior and unworthy by comparison with moral, aesthetic, and intellectual pursuits. Their depiction as good only instrumentally, as merely means to our higher calling, demeans them; it shows them as results of dirty, narrowly selfish activities. To his credit, Santayana does not go out of his way to smear commercial life, but even he fails to show adequate appreciation of the central and vital roles played by material plenty in human life. Consequently, though an immigrant himself, he does not see that work and its reward constitute the hook that brings new arrivals from overseas into the culture of English liberty. The desire for wealth reaches into the tenements that house immigrants and delivers them to be shaped into compliant members of a tolerant society.

Those critics of American culture who draw a sharp line between physical well-being and the higher purposes of life seem not to understand the intimate connection between the two. The comfort of owning a house is at once fulfillment of the obligation to take care of one's family. Saving money may seem miserly, but it translates into the ability to educate one's children. Grand financial success serves as the foundation and, astonishingly, also as the motivation for promoting good causes and helping those in need. Material means may make miserable ends, but properly used they are not only indispensable for accomplishing the good but actually inseparable from it.

The English liberty that suffuses America is an adequate antidote to the violent conflicts ravaging much of the rest of the world. But its spirit is not contagious. Immigrants to many countries live as strangers, never becoming parts of the surrounding culture; why is it that something similar doesn't happen in America? The New World may not be a melting pot, but it is remarkably efficient at assimilating individuals who hail from different traditions and are initially devoted to widely divergent values. Life in a new community visits frustrations on people and demands painful adjustments.

Like the last snow of winter, however, the misery hides new growth: the habits and values of the Old World get slowly replaced with the attitudes considered proper in the New. Over a period of difficult years, the immigrants become Americans — sometimes even without wanting or fully knowing it.

The new values arise not through force or indoctrination but by doing what others do and especially by wanting the same things they have. Most immigrants find America a land of hard work and intense desire. Hungarians who arrived in New Jersey after the 1956 revolution were dismayed at the pace of life in their new homeland and outraged at what was expected of them in their jobs. Some of them grumbled that Soviet repression may have been preferable to having to expend so much energy every day. Yet within a few years, they were taking trips to Bermuda, saving money for houses, and working their hearts out to get promoted. They realized that devoted labor brings results and that desires they would not have dared to frame in their old homes could be readily satisfied with enough of their new country's money.

The ultimate motivation of the vast majority of immigrants for becoming Americans is the promise of a materially rich existence. They want money and all that it will buy: fine food, large houses, new automobiles, designer clothing, and travel. Such desires may seem superficial, but they serve as the wellspring of the perpetual striving of animals in this cruel and deadly world. Material comfort is what we lost as a result of the misstep of Adam and Eve in the Garden. America provides the antidote: it offers the possibility of a fulfilled and carefree life. The significance of this can be understood only by those who have known need and hunger; they find it unnecessary to present excuses for wanting the good things in life and wanting more and more of them. Highbrow intellectuals, in particular, encounter difficulty in grasping the legitimacy and value of seeking the good in the quest for goods. They seem to believe that there is something wholesome about poverty, that misery builds character, and that turning away from the material world supplies people with spiritual substance.

In reality, however, there is not a shred of truth in these convictions. Need fills the mind with anxiety and resentment and, except in unusual circumstances, wretched lives make people selfish and narrow. Hunger and sorrow are not sources of great ideas, and self-abnegation shrivels the soul. Worse, destitute individuals are easily captured by vicious ideologies; they look for an easy explanation of their desperate condition and find it in some twisted set of concepts focused on available scapegoats. The result is what we have seen in Europe in the twentieth century and in the Middle East in the twenty-first: grotesquely primitive ideas propelling mass movements of violence in the name of purity, utopia, or salvation.

The values underlying the pursuit of economic well-being are, at least, this-worldly and non-ideological: they turn the mind away from unproductive mischief and mayhem toward what others find constructive enough to support with their money. People who are well off tend not to fall victim to ideologies. They prefer to avoid wars and internal turmoil because they have something to lose. They like prosperity and the stability that underlies it, and they reject the cheap satisfaction of making themselves better off by expropriating others. The high priests of morality ought to embrace affluence because it reduces human suffering and eliminates one of the great causes of war. Instead, they heap scorn on trade and consumption, overlooking the fact that the affirmation of human dignity through freedom of contract is the ground of commercial life and the reduction of suffering through plenty is its product. They think it lamentable that people embrace the values of physical satisfaction, forgetting that the choice is free and that possession of the goods of this world is both essential and serves as an incentive to doing good in the world.

Immigrants to America appropriate local ideas of success with astonishing fervor. They work hard, seek advancement, buy cars and houses, save money for their children, and commit themselves to useful civic labors. The premise behind such actions and values is social stability, the expectation that possessions are secure and long-term plans can be effective. This means that one can reasonably hope that next year will be better than the last has been. Such hopes pervade American life and add structure, meaning, and justification to what people do. The future thus becomes an ever-present reality that offers rewards to the industrious. The conviction that tensions can be defused, problems solved, and every product and human situation improved turns the mind away from grief over the past and toward concrete steps of amelioration.

Recognition that human relations do not have to constitute a zero-sum game is near the heart of American beliefs. Warfare, violence, and persecution are zero-sum activities in which some win and others lose, perhaps everything. Commerce, cooperation, and even friendly competition are, by contrast, modes of action from which all participants can profit. Tacitly or implicitly, immigrants adopt this stance or at least come to believe that they can flourish. The consequent redirection of effort and exhaustion of energy in productive labors is the best explanation why in America immigrants lose interest in persecuting their neighbors.

The difference between past-directed retaliatory and future-directed

ameliorative activities plays a central role in American philosophy. Pragmatists such as John Dewey and William James extol the value of human
actions focused on influencing the future, which alone is open to improvement by our efforts. Even Royce, who recognizes the importance of communities of memory, places them in the broader context of communities of
hope, suggesting that the negativities of the past must be submerged in the
cleansing improvements we can make from here on. Such philosophical
advice is a reflection of the broader culture, but it has the advantage of
capturing in precise conceptual terms what is otherwise a prevalent though
unarticulated attitude.

Is this attitude unique to the United States? It neither is nor has to be. It
pervades any nation that gives up its absolute liberty and focuses on providing socio-political stability and the hope of material improvement to its
citizens. Prosperity undercuts the complex causes of religious intolerance
and nationalist fervor: envy and destructive anger are less likely to gain a
foothold among people who enjoy the present and see a happy future than
among those who are hungry and destitute of hope. Even plausible ideologies find it difficult to sprout roots among individuals who have enough;
such people display an interest in politics mainly to protect their happy lives
rather than to impose their will on others. The Old Testament speaks of a
promised land which, if already occupied by others, can become the source
of endless conflict. What people need instead is a land of promise, of
actualizable hope for peace and the enjoyment of material goods, which
America has been for a long time and other nations are now becoming.

A united Europe in which cooperation and growing prosperity elimi-
nate borders, and with them ethnic hatred, offers the possibility of another
America. Some Asian nations are also working hard to provide opportunities for their citizens. Although affluence in a commercial world brings
with it all the problems of overconsumption, there is in the end no alternative way to eradicate nationalist, ethnic, and religious violence.

If this analysis of what makes immigrants to the New World overcome
their Old World hatreds is anywhere near right, it uncovers the secret of
what will make it unnecessary for people to immigrate at all. They need
hope in their own lands for a better life for themselves but especially for
their children.

Not many philosophers have come out in defense of an existence of
comfort and prosperity. Superbly cognizant of divergent perspectives and
alternative values, Santayana comes close to appreciating the virtues of
business, but in the end veers off to praise ideal objectives and the activity
of production rather than the joys of consumption. In America, "the ruling

passion is the love of *business*,"[1] and not the love of money, he says. He reminds us that "business . . . will, as things now stand, look chiefly to material results"[2] and readily admits that material well-being is a necessary condition of the higher functions of human life. But he continues with the admonition that "the material basis is a basis only" and requires completion in the form of "moral and intellectual functions."[3] In the end, only speculation, the abstraction possible in solitude and thoughts "deeper and higher" than ordinary ones justify material comfort and consumption.

That such "deeper and higher" thoughts come naturally to some people is an obvious fact. It may even be true that in certain respects the world would be a better place if more people entertained such ideas. But I cannot imagine what would justify the conclusion that a materially satisfying existence *requires* completion in the form of deep thoughts. Life is short and after it is over nothing remains of it, so it cannot be the enduring value of mentation that justifies our passing pleasures. If it were, given how few individuals choose to think deep thoughts, the lives of the vast majority of people would be pointless and vain. But this is elitist foolishness. If there is anything self-justifying, it is a good and satisfying life, even if it consists of little beyond consumption and work. Philosophers, devoted to thinking, charge shoppers with superficiality. Rightly, the shoppers have been too busy to reply.

NOTES

1. George Santayana, "Tradition and Practice," in *Animal Faith and Spiritual Life*, ed. John Lachs (New York: Appleton-Century-Crofts, 1967), p. 457.

2. Ibid., p. 458.

3. Ibid.

The Genteel Tradition
and English Liberty

JAMES SEATON

Those who know George Santayana's "The Genteel Tradition in American Philosophy" only by its title may be forgiven for assuming that the essay has little to contribute to an understanding of American culture and society today, however illuminating it might have been when first delivered as a lecture at the University of California in 1911. The genteel tradition Santayana analyzed surely lost its power to stifle or censor long ago. The crucial decade was the 1920s, after the passage in 1920 of a constitutional amendment prohibiting alcohol consumption roused a generation to combat Puritanism in all its forms. Critics like H. L. Mencken and Van Wyck Brooks and writers like Sinclair Lewis led a rebellion against all the old pieties, skewering what Lewis in his 1930 Nobel Prize address called "tea-table gentility" wherever they found it.[1] The rebels were successful; the power of the genteel tradition was destroyed, and the tradition itself was lost. There may be many things to criticize about contemporary American society, but excessive gentility is not one of them. Why then should one turn to "The Genteel Tradition in American Philosophy" for insights about American culture today?

One might begin to answer that question by distinguishing Santayana's critique from the typical attack on gentility led by writers like Lewis, Mencken, and Brooks. In his Nobel lecture Sinclair Lewis lamented the influence of William Dean Howells on literature because, although Howells "was one of the gentlest, sweetest, and most honest of men . . . he had the code of a pious old maid whose greatest delight was to have tea in the vicarage" (15). H. L. Mencken claimed that Puritan prudishness about sex discouraged free thought in general: "It is on the side of sex that the appointed virtuosi of virtue exercise their chief repressions, for it is sex that especially fascinates the lubricious Puritan mind; but the conventual reticence that thus becomes the enforced fashion in one field extends itself to all others."[2] Van Wyck Brooks argued that Mark Twain had never fulfilled his great promise because he had "abdicated his independence as a creative spirit" when he became a "candidate for gentility."[3] In *After the Genteel*

Tradition, Malcolm Cowley described the effect of the genteel tradition on literature: "Every book or magazine intended to appear on the center table in the parlor was kept as innocent as milk. American women of all ages, especially the unmarried ones, had suddenly become more than earthly creatures; they were presented as milk-white angels of art and compassion and culture."[4] These writers, like most of those who condemned the genteel tradition, thought of it as simply a polite, upper-class version of Puritanism, whose most typical act was sexual repression. Santayana himself did not condemn Puritanism, and for him Puritanism or Calvinism was in any case only one component of the genteel tradition. Unlike Lewis, Mencken, Brooks, and Cowley, Santayana was not a combatant in the culture wars of his time. In "The Genteel Tradition in American Philosophy" he follows the example of Henry James. For Van Wyck Brooks, Henry James, like Mark Twain, was a writer of great promise who was unable in his maturity to fulfill that promise because he was unwilling or unable to break free from Puritanism and the genteel tradition. James, like Mark Twain before him — the one a "candidate," the other a "probationer" — had given up his creative independence and submitted to the standards of genteel society: "had he not subscribed, as only a probationer can subscribe, to the codes and scruples, the conventions and prejudices, the standards (held so lightly by everyone else) of the world he longed to possess?"[5] Santayana, however, argues that Henry James did indeed free himself from the genteel tradition, not by breaking its rules but "by turning the genteel American tradition, as he turns everything else, into a subject-matter for analysis." James in his fiction has accomplished what Santayana aims for in his essay: "he has overcome the genteel tradition in the classic way, by understanding it" ("The Genteel Tradition in American Philosophy," 13).

To understand Santayana's overall judgment of American society, one must study not only "The Genteel Tradition in American Philosophy" but also his 1920 book *Character and Opinion in the United States* and especially its last chapter, in which Santayana, after pointing out the limitations and blind spots of high culture in the United States, argues that the American way of life, with all its flaws, nevertheless provides an example worthy of emulation throughout the world. A reconsideration of both Santayana's original conception of the "genteel tradition" and his notion of "English Liberty" leads to a renewed appreciation of the fruitfulness of the two ideas and of Santayana's stature as a critic of American culture.

In his 1911 lecture Santayana contrasted the genteel tradition, "the traditional mentality," with a "fresh mentality" expressing "the instincts, practice, and discoveries of the younger generations," a contrast, that is, between the "American Will" and the "American Intellect": "The American Will inhabits the sky-scraper; the American Intellect inhabits the colonial mansion. The one is the sphere of the American man; the other, at least predominantly, of the American woman. The one is all aggressive enterprise; the other is all genteel tradition." "The Genteel Tradition in American Philosophy," as this passage makes clear, is no wholesale condemnation of all things American. Even as Santayana criticizes the side of American society in which he himself is a leading participant, the side of high culture and "Intellect," he distinguishes himself from the long list of critics denouncing capitalism and modernization by his acknowledgment of American creativity "in invention and industry and social organization" (4). (The last chapter of *Character and Opinion in the United States,* "English Liberty in America," explains what Santayana has in mind in praising American accomplishment in "social organization.")

Santayana begins not by discussing the Protestant denominations whose theology is derived from the teachings of John Calvin but by addressing what he calls "the philosophical principle of Calvinism" (4). This philosophical principle, according to Santayana, has no necessary relation with Protestant Christianity, but "appears also in the Koran, in Spinoza, and in Cardinal Newman," and also in thinkers like Thomas Carlyle and Josiah Royce, both of whom could be considered "philosophically, perfect Calvinists" (4–5). This list of names, and especially the inclusion of Spinoza, the modern philosopher whom Santayana honored above all others, makes it clear that Calvinism in his view deserves to be taken seriously as a philosophical doctrine. Calvinism so understood is "one of the radical points of view in philosophy" that can never be regarded as outdated or surpassed, since it can never "cease to be possible" (6).

It is true, Santayana observes, that Calvinism is no longer intellectually vigorous in the United States, but that is not because its doctrines have been defeated by more sophisticated or more comprehensive ideas. Instead, the frame of mind it expresses is no longer typical. Philosophical Calvinism, Santayana explains, "is an expression of the agonized conscience" (5) and gains wide acceptance only in a society where that attitude is encouraged by circumstances. The United States was once such a society, "small and isolated . . . under pressure and constant trial," a nation where "vigilance over conduct and an absolute demand for personal integrity" were requirements for survival. Calvinism was then a living philosophy. The very success of the Calvinists and of the United States, however, "relax[ed] the pressure of external circumstances, and indirectly the pressure of the agonized conscience within" (5). Americans no longer believed that God was angry with them but instead felt they had been especially blessed. The sense that oneself and one's country were "victorious and blameless" (6) found expression in the essays of Ralph Waldo Emerson, whose transcendentalism rejected the insistence on the reality of original sin that marked the Puritanism of a Calvin or a Jonathan Edwards.

Just as Santayana is able to respect the radical logic of Calvinism even though he himself does not suffer from an "agonized conscience," so he is able to appreciate Emerson's integral sincerity, even while noting how much was excluded from the vision of Emerson's "cheery, child-like soul, impervious to the evidence of evil" (9). Emerson, Santanaya observes approvingly, constructed no system that required defending; he was thus free to "covet truth" (10), even if the truths he discovered were true for him only and only for a time. In examining first and above all his own thoughts, Emerson made use of transcendentalism as a method, and as a method Santayana commends it "as correct and . . . the chief contribution made in modern times to speculation" (7–8). There is nothing wrong and a good deal right with the desire to learn as much as one can about the workings of one's own perceptions. The transcendental method, when worked out through repeated close analyses and regularized, "is the critical logic of science" (7). Because it tests everything, no matter how old or authoritative, by reference to the self, transcendentalism had a special attraction for Americans building a new society and a special appeal to "the individualistic and revolutionary temper of their youth" (8).

Americans, however, did not simply give up their Calvinist beliefs and embrace Emerson's transcendentalism. Instead, they — or the New England Protestants whom Santayana has in mind when he speaks of Americans in the "Genteel Tradition" essay — continued to profess belief in Calvinist doctrines while interpreting them in a transcendentalist fashion. The Calvinism of Calvin stressed a belief in the sinfulness of the individual soul, which could be saved only by the entirely unmerited grace of God. Emerson's transcendentalism, on the other hand, had no place for the concept of sin and emphasized "self-reliance," certain that the self was ultimately divine. The two ways of thought could be united only by diluting and distorting both. The austere logic of Calvin's theology had to be ignored so that religion could be based only on emotion, "on one's fine feelings, on one's indomitable optimism and trust in life" (*Character and Opinion,* 30). Transcendentalism's skepticism about the possibility of obtaining real knowledge about anything beyond the self could be used to justify a rejection of belief in both an external material world and in orthodox Calvinist doctrine on predestination and eternal damnation. On the other hand, support for belief in some sort of God, if not exactly the God of the Bible or the Nicene Creed, could be found by taking the epistemological starting points of the transcendental method for metaphysical conclusions; in so doing, however, what had been "a conscientious critique of knowledge was turned into a sham system of nature" (8).

Santayana's objection to the genteel tradition is thus based on an immanent critique. He does not denounce either Calvinism or transcendentalism but instead points out the fundamental disagreement that makes the attempt to unify the two intellectually dishonest. Santayana does not object to the moral code of the "genteel tradition" but observes that the moral authority associated with Christianity was purchased without paying the price of actual belief in Christian doctrine. Adherents of the tradition could claim moral and social respectability as Christians and also intellectual status as up-to-date philosophical idealists and epistemological skeptics.

On this reading, the parallel to the genteel tradition today is not with those whose moral views are based on their religious faith but rather with the postmodernist academic left, which has reprised the genteel tradition's convenient but incongruous alliance of epistemological skepticism with moral certainty. On balance, the intellectual contradictions and difficulties ignored and smoothed over by the genteel tradition are less glaring than those that characterize contemporary postmodernism. The philosophical basis of the genteel tradition was an idealism that denied the reality of matter in favor of the reality of mind or spirit. The philosophical basis of postmodernism is an epistemological skepticism so absolute that it denies the very concepts of "reality" or "truth." Both theories are at odds with common sense, the latter even more than the former. As Santayana observed in *Scepticism and Animal Faith*, "total dogmatic skepticism is evidently an impossible attitude. It requires me to deny what I assert, not to mean what I mean, and (in the sense in which seeing is believing) not to believe what I see."[6] The adherents of the genteel tradition derived their moral authority from a Calvinism in which they no longer believed but were not ready to condemn, while today's postmodernists derive the moral concepts that fuel their anger from the same Western culture they are more than ready to condemn as irremediably logocentric, imperialist, and racist.

Santayana saw the same anger and the same rejection of common sense in German romanticism. His characterization of the attitudes encouraged by romantic philosophy would have to be revised only slightly to accurately describe the postmodernist outlook today: "In various directions at once we see to-day an intense hatred and disbelief gathering head against the very notion of a cosmos to be discovered, or a stable human nature to be respected. Nature, we are told, is an artificial symbol employed by life; truth is a temporary convention."[7] Romanticism in Germany was underwritten by idealist philosophers like Fichte and Schelling, and it was the importation of the German idealist tradition from Kant through Hegel to American departments of philosophy that allowed Emerson's intuitive transcendentalism to be systematized and taught in the schools. In the United States, however, the romantic fervor of a Fichte or Schelling was transmuted into earnest attempts to make belief in the God of Christianity compatible with the current philosophical trends.

The most ambitious of such attempts was carried out by Santayana's colleague Josiah Royce, whose intellectual portrait in the fourth chapter of *Character and Opinion* matches the chapter on the better-known William James in its union of sympathetic understanding and devastating analysis. Royce was an idealist in the German tradition, whose metaphysics amounted to a kind of "grammatology," to use a term made famous by the master of deconstruction.[8] This idealism, in Santayana's words, "regards all objects, including the universe, as merely terms posited by the thinker, according to a definite grammar of thought native to his mind" (70). Such a rejection of "the incubus of an external reality or truth" (70) stimulated the romantic philosophers to visions of a godlike freedom for the individual soul. Royce, however, was unwilling to accept entirely the romantic view of life, with its advocacy of "action and stress for their own sake" (73), despite his idealist metaphysics. Santayana argues that it was the influence of "the democratic and American spirit of service" (74) that prevented Royce from accepting the full consequences of his philosophical romanticism. Royce, for example, refused to consider the German sinking of the American ship *Lusitania* from the romantic philosophical perspective according to which it could be considered "a providential act, requisite to spread abroad a vitalising war" (75). As a romantic idealist philosopher, he should have looked beyond the deaths of the individual human beings caused by the sinking and reflected that "the Universal Spirit [was] compelled to bifurcate into just such Germans and just such Americans, in order to attain self-consciousness by hating, fighting against, and vanquishing itself" (74). But Royce instead was appalled by the sinking of the *Lusitania,* condemning it as "a crime to execrate altogether" (75); although he was certainly a romantic idealist philosopher, he was also an American, and "the deepest thing in him personally was conscience, firm recognition of duty, and the democratic and American spirit of service" (74).

Santayana's evident preference in his discussion of Josiah Royce for the "American spirit of service" over the seeming profundity of romantic idealism anticipates the measured but far-reaching affirmation of American life that he offers in "English Liberty in America," the last chapter of *Character and Opinion.* Perhaps even more relevant today than his critique of the genteel tradition, Santayana's final judgment on American culture is breathtaking in its implications, the scope of which is easily missed, since Santayana's rhetoric is sober rather than soaring, reflective rather than inspirational. Santayana goes out of his way to make it clear that he himself feels little personal affinity for the American way of life. His affinities are instead with the sort of "luckless American" who feels out of place, the kind "who is born a conservative, or who is drawn to poetic subtlety, pious retreats, or gay passions" (166). (Santayana is of course using "gay" in its traditional sense to mean "merry," not to mean "homosexual," a usage that did not become widespread until long after his death.) Santayana the philosopher has little in common with the typical American who "can conceive of no more decisive way of recommending an opinion or a practice than to say that it is what everybody is coming to adopt" (93). "To the good American," Santayana observes, "many subjects are sacred: sex is sacred, women are sacred, children are sacred, business is sacred, America is sacred, Masonic lodges and college clubs are sacred" (94) — a list whose anomalies already make Santayana's point that "if he [the good American] did not regard all these things as sacred he might come to doubt sometimes if they were wholly good" (94). Perhaps Santayana's most serious criticism of American culture is that the typical American "is a materialist in morals; he esteems things, and esteems himself, for mechanical uses and energies" (99). Santayana, a philosophical materialist in the tradition of Democritus and Lucretius, deplores the "moral materialism" of the American, "his singular preoccupation with quantity" (100), a preoccupation by no means confined to businessmen or manufacturers. When the president of Harvard, Charles Eliot, once asked Santayana how his classes "were getting on" and was told "my men seemed to be keen and intelligent," the President quickly informed Professor Santayana that "I meant . . . *what is the number* of students in your classes" (100; italics in original).

A materialist who rejected the possibility that natural forces might be governed by any moral criteria at all, Santayana thought the "laws of Nature and Nature's God" cited in the Declaration of Independence were not "unalienable truths" but evidence that the Declaration was "a salad of illusions."[9] Never a believer in American exceptionalism, Santayana agreed with William James that the Spanish-American War demonstrated that the United States was becoming an imperial power, but unlike James he did not worry that in doing so the United States was unfaithful to its animating ideals. The history of the United States could be compared to that of Spain, which had risen to become a great empire and then eventually lost that empire, parts of which the United States in its turn had seized. Eventually, no doubt, the United States itself would go through the same sort of decline that Spain had undergone.

All the more striking, then, that Santayana came to believe that the American way of life, what Santayana calls "English liberty in America," might be worthy of emulation throughout the world for the indefinite future. Without making any predictions about the future of the United States itself, Santayana speculates that the way of life he describes as English liberty in America "may last indefinitely, and can enlist every reasonable man and nation in its service" (118). It may do so because it allows the individual a full measure of freedom or "liberty," and "calls only for a partial and shifting unanimity among living men" (118). In America even more than in England, the conformity that in other countries is enforced by the authority of laws, custom, and social hierarchy is countered by a "free individuality" that, remarkably, does not result in anarchy but is imbued with "the spirit of free co-operation" (103). Santayana observes that this cooperation without coercion is possible because "there is no country in which people live under more overpowering compulsions. . . . Even what is best in American life is compulsory" (109–110). All Americans, it seems, must share "the gospel of work and the belief in progress"; "otherwise you will feel like a traitor, a soulless outcast, a deserted ship high and dry on the shore" (110).

Other commentators have made similar observations and drawn drastic conclusions. Describing American society as a "totalitarian democracy," Herbert Marcuse argued that true freedom could be attained only by what he called a "liberating tolerance" that "would mean intolerance against movements from the Right," including "the withdrawal of tolerance before the deed, at the stage of communication in word, print, and picture."[10] Santayana, however, believes that no such radical measures are necessary: "American life *is* free as a whole" (110). The "constitutional religion" that assures "moral cohesion" (105) is indeed all-encompassing, but its directives are vague and general; they do not issue from the top down and they leave room for individual initiative and experiment: "the American orthodoxy, though imperious, is not unyielding. . . . It is confident of a happy and triumphant future, which it would be shameful in any man to refuse to work for and to share; but it cannot prefigure what that bright future is to be" (111). The readiness to experiment and the ability to learn from experience give English liberty its "great advantage"; it is not merely in accord with the history and customs of a certain nationality at a particular historical moment, but "it is in harmony with the nature of things" (116). In making this strong claim, Santayana is far from suggesting that English liberty is in accord with either natural law or with God. He does not even suggest that the English and the Americans have somehow stumbled upon the one right way to live. His point is rather that just because human beings are necessarily ignorant about most aspects of a constantly changing universe, it is only the sort of trial and error fostered by English liberty that makes adaptation possible: "In the end, adaptation to the world at large, where so much is hidden and unintelligible, is only possible piecemeal, by groping with a genuine indetermination in one's aims" (106).

Santayana's case for English liberty includes not only an explanation of its practical success but accounts as well for its failure to fire the imagination. English liberty, he observes, is indeed "a positive infringement and surrender of the freedom most fought for and most praised in the past" (112). The martyrs of Christianity died and the revolutionaries of left and right killed and died rather than cooperate and get along in the spirit of English liberty; the martyr or revolutionary is determined "to live absolutely according to his ideal, and no hostile votes, no alien interests, must call on him to deviate from it by one iota" (112–113). This unwillingness to compromise, this insistence on sacrificing all, including oneself and often others, for an impossible ideal, has been celebrated in song and story as English liberty will never be. English liberty leads ineluctably to a bourgeois society, and the bourgeois way of life has been condemned by artists and writers for its lack of aesthetic appeal as strongly as Marxists have condemned it for preventing the triumph of socialism. There is little that is romantic or exciting about the "broad-based, stupid, blind adventure, groping toward an unknown goal" (112) to which English liberty is committed.

Not only is a society founded on English liberty likely to be criticized from within by writers and artists disdaining the middle class and intellectuals looking for a cause, Santayana warns that English liberty will not be welcomed by peoples who are interested only in maintaining the "fierce liberty" (118) to live as they have always lived. This "fierce liberty" or "absolute liberty" means the ability of every society founded on custom or religion or tribal or clan allegiances "to be just so, and to remain just so forever" (113). No matter how irrational or unproductive such a way of life might appear to those enjoying the benefits of English liberty, one should not assume that those who live according to other customs and allegiances will be eager to give them up. Santayana issues an eloquent, prophetic warning: "Enthusiasts for democracy, peace, and a league of nations should not deceive themselves; they are not everybody's friends; they are the enemies of what is deepest and most primitive in everybody. They inspire undying hatred in every untamable people and every absolute soul" (113).

Santayana's very eloquence, however, lends itself to misunderstanding. If this passage were taken out of context and its author were unknown, it would be natural to suppose that he or she wanted the reader to oppose the repression of "what is deepest and most primitive in everybody" and to admire "untamable people" and the "absolute soul." For a romantic sensibility, it is surely admirable to be "untamable" — readers of Shelley's "Ode to the West Wind" are meant to be impressed when the poet describes himself as, like the West Wind, "tameless, and swift, and proud." Similarly, those who prize authenticity in literature and life are likely to think that it would be a better world if "what is deepest and most primitive in everybody" would be allowed to express itself. Santayana himself feels otherwise. A willingness to be "tamed" demonstrates not weakness but awareness. Docility is for him a quality to praise. The Greeks deserve admiration because they "were singularly docile . . . to the proved limitations and resources of human life" (*Egotism,* 234). For Santayana the ability to learn from experience what is possible and what is not and the readiness to adapt oneself to the possible constitute wisdom. To be "tamed" does not mean, as Nietzsche suggests, that one's selfhood is crushed but rather that one has learned the ways through which that self may be fulfilled and find happiness; thus to be "tamed" means to live the life of reason: "To be happy, even to conceive happiness, you must be reasonable or (if Nietzsche prefers the word) you must be tamed. . . . To be happy you must be wise" (*Egotism,* 239). In Santayana's view an "untamable people" is one unwilling to learn from experience, one that refuses to be guided by the wisdom of the past and thus earns the appellation of "heathen," regardless of their religion or lack of one: "the morally and essentially heathen are those who possess no authoritative wisdom, or reject the authority of what wisdom they have; the untaught or unteachable who disdain not only revelation but what revelation stood for among early peoples, namely, funded experience" (*Egotism,* 234). In Santayana's view a rejection of the compromises endemic to English liberty, an insistence on having one's way completely and absolutely, is not a sign of strength but of weakness: "the feebler, more ignorant, and more childlike an impulse is, the less it can restrain itself or surrender a part of its desire in order the better to attain the rest" (114).

The opposing concepts of "English liberty" and "absolute" or "fierce liberty" are fruitful not only in regard to relations between the United States and the rest of the world but also in coming to terms with tensions within the

United States itself, including the central tension of race. It is true that Santayana's own reflections abstracted from issues of race. His "universal American" was white. Although "largely adequate to the facts," his "symbolic American" could not be entirely representative, since "there are immense differences between individual Americans — for some Americans are black" (93). Santayana's distinction between "English liberty" on the one hand and "fierce" or "absolute liberty" on the other clarifies what was — and is — at issue in the struggle for racial equality. When George Wallace in his 1963 inaugural speech as governor of Alabama presented himself as a champion of "freedom" and an opponent of "tyranny" while defending racial segregation, he was speaking on behalf of the "fierce liberty" of white Southerners: "It is very appropriate then that from this Cradle of the Confederacy, this very Heart of the Great Anglo-Saxon Southland, that today we sound the drum for freedom as have our generations of forebears before us done, time and time again through history. Let us rise to the call of freedom-loving blood that is in us and send our answer to the tyranny that clanks its chains upon the South. In the name of the greatest people that have ever trod this earth, I draw the line in the dust and toss the gauntlet before the feet of tyranny . . . and I say . . . segregation today . . . segregation tomorrow . . . segregation forever."[11]

In calling for "segregation today . . . segregation tomorrow . . . segregation forever," Wallace is certainly championing the subjugation of African Americans, but he is able to present himself as a champion of freedom because he is also defending the "fierce liberty" of the white South "to be just so, and to remain just so for ever." His speech expresses the characteristic attitude of embattled defenders of "fierce liberty": "the most vehement defiance of anybody who might ask them, for the sake of harmony, to be a little different" (113). This defiance, so impressive when expressed by "the Christian martyrs in the arena" (112), seems perverse obstinacy or worse when voiced by George Wallace in 1963. Yet Santayana's contrast between "English liberty" and "absolute liberty" depends on the recognition that extremism itself is the identifying quality of the latter, not the moral character of the causes for which it is enlisted.

Santayana's belief that "English liberty," not "absolute" or "fierce" liberty, is the dominant spirit of the United States is borne out by the history of the civil rights movement. Despite bitter-enders and would-be secessionists, the nation has moved toward greater equality; nobody is entirely satisfied, since change has occurred "by a series of checks, mutual concessions, and limited satisfactions" (112), but real change has taken place nonetheless. Ralph Ellison, one of the most perceptive analysts of the tension between American ideals and American racial reality, confirms Santayana's observation that "in each of us there is a little absolute will" (117) when he notes that, whatever our ethnicity, "we are all at some point or other secessionists,"[12] ready to give up on the national experiment if we can't have our way. But Ellison also shares Santayana's belief in the vitality of the spirit of "English liberty," though he refers instead to the "underground logic of the democratic process." This "underground logic" or "unwritten history" includes "unremarked contacts between individuals of differing status and background" and "the sharing of bloodlines and cultural traditions by groups of widely different ethnic origins"; in Ellison's view this "unconscious logic" is an "irresistible force" moving "all too slowly, but steadily, against and around those forces which would thwart our progress toward the fulfillment of the democratic ideal."[13] Santayana, it is true, thinks of English liberty as "groping toward an unknown goal," while Ellison sees a zigzag movement "toward the fulfillment of the democratic ideal." The difference, however, is not so great as it seems, since Ellison's "democratic ideal" includes individual liberty as a central component, while the "groping" of Santayana's English liberty in America assumes American democracy as its starting point and field of action.

Although English liberty fosters a way of life in which Santayana himself cannot feel at ease, he nevertheless recognizes, with philosophic disinterestedness, that it has one "great advantage": "it is in harmony with the nature of things" (116). Human beings and human societies do not have the absolute knowledge necessary to make absolute liberty practicable, and thus "the life of reason, like English liberty, is a perpetual compromise" (117). The absolute liberty demanded by martyrs and revolutionaries may be thrilling, and one may well admire the courage of those who insist on having their way no matter what, but it also requires courage to recognize that neither the intensity of our desires, nor even the certitude of our own righteousness, provides any guarantee of triumph or even survival for an individual or a society. Santayana concludes that English liberty must ultimately take hold throughout the world, if civilization of any kind is to continue. Yes, absolute liberty is sometimes "beautiful," but sober judgment must acknowledge that it is ultimately "impracticable" (117). Santayana's verdict deserves to be taken seriously, all the more because declaring it gives him no occasion for celebration: "Absolute liberty and English liberty are incompatible, and mankind must make a brave choice between them. The necessity of rejecting and destroying some things that are beautiful is the deepest curse of existence" (119).

Santayana's cultivation of detachment, which allowed him so many insights, also on occasion played him false. His philosophic disinterestedness allowed him to appreciate the virtues of English liberty even though he himself found the way of life it fostered antipathetic. Sometimes, however, Santayana's stance as a mere observer encouraged him to judge societies and governments by the interest they were capable of arousing in an onlooker rather than the kind and degree of fulfillment they made possible for those affected by them. Criticizing the New Humanists as the last expression of the genteel tradition, he urged Irving Babbitt and Paul Elmer More to stop their worried moralizing and, like Santayana, "frankly rejoice" in a modern world that includes "at least (besides football) . . . Einstein and Freud, Proust and Paul Valéry, Lenin and Mussolini."[14] It was enough, apparently, that Lenin and Mussolini, like the writers and thinkers listed first, provided food for thought and speculation. Whether the rule of the dictators promoted liberty or made life more tolerable for those under their power was apparently beside the point, at least when Santayana was out to score a polemical point.

This passage, however, is not nearly as disturbing as Santayana's declaration, in the preface to his last published work, as to "the moral light in which I am accustomed to see the world." This "moral light" includes, he writes six years after the near-success of the Nazi's Final Solution, a willingness to "gladly extirpate all the crawling ugliness in the world" if doing so would allow one "to obtain anything lovely."[15] It is not clear what the political implications of this remark might be, although "extirpate" seems a sinister concept in a world where genocide had just been attempted. One's doubts are not eased by the previous sentence, in which Santayana announces that "I prefer the rose to the dandelion; I prefer the lion to the vermin in the lion's skin." There are no obvious political associations with the terms "rose" and "dandelion," or for "lion," either, unless one thinks of the British lion. In the decades before the preface, however, "vermin" was a common term of abuse applied by Nazis in Germany to Jews and by Communists in the Soviet Union to those of the wrong class or ideology. In the same preface, writing just after the defeat of Nazism, fascism, and Japanese imperialism and while Stalin's dictatorship remained in power, Santayana singled out "liberalism" for condemnation, apparently on aesthetic criteria: "if one political tendency kindled my wrath, it was precisely the tendency of industrial liberalism to level down all civilizations to a single cheap and dreary pattern" (xxi). No doubt such a passage in the preface to his last book played its part in the decline in Santayana's influence and reputation that began in the 1950s and has been reversed only recently. Indeed, when Santayana allows himself to make judgments about political and social matters on the basis of their capacity to provide aesthetic pleasure, entertainment, or even intellectual stimulation for the observer rather than by their impact on the moral, political, and economic well-being of those affected, he deserves to be criticized and those judgments rejected.

Yet an awareness of Santayana's tendency to substitute aesthetic for political or social criteria serves to clarify the extent to which Santayana's analysis of English liberty in America is not only an intellectual accomplishment, a brilliant cultural analysis, but also a moral achievement, a striking instance of a philosopher's ability to remain true to the implications of his thinking, even when his own inclinations and affinities lead elsewhere. The insights made available by Santayana's philosophic disinterestedness are also demonstrated in his analysis of the genteel tradition, which remains pertinent in a new century, while the many denunciations of the tradition, lively reading in their own day, are no longer interesting except as historical documents. A reconsideration of George Santayana that places his writings on the United States at the center, especially "The Genteel Tradition in American Philosophy" and *Character and Opinion in the United States,* in particular its last chapter on "English Liberty in America," leads, I believe, to a recognition of the philosopher as one of those few critics of American culture whose insights remain permanently valuable.

NOTES

1. Sinclair Lewis, "The American Fear of Literature," *The Man from Main Street: A Sinclair Lewis Reader,* ed. Harry E. Maule and Melville H. Cane (New York: Random House, 1953), 3–17, p. 16. The following quotation from this work is cited by page number in the text.

2. H. L. Mencken, "Puritanism as a Literary Force," *A Book of Prefaces* (New York: Knopf, 1918), 197–283, p. 275.

3. Van Wyck Brooks, *The Ordeal of Mark Twain* (London: Heinemann, 1922), p. 100.

4. Malcolm Cowley, "The Revolt against Gentility," *After the Genteel Tradition: American Writers 1919–1930,* ed. Malcolm Cowley (Carbondale, IL: Southern Illinois University Press, 1964), 3–20, p. 10. First published in 1937.

5. Van Wyck Brooks, *The Pilgrimage of Henry James* (New York: E. P. Dutton, 1925), p. 105.

6. George Santayana, *Scepticism and Animal Faith: Introduction to a System of Philosophy,* The Works of George Santayana, Triton Edition, Vol. XIII (New York: Charles Scribner's Sons, 1937), 1–275, pp. 153–54.

7. George Santayana, *Egotism in German Philosophy,* The Works of George Santayana, Triton Edition, Vol. VI (New York: Charles Scribner's Sons, 1936), 143–249, p. 236. First published in 1916. Hereafter cited as *Egotism.*

8. Jacques Derrida, *Of Grammatology,* trans. Gayatri Chakrovorty Spivak (Baltimore: Johns Hopkins University Press, 1976), p. 158. Published as *De La Grammatologie* in 1967.

9. George Santayana, *Persons and Places: Fragments of Autobiography,* ed. William G. Holzberger and Herman J. Saatkamp, Jr., The Works of George Santayana, Vol. I (Cambridge, MA: MIT Press, 1987), p. 404. Hereafter cited as *Persons.*

10. Herbert Marcuse, "Repressive Tolerance," *A Critique of Pure Tolerance* (Boston: Beacon Press, 1965), 81–117, p. 109.

11. George Wallace, "The 1963 Inaugural Address." Lloyd Rohler, *George Wallace: Conservative Populist* (Westport, CT: Praeger, 2004), 111–20, p. 113. Ellipses in original. Available online from the Alabama Department of Archives and History under the title "The 1963 Inaugural Address of Governor George Wallace" at ⟨http://www.archives.state.al.us/govs—list/inauguralspeech.html⟩.

12. Ralph Ellison, "Presentation to Bernard Malamud of the Gold Medal for Fiction," *The Collected Essays of Ralph Ellison,* ed. John F. Callahan (New York: Random House, 1995), 461–67, p. 465. Ellison thought of "black separatism" as "really another version of secessionism" ("Haverford Statement," *The Collected Essays of Ralph Ellison,* 427–32, p. 432).

13. Ralph Ellison, "Going to the Territory," *Going to the Territory* (New York: Random House, 1986), 120–44, pp. 125–26.

14. George Santayana, *The Genteel Tradition at Bay,* The Works of George Santayana, Triton Edition, Vol. VIII (New York: Charles Scribner's Sons, 1937), 131–69, p. 140.

15. George Santayana, *Dominations and Powers: Reflections on Liberty, Society, and Government* (New Brunswick, NJ: Transaction Publishers, 1995), p. xxiii. Originally published in 1950.

Mental Hygiene and Good Manners
The Contribution of George Santayana

ROGER KIMBALL

"Americans go deeply into the surface of things."
— Geoffrey Madan, *Geoffrey Madan's Notebooks*

"America is a young country with an old mentality."
— Santayana, "The Genteel Tradition in American Philosophy"

"To be an American is of itself almost a moral condition, an education, and a career."
— Santayana, *Character and Opinion in the United States*

"[I]n renouncing everything else for the sake of English letters I might be said to have been guilty, quite unintentionally, of a little stratagem, as if I had set out to say plausibly in English as many un-English things as possible."
— Santayana, "A General Confession"

George Santayana was one of the most urbane philosophers ever to put pen to paper. He was also one of the sanest practitioners of the philosopher's craft and (as it often is) sullen art.

Admittedly, that may not be saying a great deal. You do not have to read far in the corpus of philosophical speculation to appreciate that neither urbanity nor sanity — especially not sanity — has generally been much prized by *homo philosophicus*. There are exceptions, of course. Plato and Descartes were nothing if not urbane; Hume was commendably sane. But as a rule philosophers have demonstrated by their practice — if not always by their prescriptions — that they adulate other mental and moral qualities: profundity, for example, or at least the appearance thereof, as well as a certain ferocious verbal dexterity and obtuse cleverness in the juggling of concepts. ("Anyway, I'd rather be right than clever," said a brittle English clubman. "I'd rather be both than neither," came the withering rejoinder.)

Whether all this speaks well of philosophy is a question that we can (as the phenomenologists say) bracket. My point is only that Santayana — the Spanish-born, Boston-bred, Harvard-educated cosmopolite — stands out as an unusual specimen in the philosophical fraternity. He wrote beautifully, for one thing, commanding a supple yet robust prose that was elegant but rarely precious or self-infatuated.

There was a time when Santayana's work was part of the normal furniture of educated discourse. His poetry, essays, and wide-ranging philosophical writings were eagerly read and digested, flowering in turn in the sentiments and opinions of several generations of readers. At Harvard, where he taught from 1889 until 1912, Santayana's official and unofficial students included Conrad Aiken, Robert Frost, T. S. Eliot, Witter Bynner, Walter Lippmann, Wallace Stevens, Scofield Thayer, Max Eastman, Van Wyck Brooks, Felix Frankfurter, and James B. Conant, many of whom (conspicuously excepting Eliot) registered their profound debt to his teaching. Until yesterday, it seems, Santayana's influence was woven into the living tapestry of intellectual life. In our amnesiac day, his influence seems to have been reduced to the literary equivalent of a geometric point: a single epigram, to wit, "Those who cannot remember the past are condemned to repeat it." [1]

Not a great deal else survives from Santayana in the chapbook of public memory. More's the pity, for he is deliciously quotable, nowhere more piquantly than in *Character and Opinion in the United States*:

> The milk of human kindness is less apt to turn sour if the vessel that holds it stands steady, cool, and separate, and is not too often uncorked. (94)

> Free government works well in proportion as government is superfluous. (109)

> The romanticist thinks he has life by virtue of his confusion and torment, whereas in truth that torment and confusion are his incipient death, and it is only the modicum of harmony he has achieved in his separate faculties that keeps him alive at all. (74)

Santayana was often at his most memorable not in his "official" philosophical works — the five-volume *Life of Reason*, for example, or *Scepticism and Animal Faith* — but in more avocational endeavors: the poignant *Soliloquies in England*, say, or *The Last Puritan*, his "memoir in the form of a novel." Santayana's letters — he was a tireless and engaging correspondent — also sparkle with that dry but tonic light. *Character and Opinion* and "The Genteel Tradition in American Philosophy" belong to this exalted company. If they lack the sweep and political urgency of Tocqueville's *Democracy in America*, they make up for it in charm and mental buoyancy. Together, they stand as one of our most penetrating reflections on what is American about the American spirit.

As far as I have been able to determine, Santayana never met the English aesthete Geoffrey Madan (1895–1947). But he would have delighted in Madan's observation, quoted above, that "Americans go deeply into the surface of things."[2] But where Madan would have meant it to sting, Santayana would have extracted an element of compensating commendation. Only a very shallow person, Oscar Wilde once observed, doesn't judge things by appearances. A typical Wildean quip, true, but how loaded with wisdom!

Hegel said that Minerva's owl flew only with the coming of the dusk. But Santayana's America — he lived here from 1872, when he was nine, until 1912 — was (is it still?) a country of the morning. Morning may be a time for thoughts, but few second thoughts, which is where Minerva comes in. "Until yesterday," Santayana wrote in *Character and Opinion*, America "believed itself immune from the hereditary plagues of mankind" (83). Tocqueville had long before noted that Americans paid less attention to philosophy than any civilized country in the world. Yet nowhere, he said, were the precepts of Descartes more widely applied. What Tocqueville had in mind was less the speculative than the practical side of Descartes. Not "cogito ergo sum" but that simple yet powerful method that would render man "the master and possessor of nature."[3] How much thought, and how much deliberate thoughtlessness, must be taken on board to prosecute such a plan? In America, Santayana wrote, "Every system was met with a frank gaze. 'Come on,' people seemed to say to it, 'show us what you are good for. We accept no claims; we ask for no credentials; we just give you a chance. Plato, the Pope, and Mrs. Eddy shall have one vote each' " (83).

Do we still live in the America Santayana described? An American's instinct, Santayana said, "is to think well of everybody, and to wish everybody well, but in a spirit of rough comradeship, expecting every man to stand on his own legs and to be helpful in his turn. When he has given his neighbour a chance he thinks he has done enough for him; but he feels it is an absolute duty to do that. It will take some hammering to drive a coddling socialism into America" (94). Tocqueville, in his famous paragraphs on Democratic Despotism, showed how the hammering would proceed. It was left to the later twentieth century to forge the instruments and the policies that prescribed their use.

But already in the early part of the last century Santayana discerned other, contrasting currents in American culture. Mornings come in autumn as well as spring. At the beginning of "The Moral Background," the opening chapter of *Character and Opinion*, he evokes the fragile, evanescent, and barren beauty of an Indian summer. In the middle of the nineteenth century, he writes, "New England had an Indian summer of the mind; and an agreeable reflective literature showed how brilliant that russet and yellow season could be. There were poets, historians, orators, preachers, most of whom had studied foreign literatures and had travelled; they demurely kept up with the times; they were universal humanists. But it was all a harvest of leaves; these worthies had an expurgated and barren conception of life; theirs was the purity of sweet old age" (25). What follows is a quiet tour de force of intellectual portraiture, wry and dispassionately affectionate.

Well, partly affectionate. It is also partly admonitory. Santayana wrote *Character and Opinion* in England in the immediate aftermath of the First World War, not exactly an allegro moment. Casting his glance not only at America but also at the civilization of which it was the latest outcrop and heir, Santayana speculated that "Civilisation is perhaps approaching one of those long winters that overtake it from time to time. A flood of barbarism from below may soon level all the fair works of our Christian ancestors, as another flood two thousand years ago levelled those of the ancients. Romantic Christendom — picturesque, passionate, unhappy episode — may be coming to an end" (24).

The jury is still out on that prognostication, but it is worth noting that Santayana's assessment of the American temper did not require the displacement of war to wax somber. Something of the sere and russet quality he diagnosed in 1918 was already part of what he called, in 1911, "the genteel tradition," one of the most mellifluous phrases ever to have been enlisted in the armory of rhetorical diminishment. That enlistment, it is worth noting, represents a curious semantic shift. To judge from the dictionary, "genteel" is largely a flattering adjective. "Refined in manner, polite": nothing wrong with that. "Free from vulgarity or rudeness": OK there, too. "Elegantly fashionable or stylish in manner or appearance": who could object? Only the last definition in my dictionary — "Marked by affected and somewhat prudish refinement" — would give most of us pause.

And yet "the genteel tradition," a lecture title that matured into an all-purpose intellectual indictment (and wore itself out in the process), is no commendation. We have Santayana to thank for that: or maybe we should thank the many who came after him and gleefully seized upon the phrase to decry whatever they thought vulgar, stuffy, philistine, or behind-the-times. But it is worth noting that, although Santayana speaks of "The Genteel Tradition in American Philosophy," the tradition he invokes is neither peculiarly philosophical nor distinctively American. The "genteel tradition" is the dominant tradition of establishment opinion, whatever it may happen to be at a given time. Thus Santayana speaks of the genteel tradition in Europe that was "handed down since Socrates." Surely that yawning historical vista puts a crimp in the criticism the phrase is meant to imply. In his famous essay — and twenty years later in "The Genteel Tradition at Bay" — Santayana provides an anatomy of received opinion as it then operated in American culture. It is part of what he meant when he said (and said more than once) that "America is a young country with an old mentality" (3). Commercially, in practical matters, America was vibrant, adventurous, "masculine." In matters of culture she was cautious, "feminine," not "high-and-dry, but slightly becalmed."

But the irony is that the genteel tradition need not be genteel, that is, polite, refined, circumspect. Today, for example, the genteel tradition in American academic and cultural life thrives by repudiating those very virtues. It is an irony that Santayana would have savored even as he would have disapprobated the behavior and attitudes that made the irony so pointed. As the historian Robert Dawidoff noted in a perceptive essay on "The Genteel Tradition," Santayana "would have been amused but unsurprised that . . . the genteel ended up endorsing free-speech relativism, obscenity, and anti-social behavior (and many other things) in its helpless pursuit of cultural control through misapplied moralizing."[4] The indispensable thing about the genteel tradition turns out to be the moralizing pressure toward conformity, not the substance of the governing strictures.

Although Santayana thrived on such vertiginous reversals, he did so quietly, with the utmost discretion. Santayana never hectored. Indeed, he rarely even bothered to argue. Instead, he observed; he described; he slyly took readers into his confidence. This is not to say that there isn't a didactic side to Santayana's philosophy. There is. It is just that, like all the best teachers, Santayana understood that arguments are a less effective catechism than a vision of the world. ("Men," wrote Cardinal Newman, "are guided by *type*, not by argument.")[5] Most modern philosophy puts a premium on argument and analysis. But the Australian philosopher David Stove was right when he noted that "Some of the best philosophers never argue, or even pretend to. Santayana, for example. He simply tells you how he thinks the world is, and delicately makes fun of some other philosophers, almost always unnamed, who think there is more to the world, or less, than he does."[6]

Santayana was a curiously amphibious creature. He tarried more as a guest than a citizen in institutions, in countries, even in the world at large. He titled the last section of *Persons and Places*, his posthumously published memoir, "My Host, the World." What does that tell us? In the fall of 1911, Santayana traveled to California to gaze upon the Pacific and deliver his famous lecture on the genteel tradition at Berkeley. The following year, he left for Europe and never set foot in the United States again. Santayana was not without affection for America — he endeavored, he said, to understand it "as a family friend . . . who has a different temperament" (*Character and Opinion*, 23) — but he liked to say that his love for it, like his love for Spain, was "manifested . . . by living there as little as possible."[7]

Santayana enjoyed aspects of college life. He liked the semi-cloistered existence, the intellectual intimacy with burgeoning young minds, the easy proximity to handsome young faces. But he always loathed the academic industry. Indeed, no sooner had he started teaching than he began plotting his escape. Being a teacher, he remarked in *Persons and Places*, was forced upon him by the necessity of earning a living, "but being a student was my vocation."[8] He lived frugally, saved diligently, and was finally able to announce his departure in 1912, just shy of fifty, when his mother died leaving him a legacy of $10,000 (more than $200,000 today). At Harvard, too, he was always more a tourist than a citizen. The university, Santayana thought, had been ruined by people like Charles Eliot, the ambitious president from 1869 to 1909, who strove to transform Harvard College into a great modern — which meant Germanic — university. Eliot and Santayana were like oil and water. Early in his teaching career, Santayana chanced to encounter the president; asked about the progress of his classes, Santayana explained that he had finished with Plato and was moving on to Aristotle. "No, no, Santayana," Eliot said, "what I mean by my enquiry is, *how many* students have enrolled for your lectures?"[9]

It wasn't just a matter of administrative expansionism that bothered Santayana, though. The very discipline of academic philosophy rubbed him the wrong way. "That philosophers should be professors is an accident," he wrote, "and almost an anomaly. Free reflection about everything is a habit to be imitated, but not a subject to expound; and an original system, if the philosopher has one, is something dark, perilous, untested, and not ripe to be taught, nor is there much danger anyone will learn it" (39).

Looking back on his Harvard days in *Character and Opinion*, he spoke of the new breed of philosophy professor who was "very professional in tone and conscious of his *Fach*," "open-minded, whole-hearted, appreciative," but also — scarifying phrase — "toasted only on one side." It is a devastating portrait:

His education has been more pretentious than thorough; his style is deplorable; social pressure and his own great eagerness have condemned him to overwork, committee meetings, early marriage, premature authorship, and lecturing two or three times a day under forced draught. He has no peace in himself, no window open to a calm horizon, and in his heart perhaps little taste for mere scholarship or pure speculation. Yet, like the plain soldier staggering under his clumsy equipment, he is cheerful; he keeps his faith in himself and in his allotted work, puts up with being toasted only on one side, remains open-minded, wholehearted, appreciative, helpful, confident of the future of goodness and of science. In a word, he is a cell in that teeming democratic body; he draws from its warm, contagious activities the sanctions of his own life and, less consciously, the spirit of his philosophy. (82–83)

It is sometimes suggested that William James, Santayana's teacher and then colleague at Harvard, had been instrumental in poisoning the academic atmosphere for Santayana. This is emphatically not the case. Everyone quotes James's description of Santayana's early work as exhibiting a "perfection of rottenness" and "moribund Latinity." Few supply the context: "The great event in my life recently," James wrote to a colleague in 1900, "has been the reading of Santayana's book [*Interpretations of Poetry and Religion*]. Although I absolutely reject the platonism of it, I have literally squealed with delight at the imperturbable perfection with which the position is laid down. . . . I now understand Santayana, the man. I never understood him before. But what a perfection of rottenness in a philosophy! I don't think I ever knew the anti-realistic view to be propounded with so impudently superior an air. It is refreshing to see a representative of moribund Latinity rise up and administer such reproof to us barbarians in the hour of our triumph."[10] James ends by asking that his letter be passed along to Santayana, adding: "He is certainly an *extraordinarily distingué* writer. Thank him for existing!"

Temperamentally, the two men were complete opposites — James bluff, hearty, the thorough New England pragmatist in manner as well as philosophical outlook; Santayana the super-refined, sonnet-writing, exquisitely disillusioned Catholic Spaniard. In many ways, Santayana was closer in spirit to William's brother Henry. They met only once, in England, toward the end of Henry's life. "In that one interview," Santayana recalled — sadly, I think — he "made me feel more at home and better understood than his brother William ever had done in the long years of our acquaintance. Henry was calm, he liked to see things as they are, and be free afterwards to imagine how they might have been."[11] High praise from that apostle of clarity animated by subjunctive dispensation.

Despite their differences, however, there was no contemporary to whom Santayana owed more, intellectually, than William James, whose "sense for the immediate," "for the unadulterated, unexplained, instant fact of experience"[12] Santayana celebrated. The problem with Harvard was not William James but the increasing professional drift of the institution.

Santayana regularly allowed his gaze to wander toward the empyrean. But his feet, and his allegiance, he kept anchored firmly on the ground. In one sense, he was the most worldly of philosophers — worldliness, in fact, was one part of his urbanity. By the same token, "superstition" was one of his favorite deflationary epithets. But his worldliness was highly, exquisitely cultivated. There was nothing gross, reductive, or triumphalist about it. He was vigorously, even brutally, disillusioned, yet with an irony so scrupulous that his chilliness seems Olympian, not cruel or self-serving. As Robert Dawidoff noted, he was "as detached from what he cherished as from what he criticized."[13]

Many people who know Santayana only from anthologies are surprised to discover how thoroughly naturalistic a thinker he was.[14] Santayana's naturalism — what he describes in one essay as "the open-air materialistic setting"[15] of his philosophy — was the well-spring of the great attribute that complemented his urbanity: his unshakeable sanity. It somehow seems strange for a poet of his sometimes trembling fervency. But right from the start Santayana's primary philosophical inspirations were radical materialists like Lucretius and Spinoza (Spinoza, he said, "in several respects laid the foundation of my philosophy").[16]

Santayana's naturalism assured his implacable hostility to supernaturalism: the patent variety — his native Roman Catholicism, for example — as well as the covert versions populating many schools of philosophy — German idealism, say, in both its original and transplanted-to-England-and-America forms.

In 1890, when he was in his late twenties, Santayana wrote to William James that "I doubt whether the earth supports a more genuine enemy of all that the Catholic Church *inwardly* stands for than I do,"[17] and he later noted that he had "never been what is called a practising Catholic."[18] It was a position from which he never wavered. It is worth stressing this. Santayana spent the last twelve years of his life at the Blue Nuns' clinic in Rome. This has tempted some commentators to suggest that his atheism softened or even evaporated with age. But this was not the case. During his last illness, Santayana took pains to advise his friend Daniel Cory that if he were unconscious and the sacrament of Extreme Unction were administered, no one should interpret that as a deathbed conversion.

Santayana's philosophical sanity, delicately on view throughout *Character and Opinion*, is somewhat more bluntly stated in *Egotism in German Philosophy*, first published in 1916. In one central passage, writing about thinkers like Kant, Hegel, and Nietzsche, Santayana notes that "the more profound they are the more content and even delighted they are to consider nothing but their own creations. Their theory of knowledge proclaims that knowledge is impossible. You know only your so-called knowledge, which itself knows nothing; and you are limited to the autobiography of your illusions."[19] Santayana's description of Hegel's dialectic as a futile attempt to make "things conform to words, not words to things"[20] says everything one needs to know about that intellectual monstrosity.

In *Character and Opinion*, Santayana extends that criticism to Transcendentalism — that odd confect of displaced religious yearning and psychological boisterousness — as well as the two great streams of nineteenth-century American philosophy: empiricism and idealism. It was Santayana's singular achievement to perceive the manifold ways in which these schools, so different in tone and the "face" they presented to the world, were in fact children of the same parent. "Even the most emancipated and positivistic of the latest thinkers — pragmatists, new realists, pure empiricists — have been bred in the atmosphere of German idealism; and this fact should not be forgotten in approaching their views" (83). This paternity is obvious in a self-declared idealist like Emerson or Santayana's Harvard colleague Josiah Royce, whose maddening prolixity was a matter of substance as well as style: "in spite of his comprehensiveness, he seemed to view everything in relation to something else that remained untold" (64). The afterlife of idealism was less obvious in James, whose studied posture of hard-headedness concealed the many filiations that his brand of "radical empiricism" maintained with idealism.

The key, Santayana saw, was James's understanding of experience, which had the effect of "turning psychology into metaphysics" (33). "Experience," Santayana wrote, "seems to most of us to lead to conclusions, but empiricism has sworn never to draw them" (58). If, as James argued, "experience is taken to be in itself the only real existence" then we come to "the remarkable conclusion that the human spirit was not so much the purpose of the universe as its seat, and the only universe there was" — a conclusion, Santayana observes, that "sums up idealism" (33).

Given his patent aversion to idealism and all its works, it is curious that, in "The Genteel Tradition," Santayana should pause to caution readers that he regarded transcendentalism (a.k.a. "systematic subjectivism," a.k.a. idealism) not only as something "unforgettable," "the chief contribution made in modern times to speculation," but also, considered "as a method," "correct" (7–8). Perhaps he meant nothing more than the tautology that our experience of the world is, after all, our experience of the world. But if transcendentalism "as a method" is somehow "correct," as a matter of substance it is something perilous indeed, for it inculcates the "the conceited notion that man, or human reason, or the human distinction between good and evil, is the center and pivot of the universe" (19). (It is also worth pausing over his observation that "Incapacity for education, when united with great inner vitality, is one root of idealism" [97].)

Santayana provides a bracing hygienic antidote to the intellectual virus of idealism. His inestimable contribution is to remind us, *pace* idealists of whatever stripe, that when we speak of trees, it is trees of which we speak: not "trees in the mind," consciousness or experience of trees. In the end, his interest in philosophy was for the reality it revealed — and for the relief that it promised. In an important reply to his critics from 1940, Santayana summed up the nature of his interest in philosophy:

> I have never been curious to make more accurate the rough views that common information gives us of the physical world and of human history. Increase in such world knowledge may enlarge and strengthen the mind, or may distract and confuse it. The use of philosophy . . . is to distil the wine out of those trodden grapes, in order that in whatever kind of world we may be living, we may live freely in the spirit. The relief that I find . . . does not come, as in religious faith, through trust in any higher facts. It comes through liberation from anxiety, from the need of faith, and from the very problem of knowledge. I then espouse precisely the transcendental logic that [one of Santayana's interpreters, Antonio] Banfi recommends; only it never crosses my mind to mistake this play of ideas for *knowledge*, or to suppose that it miraculously reveals to me the logic of history or the necessary problems of all thought.[21]

Santayana was a generous purveyor of that most uncommon benefice, common sense. But if in his metaphysics he was a thoroughly naturalistic thinker, he came armed with a remarkable aesthetic sensibility and native appreciation of the imaginative resources that religion offered. Religions, he insisted, "are the great fairy-tales of the conscience."[22] Nevertheless he also believed that religions are indispensable, not least because they nurture the emotion of piety, "Man's reverent attachment to the sources of his being and the steadying of his life by that attachment."[23] Santayana was the

enemy of religion considered as dogma, as a repository of moral command-
ments or "literal" truth. (Santayana had little time, probably too little time,
for what he dismissed as "literal truth." "My matured conclusion," he
wrote, "is that no system is to be trusted, not even science in any literal or
pictorial sense.")[24]

But he also saw in religion an irreplaceable friend of human yearning. Its
disappearance, hailed as an emancipation, actually brought forth new forms
of bondage. "The absence of a positive religion," he wrote in "A General
Confession," a late summary of his philosophy, "was very far from liberating the spirit for higher flights: on the contrary, it opened the door to the
pervasive tyranny of the world over the soul."[25] When he looked around at
the increasing secularization of the modern world, Santayana saw that the
degradation of religion went hand-in-hand with the diminishment of culture. In "The Intellectual Temper of the Age," Santayana forlornly describes the dissolution of Christianity and the rise of "an emancipated,
atheistic, international democracy": "In vain do we deprecate it; it has
possession of us already through our propensities, fashions, and language.
Our very plutocrats and monarchs are at ease only when they are vulgar.
Even prelates and missionaries are hardly sincere or conscious of an honest
function, save as they devote themselves to social work."[26] It goes without
saying that he did not regard this development as a sign of spiritual health.

Santayana seems to have had an ingrained suspicion of almost everything
beginning with "pro": "professors," as we've seen, but also "Protestantism," "protégés," "prophets," and, above all, perhaps, "progress." "Those
who speak most of progress," he wrote, "measure it by quantity and not by
quality; how many people read and write, or how many people there are, or
what is the annual value of their trade; whereas true progress would rather lie
in reading or writing fewer and better things, and being fewer and better men,
and enjoying life more."[27] At a time when nearly everyone — conservative
as well as liberal — has difficulty dissociating the ideas of "more" and
"better," Santayana's unorthodox remarks are worth pondering.

The philosopher Frederick Olafson noted that there exists in Santayana's
thinking "a pervasive animus against democracy and liberalism."[28] This
is true. And it must be said that about some political matters, Santayana
was naïve if not obtuse. In a letter of 1920, for example, he wrote to a
former Harvard colleague that "I think to be born under Bolshevism would
not be worse than to be born in Boston."[29] (Moscow, where Stalins speak
only to Lenins, and the Lenins speak only to Marx?) But in other respects,
Santayana's traditionalist temperament and passion for individual liberty
made him an astute social critic. He was especially penetrating about the

contradictions of liberalism. In "The Intellectual Temper of the Age," he noted that "Liberalism had been supposed to advocate liberty; but what the advanced parties that still call themselves liberal now advocate is control, control over property, trade, wages, hours of work, meat and drink, amusements, and in a truly advanced country like France control over education and religion; and it is only on the subject of marriage . . . that liberalism is growing more and more liberal."[30] In an important essay called "The Irony of Liberalism," Santayana dilates on the element of social presumption that stands behind the liberal's habit of coercion: "No man . . . can really or ultimately desire anything but what the best people desire. This is the principle of the higher snobbery; and in fact, all earnest liberals are higher snobs. If you refuse to move in the prescribed direction, you are not simply different, you are arrested and perverse. The savage must not remain a savage, nor the nun a nun, and China must not keep its wall. If the animals remain animals it is somehow through a failure of the will in them, and very sad. Classic liberty, though only a name for stubborn independence, and obedience to one's own nature, was too free, in one way, for the modern liberal."[31] Liberalism in the modern sense is deeply hostile not only to tradition — tradition is by definition an impediment to "progress" — but also to "the wilder instincts of man": "the love of foraging, of hunting, of fighting, of plotting, of carousing, or of doing penance."[32] (The inclusion of penance is a characteristic Santayana touch.) The perfect liberal society is one that excludes initiative.

The homogenizing imperative of liberalism has a psychological correlative in abstract moralism. Santayana memorably captures this in a vignette in *Persons and Places*. Under the rubric "A lesson in morals," he recalls an episode after lunch one day when he was a young boy. A single piece of cake remained on a plate. He asked his mother whether he might have it. "No," she said. "It is for the little birds."

> Though it was by no means a fixed habit of hers, she opened the window and spread the crumbs out for the sparrows. She did not care for sparrows, she never watched them or tried to tame them; and that day, having performed her act of zoological benevolence, she closed the window at once, and went upstairs to sit as usual in her own room. . . . I am sure that in her silence she felt that she had given me a lesson in justice and in universal love. She had kept the cake from her son and given it to the sparrows. She was a liberal in politics.[33]

One is tempted to add, after the fashion of his beloved Spinoza, Q.E.D. Another side of Santayana's criticism of "egotism" — and another example of his commendable sanity — shows itself in his discussion in the last chapter of *Character and Opinion* of "English Liberty in America." Just as idealism makes extravagant but unfulfillable claims about metaphysics, so in its understanding of freedom it ups the ante but lacks currency when the bet is called. What Santayana calls "English liberty" is "vague," "reticent," and involves "perpetual compromise." It recognizes that "In the end, adaptation to the world at large, where so much is hidden and unintelligible, is only possible piecemeal, by groping with a genuine indetermination in one's aims" (106). "Absolute liberty," by contrast — "a foolish challenge thrown by a new-born insect buzzing against the universe" — is reckless, unwavering, and dangerously impatient. The partisans of absolute liberty, Santayana writes, "summoned every man to become free in exactly their own fashion, or have his head cut off" (113).

As a quick summary of revolutionary ambition, that would be hard to improve upon. What Santayana saw with unusual clarity was that the actual practice of "English liberty" required a widely recognized commonality of interest. "In a hearty and sound democracy," he notes, "all questions at issue must be minor matters; fundamentals must have been silently agreed upon and taken for granted when the democracy arose" (108). This is, Santayana saw, an unheroic view of freedom. But it was a stock that had the advantage of offering real dividends as distinct from speculative capital appreciation. English liberty "makes impossible the sort of liberty for which the Spartans died at Thermopylae, or the Christian martyrs in the arena, or the Protestant reformers at the stake" (112). But then, Santayana drily notes, while martyrs may be heroic, "unless they have the nature of things on their side and their cause can be victorious, their heroism is like that of criminals and madmen, interesting dramatically but morally detestable" (117).

And what of Santayana's own view of freedom and the meaning of life? Santayana was a curious hybrid. In one way, he was every bit as radical a thinker as Schopenhauer (whom he greatly admired) or Nietzsche (whom he did not). Ultimately, though, he was the cheerful, affirmative figure that Nietzsche pretended to be but wasn't. (No one, I think, ever accused Schopenhauer of being cheerful.) What Santayana described as his "scepticism" ran very deep indeed. "The truth is a terrible thing," he has the vicar of Iffley say in *The Last Puritan*. "It is much darker, much sadder, much more ignoble, much more inhuman and ironical than most of us are willing to admit, or even able to suspect."[34]

That is just the sort of thing one might expect to find in Nietzsche ("Truth is ugly," he declared in *The Will to Power*). But where Nietzsche engaged in unending histrionics ("God is dead," Zarathustra, the *über-mensch*), Santayana behaved like a gentleman. Nietzsche described himself as "the Antichrist," said he was "dynamite," and presumed to instruct us about "how to philosophize with a hammer." Santayana was much calmer. He sought no detonations. He wished to smash no idols. He came much closer, in fact, to being the disabused spiritual aristocrat that Nietzsche admired but sweated too much to resemble. "Criticism," Santayana said, "must first be invited to do its worst."[35] But only for the indelicate, he thought, did thoroughgoing criticism lead to nihilism or madness. Out of skepticism came faith, but it was an *animal* faith, modest, grateful, thoroughly materialistic: disillusioned but also at peace.

There were two interrelated sources of Santayana's calm. One was his aestheticism. Santayana strove to regard the entire world as a thing of beauty, which is to say a source of pleasure. (In his early book *The Sense of Beauty* he defined beauty as "pleasure objectified"[36]: inadequate as a definition, no doubt, but useful as a barometer of temperament.) "I can draw no distinction," he wrote in a mature summing-up, " — save for academic programmes — between moral and aesthetic values: beauty being a good, is a moral good; and the practice and enjoyment of art, like all practice and all enjoyment, fall within the sphere of morals — at least if by morals we understand moral economy and not moral superstition."[37]

Santayana attempted to provide a philosophical justification for this thoroughgoing aestheticism with what he called his doctrine of "essences." How do we know that what we believe is true is true? what we find beautiful is in fact beautiful? Are we not everywhere besieged by error and illusion? Yes, but Santayana proposes "to entertain the illusion without succumbing to it, accepting it openly as an illusion, and forbidding it to claim any sort of being but that which it obviously has; and then . . . it will not deceive me. What will remain of this non-deceptive illusion will then be a truth, and a truth the being of which requires no explanation, since it is utterly impossible that it should be otherwise."[38] How convincing is this? Not very. The fact that we embrace an illusion as an illusion does not automatically grant it the patent of truth. But it is worth noting that Santayana's criterion of trustworthiness is a quality often accorded to aesthetic and religious experience, namely the conviction that contingency, if but momentarily, had been defeated. It is also worth noting that it is not an attitude peculiar to Santayana. His former student Wallace Stevens, for example, advocated something similar when he wrote that "The final belief is to believe in a fiction, which you know to be a fiction, there being nothing else. The exquisite truth is to know that it is a fiction and you believe in it willingly."[39]

There are many problems with Santayana's (and Stevens's) aestheticism. The chief problem is its subjectivity. By locating the criterion of morality and truth in a species of pleasurable sensation, Santayana in effect denies them any public measure. This means that—I won't call it the validity, but—the attractiveness of Santayana's ideal depends largely on the quality of the individual espousing it. In the delicate hands of a Santayana this doctrine might provide a workable philosophy of life. Not everyone has the sensibility, the discipline, the restraint to make "all practice and all enjoyment fall within the sphere of morals."

The relation between enjoyment and restraint brings us to the other source of Santayana's calm, his Epicureanism. Colloquially, "epicurean" is often used to mean "devoted to sensuous pleasure." In fact, though, Epicureanism is a deeply ascetic philosophy. It is devoted to pleasure, but pleasure understood as the absence of pain. The goal is *ataraxia*: privative tranquillity: at peace because *not* disturbed by emotional tumult. Not so much happiness as invulnerability. "I have the Epicurean contentment," Santayana wrote to one of his correspondents in 1936, "which is not far removed from asceticism."[40]

Santayana early on learned to regard the world as a threat that could be best countered by holding it at bay. The phrase "a detached observer" recurs frequently in his writings. It names not simply an intellectual ideal but an emotional imperative. "The moral pageantry of this world," Santayana wrote, "is calculated wonderfully to strengthen and refine the philosophy of abstention suggested to Epicurus by the flux of material things and by the illusions of vulgar passions."[41]

Which passions were not vulgar? Those that did not collude to involve us emotionally—the dispassionate passions of observation, retrospection, and amused noninvolvement. In the 1890s, one of Santayana's colleagues at Harvard noted that "Santayana impressed us as an onlooker in the world more than a sharer in its struggle."[42]

It was an impression that Santayana was careful to cultivate, and it nurtured the reputation he had (despite his conspicuous financial generosity) for emotional chilliness. Daniel Cory reports that in 1931 when he told Santayana about the death of his old friend Frank Russell, the philosopher "reacted not at all." Taken aback, Cory asked: "Mr. Santayana, if I dropped dead in front of you at this moment, would you be emotionally moved at all?" To which Santayana replied: "You should not ask me personal questions."[43] Santayana later added that he had known Russell "long ago," but the impression of glacial *noli me tangere* persisted.

Santayana's distance from involvement was a leitmotif of his character.

By disposition, he was homosexual, though it is not clear that he was ever sexually involved with anyone. Reflecting on a meeting he had with A. E. Housman, Santayana mused to Cory that "I think I must have been that way in my Harvard days — although I was unconscious of it at the time."[44]

Santayana's biographer, John McCormick, regarded that as deliberately coy, but he supplied no evidence to gainsay it. Santayana regarded sex the way he regarded emotional entanglements generally, as temptations to be avoided. "Carnal pleasures," he wrote, "are but welcome pains, [they] draw the spirit inwards into primal darkness and indistinction."[45] Perhaps it was fortunate that Santayana was, or made himself, unsusceptible to such pleasures. "Love has never made me long unhappy, nor sexual impulse uncomfortable," he wrote in a letter of 1924.[46] Burdens, responsibilities, emotional ties: these sutures of ordinary life are among the chief evils in the Epicurean's lexicon. Disturbing tranquility, they remind us of our essential poverty, our lack of self-sufficiency. But of course such entanglements are also our most reliable sources of joy. I suspect that this is something that Santayana understood, even if he refrained from indulging it. "It takes patience to appreciate domestic bliss," he wrote in *The Life of Reason*; "volatile spirits prefer unhappiness."[47]

Santayana did not at all prefer unhappiness. But he was reluctant to wager on a bliss burdened with the imperfections of the domestic. In a letter of 1924, Oliver Wendell Holmes, Jr., put his finger on something essential about Santayana. "In a general way," Holmes wrote, "his thinking more than that of other philosophers coincides with mine. But he has a patronizing tone — as of one who saw through himself but didn't expect others to."[48]

NOTES

1. *The Life of Reason*, vol. 1 (Scribners: New York, 1905), 12.

2. *Geoffrey Madan's Notebooks*, edited by J. A. Gere and John Sparrow (Oxford University Press: Oxford, 1981), 120.

3. *Discourse on Method*, part 6.

4. Robert Dawidoff, Introduction to the Bison Books edition, *The Genteel Tradition: Nine Essays by George Santayana*, edited by Douglas L. Wilson (University of Nebraska Press: Lincoln, 1998), vii–xx, x.

5. Quoted from Walter Bagehot, *Physics and Politics: Or: Thoughts on the Application of the Principles of "Natural Selection" and "Inheritance" to Political Society*, edited with an introduction by Roger Kimball (Ivan R. Dee: Chicago, 1999), 83.

6. David Stove, "Idealism: A Victorian Horror-Story (Part One)," *The Plato Cult and Other Philosophical Follies* (Basil Blackwell: Oxford, 1991), 100.

7. *The Letters of George Santayana*, The Works of George Santayana, Volume V, Book Five, 1933–1936, edited by William G. Holzberger (Cambridge, MA: MIT Press, 2003), 284.

8. *Persons and Places: Fragments of Autobiography*, edited by William G. Holzberger and Herman J. Saatkamp, Jr., The Works of George Santayana, Vol. I (Cambridge, MA: MIT Press, 1987), 423.

9. John McCormick, *George Santayana: A Biography* (Knopf: New York, 1987), 96.

10. McCormick, *George Santayana*, 56.

11. Quoted from Leon Edel, *Henry James: The Master: 1901–1916* (Lippincott: Philadelphia, 1972), 493.

12. "A General Confession" in *The Philosophy of George Santayana*, edited by Paul Arthur Schlipp (Tudor: New York, 1951), 15.

13. Dawidoff, *The Genteel Tradition*, xiv.

14. I draw in this section and later on my essay "George Santayana" in Roger Kimball, *Lives of the Mind: The Use and Abuse of Intelligence from Hegel to Wodehouse* (Ivan R. Dee: Chicago, 2003), pp. 178–200.

15. "Apologia Pro Mente Sua," in *The Philosophy of George Santayana*, 530.

16. *Persons and Places*, 234.

17. McCormick, *George Santayana*, 56.

18. "A General Confession," 7.

19. *Egotism in German Philosophy* (Scribners: New York, 1940), 14–15.

20. *Egotism in German Philosophy*, 89.

21. "Apologia Pro Mente Sua," 532–533.

22. "A General Confession," 8.

23. *Reason in Religion*, vol. 3 of *The Life of Reason* (London: Constable, 1912), 179. *Reason in Religion* first published by Scribner's in 1905.

24. "A General Confession," 8.

25. "A General Confession," 12.

26. "The Intellectual Temper of the Age" in *Winds of Doctrine: Studies in Contemporary Opinion* (Scribners: New York, 1926), 5.

27. "The Intellectual Temper of the Age," 8.

28. *The Encyclopedia of Philosophy*, Vol. 7 (Macmillan: New York, 1967), 285.

29. McCormick, *George Santayana*, 244.

30. "The Intellectual Temper of the Age," 8.

31. "The Irony of Liberalism," in *Soliloquies in England and Later Soliloquies* (University of Michigan Press: Ann Arbor, 1967), 181–182.

32. "The Irony of Liberalism," 184.

33. *Persons and Places*, 248.

34. *The Last Puritan: A Memoir in the Form of a Novel* edited by William G. Holzberger and Herman J. Saatkamp, Jr., The Works of George Santayana, Vol. IV (MIT Press, Cambridge, MA, 1994), 242–43.

35. "A General Confession," 18.

36. *The Sense of Beauty: Being the Outline of Aesthetic Theory* (Dover: New York, 1955), 33.

37. "A General Confession," 20.

38. *Scepticism and Animal Faith* (Dover: New York, 1955), 72–73.

39. Wallace Stevens, *Opus Posthumous* (Knopf: New York, 1977), 163.

40. *Letters*, Book Five, 297.

41. *The Philosophical Poets* (Harvard University Press: Cambridge, Massachusetts, 1910), 46.

42. Quoted from Milton Bates, *Wallace Stevens: A Mythology of the Self* (University of California Press: Berkeley, 1985), 33.

43. McCormick, *George Santayana*, 122.

44. McCormick, *George Santayana*, 51.

45. *The Realm of Spirit* (Scribners: New York, 1940), 706.

46. *The Letters of George Santayana*, The Works of George Santayana, Volume V, Book Three, 1921–1927, edited by William G. Holzberger (Cambridge, MA: MIT Press, 2002), 179.

47. *The Life of Reason*, vol. 2 (Scribners: New York, 1905), 2.

48. Quoted from Edmund Wilson, *The Bit between My Teeth: A Literary Chronicle of 1950–1965* (Farrar, Straus and Giroux: New York, 1965), 79.

Index

9/11 151, 153

Agnosticism 54–57, 131
Aiken, Conrad 134–35, 176
Aristotle 37, 39, 66, 74, 77, 180
Arnold, Matthew 82
Aryan Society xxxi–xxxii,
    xxxvii*n*39
Atheism xii, 48, 67, 134, 182, 185
Avenarius, Richard 86
Avila xi, 130, 131, 137, 139

Babbitt, Irving 172
Banfi, Antonio 184
Bergson, Henri xvii, 16
Bible 30, 107, 164
Blue Nuns xix, xxx, 136, 140, 182.
    See also Clinica della Piccola
    Compagna di Maria
Borrás, Josefina xi, 129, 186
Boston xi–xii, xxi, 41, 45, 48, 128–
    32, 136, 176, 185
Brooks, Phillips 31
Brooks, Van Wyck 134, 136, 160,
    161, 176
Browning, Robert xii, xiii, 74
Burne-Jones, Edward 82
Bynner, Witter 176

Calvin, John 4, 7, 28, 68, 71, 162,
    163

Calvinism 11, 28; the genteel tradi-
    tion and xiv, 18, 30, 40–41, 161,
    163–64; philosophical principle
    of 4–5, 162; lost its basis in
    American life 6–7, 162–63; Kant
    and 8; Royce and 65, 68, 71
Cambridge, Massachusetts 13, 28,
    45, 131, 135, 136
Carlyle, Thomas 5, 74, 82, 162
Catholicism 43, 48, 150; tradition
    12; of Oxford 41; American 43–
    44; theology 81; system 116. *See
    also* Protestantism; Renaissance;
    Santayana, George
Celine, Louis Ferdinand 139
Channing, William Ellery 31
Chapman, John Jay xxxi–xxxii
Christian Science 101. *See also*
    Eddy, Mary Baker
Christianity 41, 111; as myth xiii,
    17, 129, 133; Santayana on xiii–
    xiv, xxix, 133–34, 185; Calvinism
    and 4–5, 7, 162; civilization of,
    possibly ending 24, 178; estab-
    lishment of 28; in nineteenth-
    century New England 30–31;
    conception of relations between
    God and church in 32; Reforma-
    tion and 33; William James and
    55, 59; Josiah Royce and 77, 165;
    martyrdom and 112, 168, 170,

Christianity (*continued*)
187; conflict between Muslims
and 148; genteel tradition and
164. *See also* Calvinism; Catholi-
cism; Protestantism; Reformation
Civil War, American 30, 100
Clark, General Mark 140
Clemens, Cyril 140
Clifford, W. K. xxii
Clinica della Piccola Compagna di
Maria 135. *See also* Blue Nuns
Comte, Auguste 53
Conant, James B. 134, 176
Cory, Daniel xix, 182, 189–90
Cotkin, George xxi
Cowley, Malcolm 161; *After the
Genteel Tradition* 160–61
Cultural constructivism xvi

Darwin, Charles xiii–xv, xvii, xxx,
49, 133; *Origin of Species* 49. *See
also* Evolution, theory of
Dawidoff, Robert 179, 182
Declaration of Independence xxvii,
113, 139, 166
Deconstruction xvi, 165
Democracy 58, 141–42; cultural effects of xxiv, 42, 74, 83, 86, 89,
94, 100, 165–66, 181; in Walt
Whitman 12; Josiah Royce and
74, 165; liberty and 104, 105,
108–9, 112, 113, 115–16, 168–
69, 171, 187; international 116,
185; totalitarian 167; Tocqueville
on 177; Santayana's animus
against 185
Democritus 166
Derrida, Jacques xv, 165
Descartes, René 84, 177

Dewey, John xxvii, 158
Dickens, Charles 45, 101

Eastman, Max 134, 176
Ecclesiastes 16
Eddy, Mary Baker 83, 177. *See also*
Christian Science
Education of Henry Adams, The 127
Edwards, Jonathan 4, 6, 28, 163
Egotism, philosophical 69, 92, 104,
117; philosophical idealism and
xvii, 8, 11, 19, 33, 84, 134, 183;
orthodox Western philosophy and
religion and 31–33; absolute liberty and 111, 152, 186–87
Eliot, Charles xii, 100, 132, 166, 180
Eliot, T. S. 134, 176
Ellison, Ralph 170–71
Emerson, Ralph Waldo 41, 141, 142;
loftier pedestal for xiv, 31; limited
by genteel tradition 6; philosophy
of 9–11; spontaneity of 13; originality of 28; consistency of 52;
rejection of original sin by 163;
intuitive transcendentalism of
165; self-declared idealist 183
Empiricism 34–35, 83–84, 89, 183;
of William James xxii–xxiii, 16–
18, 27, 49, 54–55, 57–58, 63, 88,
183; of English liberty 104, 106,
138
Epicureanism xii, 34, 189–90
Equality, racial 149–50, 170
Evolution, theory of xiii–xv, xvii, 8,
14, 16, 30–31, 41, 81
Exceptionalism, American 166

Fascism 172
Faust 42

Ferrer, Francisco (Guardia) xx
Fichte, J. G. xiii, 28, 34, 70, 165
Fish, Stanley xxii; "Boutique Multi-
    culturalism" xxii–xxiii
Francis of Assisi, St. 101
Frankel, Charles 142
Frankfurter, Felix 134, 176
Franklin, Benjamin 5
Freedom 92; mental xxii–xxiii; co-
    operative xxiv, 50; spiritual 26;
    nominally allowed 29; education
    in 45; official 48; illusory 70–71;
    brought by empty spaces 95;
    moral 101; land of 109; to work
    110; as absolute liberty and En-
    glish liberty 112, 119, 152, 167–
    68, 170, 187; not possible at Har-
    vard 135; individual 138; of con-
    tract 157; godlike 165; Herbert
    Marcuse on true 167; Santayana's
    view of 187
French Revolution 113
Freud, Sigmund 172
Frost, Robert 176

Gamo, Jose Maria Alonso 140
Genteel tradition 3–20, 83, 125,
    136–37, 142, 161–62, 166, 178;
    philosophical idealism and xvi;
    contrast between Santayana's cri-
    tique of and later attack on xxi,
    160–61, 164; and Puritanism xxx;
    contemporary version of xxxiii,
    164, 173, 179; American philo-
    sophic opinion rooted in 82; and
    the New Humanism 172; estab-
    lishment opinion of any time 179.
    See also Calvinism; Christianity;
    Emerson, Ralph Waldo; Idealism,

philosophical; James, William;
    Royce, Josiah
Greeks, ancient 16, 32, 59, 68, 169
Gross, Paul xvi

Hamilton, Sir William 18
Harvard 185, 189; intellectual cul-
    ture of xiii, xxi, xxx, 39–42, 44–
    45, 47–50, 100, 139, 166. See
    also James, William; Protestant-
    ism; Royce, Josiah; Santayana,
    George
Hawthorne, Nathaniel 6
Hegel, G. W. F.: philosophy of xiii–
    xv, 18, 37, 165, 177; dialectic of
    13, 183; sardonic heavens of 68;
    logic of 71; Josiah Royce and 71–
    72, 74–76; bondsman and lord in
    148
Higher Superstition xvi
Holmes, Oliver Wendell, Jr. 190
Hook, Sidney xxxi
Housman, A. E. xix, 190
Howells, William Dean 160
Humanism xvii–xviii, 25, 32–33,
    138, 172, 178
Hume, David 28, 84, 175
Huxley, T. H. xxii

Idealism, moral 94, 96–97, 99, 101–2
Idealism, philosophical xiii–xvii,
    xxvii, 17, 187; Calvinism and 7;
    academic 17, 101; critical or sci-
    entific side of 33; empiricism as a
    form of 35; Josiah Royce and 65,
    76, 78, 165; German 81, 83, 128,
    182–83; new American realism
    and 85–86; pragmatic concept of
    correctness and 87; incapacity for

Idealism, philosophical (*continued*)
education, one root of 97, 184;
technical philosophy calls itself
99, 142; basis of genteel tradition
164; romantic idealism 165–6;
transcendentalism as 183–4; intellectual virus of 184; extravagant but unfulfillable claims of
187
Imperialism 106, 139, 164, 166, 172
India, religion of 31, 66; *Upanishads*
39

James, Henry 33, 161, 181; *The
Bostonians* xxxvi*n*28
James, William xxi, 46, 49, 51–63,
64, 68, 165, 182; "The Will to Believe" xii, xxii–xxiii; on *Interpretations of Poetry and Religion*
xii–xiii, 133, 181; on Hegelian
philosophy xiii; on *The Life of
Reason* xvii; Santayana's evalua-
tion of xxiii–xxiv; and genteel
tradition 13–17, 27–28; *The Will
to Believe and Other Essays in
Popular Philosophy* 52; *Principles of Psychology* 52; *The Varieties of Religious Experience* 52,
57; *Pragmatism* 52, 88; *The Energies of Men* 58; critic of intellectualism 70; friend of Josiah Royce
77; denial of consciousness by 86;
and John Stuart Mill 88; and universal objectivism 89; and Harvard 127, 135; prose style 127–
28; Santayana's colleague 132,
181–82; on American imperialism 139, 166; increase in attention
to 141; and John Dewey 158; San-

tayana's debt to 182; concealed
idealism of 183. *See also* Empiricism; Pragmatism; Protestantism
Jesus xiv, 31
Jews, outlook of 5, 32, 43, 68, 74,
82, 106. *See also* Santayana,
George: anti-Semitism of

Kallen, Horace 134
Kant, Immanuel xiii, 8–9, 52, 71,
84, 165, 183
Kimball, Roger xxxiii
Koran 4, 162

Lachs, John xxxiii
Lenin, Vladimir 172, 185
Levitt, Norman xvi
Liberalism xxxiii, 31, 61, 133–34,
138, 172, 185–86
Liberty 8, 172, 185–86; English
xxxiii, 103–19, 138, 151–54, 161,
167–73, 187; absolute xxxiii, 106,
109, 111, 117–19, 138, 152–54,
158, 168–71, 187; romantic 61,
108; co-operative 109, 112–13,
116–18; fierce 118, 168–70; clas-
sic 186
Lippman, Walter 134, 176
Locke, John 52
Logocentrism xv
Logos xv
Lotze, Hermann 132
Lowell, Robert 140
Lucretius 132, 137, 166, 182
Lusitania, sinking of 74, 165
Lyon, Richard 140

Madan, Geoffrey 175, 177
Marcuse, Herbert 167

Maritain, Jacques 140
Marxism 168, 185
Materialism, moral xxvii, 99–101, 166
Materialism, philosophical xxiv, 35, 90, 128, 134, 142
Matthews, Herbert 140
McClay, Wilfred xxxiii
McCormick, John xxvii, 125, 139, 141, 190
Mill, John Stuart 88
More, Paul Elmer 172
Morison, Samuel Eliot 134
Multiculturalism xxii–xxiii
Munsterberg, Hugo 134
Mussolini, Benito xxxiii, 139, 140, 172

Naturalism xxix, 18, 68, 78, 141, 182
Nazism xxxi–xxxii, 172
New Humanism 172
New Realism 83–86, 90
New Thought 101
Newman, Cardinal John Henry 4, 162, 179
Nicene Creed xiv, 164
Nietzsche, Friedrich 33, 74, 91, 169, 183, 187–88
Norton, Charles Eliot 82

Olafson, Frederick 185

Palmer, George H. 132
Pantheism 12, 33, 69–71, 75
Pascal, Blaise 59
Pelikan, Jaroslav 144
Philippines xi, 129, 139
Plato: philosophy of xxx, 83, 123, 177, 180; Christianity and 32; nat-ural science of 32, 68; mythology of 37, 39; tradition of, not planted in America 41; urbanity of 175; in *Interpretations of Poetry and Religion* 181
Plotinus 66
Poe, Edgar Allan 6
Postmodernism xv–xvi, xxiv–xxv, xxxiii, 143, 164
Potter, Warwick xviii
Pound, Ezra 139
Pragmatism xviii, 67, 83, 87, 89, 128, 183; of William James xxiv, 14–15, 17, 54–55, 132, 158, 181. *See also* Dewey, John; James, William
Protagoras 87, 89
Protestantism 4, 81, 162, 185; of New England xii, 5, 45–46, 129–31, 136, 163; of Harvard xviii, 132; liberal xxiv, 29, 59, 133; William James and xxiv, 59, 139; transcendentalism and 9; and philosophical idealism 33; American Catholicism and 44, 59, Josiah Royce and 72; absolute liberty and 112, 187; American 141, 162, 163. *See also* Calvinism; Reformation
Proust, Marcel 172

Reason: secular xvii; spirit and xviii; Aryan Society and life of xxxi; pivot of universe not human 19, 136, 184; later comer into this world 31, 125–26; Harvard school of philosophy and 50; passions and 52; belief without 56; Josiah Royce on 72; future based

Reason (*continued*)
  on 96; English liberty and 105,
  111, 117–18, 171; Wallace Stevens on 127; Protestant pieties
  and 132; Nietzsche and life of
  169. *See also* Santayana, George,
  works of: *The Life of Reason*
Reformation 33, 34
Reisman, David: *The Lonely Crowd*
  125
Relativism, free-speech 179
Renaissance 12
Robinson Crusoe 117
Romanticism: German idealism and
  xxvii, 164–66; Nazism and xxxi;
  transcendentalism and 7–9, 11;
  William James and 13–17, 49, 52,
  54–56, 62; Christendom and 24,
  178; sympathy with nature of 36;
  Josiah Royce and 66–67, 70, 72–
  74; Santayana and 134; contemporary world and 138; Santayana
  on 144, 164–66, 176; sensibility
  of 169
Rome xi, xix, xxx, 33, 74, 91, 135–
  36, 140, 143, 145, 182
Rousseau, Jean-Jacques 62
Royce, Josiah xxi, xxiv, xxxvi, 64–
  80, 132; philosophical idealism of
  xiii–xv, 183; genteel tradition and
  xiv; *The Spirit of Modern Philosophy* xv, xxv; world as battlefield
  between good and evil in xxxv; as
  philosophical Calvinist 5, 162; on
  loneliness of the genuine philosopher 39; friend of William James
  49; and Harvard 64, 183; *The
  World and the Individual* 79; on
  communities of memory and hope

  158, Santayana on conflict be-
  tween romantic idealism and
  American spirit in 165. *See also*
  Calvinism; Protestantism
Russell, Bertrand xix, 10
Russell, John Francis Stanley xii,
  xix–xx, 189
Russian Revolution 113

Santayana, Agustín xi, 129–31
Santayana Edition xxxii–xxxiii, 141
Santayana, George: Spanish heritage
  of xi, xii, 125, 129, 131–32, 135,
  176; family of xi, xviii, xxvii,
  129–32, 186; student at Harvard
  xi, xix, 125, 131–32, 176, 190;
  professor at Harvard xi–xii, xviii,
  xix, xxvi, 128, 132, 134–35, 176,
  180, 181–82, 190; Catholicism
  and xii, xviii, 129, 132, 133, 134,
  140, 181, 182; aestheticism of
  xii–xiii, 173, 188–89; change of
  heart or *metanoia* xviii; and World
  War II xix, xxx, 140; at convent of
  the Blue Nuns xix, 140, 182–83;
  sexuality and xix, 190; relationship with John Francis Stanley
  Russell xix–xx, 189; and World
  War I xxvi–xxvii, xxix, 74–75,
  178; anti-Semitism of xxxi, xxx-
  viin39; philosophical reputation
  of xxxii–xxxiii, 125–26, 128,
  140–41, 128, 172–73; prose style
  of 123–24, 127–28, 175–76, 179;
  students of 134–35, 176; philosophical detachment of 137–38,
  139–40, 171–73, 189–90; failure
  to appreciate virtues of business
  158–9

Santayana, George, works of: "The Genteel Tradition in American Philosophy" xi, xxi, xxxiii, 125, 136, 160–63, 173, 176–77, 183–84; *Character and Opinion in the United States* xi, xvi, xxiv, xxvi–xxvii, xxxii, 123–25, 132, 135, 136, 151, 161–62, 165–66, 173, 176–78, 180, 183, 187; *Apologia Pro Menta Sua* xi, xvii, 182, 184; *Persons and Places* xii, xviii–xix, xix–xx, xxvii, xxxiii, 127, 132, 137–38, 143, 166, 180, 182, 186; *Sonnets and Other Verses* xii; *Lucifer: A Theological Tragedy* xii; *A Hermit of Carmel and Other Poems* xii; *Interpretations of Poetry and Religion* xii–xiii, xxxiii, 133, 181; *The Poetry of Barbarism* xiii; *The Life of Reason, or The Phases of Human Progress* xvi–xviii, 176, 190; *Reason in Common Sense* xvi, 126; *Reason in Society* xvi; *Reason in Religion* xvi; *Reason in Art* xvi; *Reason in Science* xvi; *Winds of Doctrine* xvii; *Realms of Being* xvii, xxix; *Egotism in German Philosophy* xxvi–xxvii; *Soliloquies in England* xxvi, xxvii–xxviii, 176; *Scepticism and Animal Faith: Introduction to a System of Philosophy* xxviii, 164; *Philosophical Heresy* xxviii–xxix; *The Realm of Truth* xxix; *The Realm of Spirit* xxix; *The Last Puritan* xxix–xxx, xxxiii, 127, 176, 187; *Dominations and Powers* xxxi–xxxii; *The Genteel Tradition at Bay* 138, 179; *A General Confession* 175, 182, 184–85, 188; *The Intellectual Temper of the Age* 185–86; *The Irony of Liberalism* 186

Sastre, Susana xviii, xxvii, 132

Scepticism *or* Skepticism xii, xxv, xxxiii, 34, 37, 65, 78, 163–64, 187–88. *See also* Santayana, George, works of: *Scepticism and Animal Faith*

Schelling, Friedrich xiii, 165

Schopenhauer, Arthur 187

Segregation, racial 170

Seldes, Gilbert 134

September *11, 2001* 151, 153

Shakespeare, William 52, 54; *Hamlet* 35, 107

Shaw, George Bernard 4

Shelley, Percy Bysshe: "Ode to the West Wind" 169

Social Gospel 128

Socialism 94, 168, 177

Socrates 19, 28, 32, 39, 61, 179

Spain xi, xx, xxvii, 61, 130, 135, 167, 180

Spanish-American War 166

Sparta 117; Spartans 112, 187

Spencer, Herbert 36

Spinoza, Benedict 4, 12, 23, 29, 39, 69, 70, 71, 162, 182, 186

Stalin, Joseph 172, 185

Stevens, Wallace 127, 134, 176, 188–89; "To an Old Philosopher in Rome" xxxi, 140

Stoicism 12, 71, 137

Stove, David 179

Sturgis, George xi, 129–30

Swedenborgianism 13, 60

Teresa of Avila, St. 137

Thayer, Scofield 176

Tocqueville, Alexis de 141–42, 177

Transcendentalism: Emerson and 6, 9, 11, 163, 165; as systematic subjectivism 7, 83, 184; as method 7–9; as myth 8; genteel tradition and 18–19, 163–64; vogue of 29–30; empiricism as starting point of 35, William James and 58–59; Josiah Royce and 70, 77–79; New England and 83; Santayana on 183–84

Twain, Mark 12, 160–61

Valéry, Paul 172

Wallace, George 170

Washington, George 5

Webster, Daniel 118

Whitman, Walt xiii, xxi, 12–13, 25, 62

Wilde, Oscar 177

Wilson, Edmund xxxi, 140, 192

Yale 30